"A fantastic, fun, and chilling tale." CANADIAN GEOGRAPHIC

"[Adam Shoalts] . . . continues to go where his curiosity pulls him—often into uncomfortable places we might not go ourselves—and is more than happy to bring us along in the recounting. Spine-tingling . . . captivating." SUDBURY STAR

"The place they end up is so isolated and untravelled that it could give the yips to even the most seasoned explorer. Shoalts is precise in his descriptions of setting and his writing is filled with . . . a clever, intentional use of language that heightens tension and lets a creepiness seep into the narrative." QUILL & QUIRE

"Like something out of Lovecraft. . . . He writes like an explorer of old . . . thrilling." BOOK CITY

"He's a great writer . . . enthralling . . . his use of language keeps you glued to the page." MYSTERIOUS UNIVERSE PODCAST

"Shoalts takes us deep into the heart of Labrador. Chock-full of immersive prose and captivating details, I felt as though I truly was in that canoe, ready to solve an eerie, century-year old mystery. I was left goose-bumped and utterly captivated." ERIN A. CRAIG, *New York Times* bestselling author of *House of Salt and Sorrows*

PRAISE FOR *BEYOND THE TREES*

"Beyond the Trees is a remarkable tale—and a staggering feat. . . . It's mesmerizing to be guided through Canada's wilderness through Shoalts' eyes . . . Shoalts also wields a wicked wit." ATLANTIC BOOKS TODAY

"[*Beyond the Trees*] might just soothe your need for adventure . . . wonder-filled . . . [a] beautiful book." BUZZFEED

"A wild adventure . . . riveting." MONTREAL GAZETTE

"Adam Shoalts takes readers across the rugged Canadian landscape . . . the trek was considered to be a near-impossible feat to achieve on one's own. . . . [*Beyond the Trees*] offers a beyond riveting adventure memoir that'll keep readers hooked until the very end." CNN

"Adam Shoalts does what most of us would never dare to do. . . . *Beyond the Trees* is a very readable homage to the wilds of the Canadian North." *RICHMOND NEWS*

"[A] rousing adventure story . . ." *CANADA.COM*

"Adam has a magic way of writing and making you feel like you are hiking through the wilderness with him." BOOKS WITH COOKE

" . . . the adventure of a lifetime [told] in thrilling detail." TVO

"[Shoalts] brings us along on his solo journey across the Arctic, infused with the wonder of seeing this majestic land and the urgency of making it back before winter sets in." *TORONTO STAR*

"His journey took him . . . across the terrestrial world's largest expanse of wilderness outside Antarctica . . . [an] engaging, hazard-strewn account." *NATURE*

"If you love an outdoor adventure, *Beyond the Trees* is for you." *KAMLOOPS MATTERS*

PRAISE FOR *A HISTORY OF CANADA IN TEN MAPS*

"It's an epic journey . . . Shoalts has done an elegant job of . . . reminding us of the vast and brooding influence of geography on our history." *THE GLOBE AND MAIL*

"Adam Shoalts's book is a must read for anybody with interests in Canadian history, geography, and exploration." CANADIAN GIS

"Shoalts analyzes early maps in order to paint a picture of the land that would become a nation, bringing its earliest stories, voices, and battles to life. Combining geography, cartography, history, and anthropology, Shoalts leaves no stone unturned." CBC

"A brilliant book." *CANADIAN GEOGRAPHIC*

"[A] marvel. . . . If you like maps, you'll like this book; if you like both maps and crisply recounted Canadian history, you'll love it. Shoalts . . . takes you inside [explorers'] heads as they face fear, doubt, and despair in tandem with cold, starvation, and rebellious wanting-to-turn-back companions. . . . Canadian history writ well." *WINNIPEG FREE PRESS*

"A masterful approach to mapping Canada." *TORONTO STAR*

"[O]ne fine book perfectly written for the armchair adventurer." POSTMEDIA

PRAISE FOR *ALONE AGAINST THE NORTH*

"Rare insight into the heart and mind of an explorer, and the insatiable hunger for the unknown that both inspires and drives one to the edge. Adam Shoalts . . . calmly describes the things he has endured that would drive most people to despair, or even madness." COL. CHRIS HADFIELD, astronaut, International Space Station commander

"As gripping to read as it must've been exciting to live!" LES STROUD, Survivorman

"Adam Shoalts's remarkable solo foray . . . is the kind of incredible effort that fosters legends." *WINNIPEG FREE PRESS*

"Shoalts's love of nature, cool professionalism, and almost archaically romantic spirit draw us into his adventures. . . . Shoalts is a knowledgeable and observant guide." *QUILL & QUIRE*

"Anyone who thinks exploration is dead should read this book." JOHN GEIGER, author, CEO of the Royal Canadian Geographical Society

"The more layers you peel away, the more you begin to see the quick mind and quiet intensity that helps propel Adam Shoalts." BRIAN BANKS, *CANADIAN GEOGRAPHIC*

"It is a story of brutal perseverance and stamina, which few adventurers could equal." *LIFE IN QUEBEC MAGAZINE*

"Shoalts is a fearless adventurer . . . *Alone Against the North* is a rip-roaring yarn." THE GREAT CANADIAN BUCKET LIST

"While the book is a nail-biting chronicle of polar-bear encounters, brutal swarms of black flies, and surprise tumbles down waterfalls, Shoalts also vividly describes an area of the country most of us will never witness." *METRO* (Toronto)

WHERE THE FALCON FLIES

WHERE THE FALCON FLIES

A 3,400 KILOMETRE ODYSSEY FROM MY DOORSTEP TO THE ARCTIC

ADAM SHOALTS

ALLEN
LANE

ALLEN LANE

an imprint of Penguin Canada, a division of Penguin Random House Canada Limited

Canada • USA • UK • Ireland • Australia • New Zealand • India • South Africa • China

First published 2023

www.penguinrandomhouse.ca

LIBRARY AND ARCHIVES CANADA CATALOGUING IN PUBLICATION
Title: Where the falcon flies : a 3,400 kilometre odyssey
from my doorstep to the Arctic / Adam Shoalts.
Names: Shoalts, Adam, 1986- author.
Identifiers: Canadiana (print) 20230144136 | Canadiana (ebook) 20230144160 |
ISBN 9780735241015 (hardcover) | ISBN 9780735241022 (EPUB)
Subjects: LCSH: Shoalts, Adam, 1986- —Travel—Canada, Northern. | LCSH: Canoes
and canoeing—Canada, Northern. | LCSH: Canada, Northern—Description and travel.
Classification: LCC FC3205.5 .S567 2023 | DDC 917.1904/7—dc23

Book design by Emma Dolan
Cover design by Emma Dolan
Cover images: (sunset over sea and mountains in Saguenay, Canada) © Denis Lomme /
EyeEm, (canoe) © Cultura / Benjamin Rondel, (falcon) © Andyworks, all Getty Images

Printed in the United States of America

10 9 8 7 6 5 4 3 2 1

Penguin
Random
House

ALLEN
LANE

To my family

Nunavut

Hudson Bay

Arctic

Manitoba

Subarctic
Taiga

Quebec

Ontario

Great Lakes-
St. Lawrence
Forest

Que

Montreal

Toronto

Niagara Falls

United States

Long Point

Greenland

Kangiqsualujjuaq

North Atlantic

Torngat Mountains

Boreal
Forest

Labrador City

Labrador

Newfoundland

Gulf of St Lawrence

Nova Scotia

New
Brunswick

🌀 Travel Route

🌲 Subarctic Taiga

🌲 Boreal Forest

🌳 Deciduous Forest

🔺 Mountains

N
W   E
S

Kilometres

0   400

CONTENTS

PREFACE

I WAS CLINGING to the side of a mountain, edging along a
steep cliff of the sort it's unwise to fall off. It had been three
months since I'd last seen home, and there wasn't another soul
around for miles. I was deep in one of North America's wildest
mountain ranges, a place few people ever set foot.

The high peaks around me had been shrouded in drifting
fog, making these ancient mountains feel even more mysterious
than they already did. The granite crags were thickly covered in
lichens, with little tufts of grass sprouting up wherever there was
some crack in the rock. In the shadowy crevices where the sun
couldn't reach was hard-packed snow and ice. I continued edging along, holding onto the weathered rocks to steady myself.
Hiking alone in these ultra-remote mountains, where there were
no trails and numerous loose boulders, meant I had to be extra
careful: if I slipped, my bones would become a new addition to
the landscape (until a bear found them and stripped them apart
to get at the marrow on the inside).

A momentary break in the mist allowed me a better view: ahead was a steep rockface, which seemed promising—in terms of what I was searching for, not for climbing. I strained my ears to the slight wind, hoping to catch somewhere in the mist the sound of my objective. But I heard nothing aside from the breeze around the peaks above.

Another few steps brought me to a clump of crowberries clinging to the rocks. I crouched down to pick a few and satisfy my hunger. Crowberries are a little bland, but not bad when you're half-starved. Growing next to the crowberries I came upon some juicy lingonberries, which cheered my spirits. It was only mid-July and lingonberries don't usually ripen until late August, meaning these were last year's crop of berries, which had overwintered. This gave the burgundy-coloured berries a rich, fermented taste.

Just as I was plucking another berry, I caught a flash of movement. Something had passed overhead through the fog. I froze—it was only the merest glimpse, but I thought I recognized it. It looked like the shape of a majestic bird, the monarch of the air, the world's fastest animal: *a peregrine falcon.* These amazing raptors can reach speeds of over two hundred miles an hour when they dive-bomb unsuspecting prey, and for centuries have been prized in cultures worldwide as a symbol of nobility and prowess. In my excitement, though, I couldn't be sure; it might have been a figment of my imagination or just some other bird. But if it was a falcon, there was a chance it might have a nest nearby, as falcons nest on steep, inaccessible cliffs, much like the one I'd reached, the very thing I'd been seeking all along.

From my backpack I carefully drew out my camera in the hope that the falcon—if that's what it was—might reappear. Then, camera ready, I edged closer to the precipitous cliff.

BIRDWATCHING

W E LIVED IN the little village of St. Williams, nestled on the north shore of Lake Erie, in Ontario's Norfolk County. It's a rural county with old-growth forests and deep ravines filled with ancient creaking hemlocks, giant sycamores, stately oaks, and winding little trout streams. But what really makes it a wonderful place for a nature lover to call home is that Norfolk is a haven for migratory birds of all kinds. Each spring, hundreds of different species pass through the area, heading in many cases to the far North. And it was this fact, more than any other, that set me off on perhaps the greatest adventure of my life.

I'd been looking out the porch window of our little house one early spring morning at the unplanted farmers' fields across the road, watching grey clouds passing rapidly by on a stiff breeze. Then suddenly a largish bird appeared, flapping across the distant sky. I recognized the peculiar way it flapped its wings as something out of the ordinary—not a hawk or an eagle, as I'd often seen. There was only one bird that flew like that: I'd spotted them from my canoe in the Arctic, and seeing it now reminded me of those lands and journeys. It was a peregrine falcon.

The falcon soon disappeared beyond the fields and over the edge of the woods. But I remained standing at the window a moment or two longer, staring off into the sky where it had flown. The sight of it left me with the stirrings of an idea, thinking as I did how fascinating it was that some of the birds I saw out my porch window would fly onward to the Arctic, thousands of miles away. Here in southern Ontario, the Arctic felt impossibly remote. Yet the falcon seemed to suggest an intriguing link between the faraway Arctic and my front yard.

Turning suddenly from the window, I sought out a map of Canada among the books and papers lying on my desk. When I'd found it, I traced my finger over what I thought might be the falcon's route north. Falcons nest almost all across the Arctic, but one place in particular they favour are the rugged peaks of the Torngat Mountains. In these remote and windswept mountains, high on inaccessible cliffs, falcons make their nests. I'd never been to the Torngats, but had long wanted to see these most majestic of arctic mountains. And there they were, labelled on the top right corner of the map, at the tip of Labrador and eastern Quebec. Staring at them now and thinking of the falcon I'd just spotted, a wild idea occurred to me: Why not get out my canoe, grab my backpack, and follow the falcon all the way to the Arctic?

It was true there was no obvious route from our house to the Arctic, but this small detail barely entered my head. In the moment, I was swept up with the thought of how neat it'd be to witness firsthand the gradual change in the landscape as I slowly worked my way north—from the lush Carolinian forests of southernmost Ontario, with their broad-leaved trees like hickory and sassafras, to the white pines and maples of the mixed Great Lakes forest, to the more northern boreal forest and its sombre evergreen woods, which thin eventually into the small, stunted trees of the subarctic lands, and finally, to the icy tundra and permafrost of the Arctic itself. Such a journey would furnish a unique chance to explore each of these natural regions and the gradual transitions between them, which together span Canada. I'd studied these different regions in my geography classes, but I felt it was one thing to look at them on the printed page and another to experience them in real life.

The more I thought about it, the more the idea appealed to me of this chance to observe the landscape, and to see it the same way people first had centuries ago—from the stern of a canoe. Some of the lands I'd pass through would have changed little since those days, others almost beyond recognition. Nearly everywhere, though, I could be sure of finding echoes of the past, and travelling by canoe would offer the possibility of exploring these, too.

I stood up from the desk and resolved, right then and there, to set off on a journey after the falcon to the Arctic (pending the necessary approval from my wife, Alexandria). Luckily, Alexandria, a keen birder herself, greeted my idea with her usual enthusiasm when I shared it with her over breakfast. She loves the outdoors nearly as much as I do, although she prefers to enjoy it more through backyard birdwatching and gardening.

With her help and encouragement, I began packing that very day, with the hope that I could be ready to leave before the week was out.

Alas, it was not to be. It was March 2020, and the world, or at least our corner of it, was about to be put on hold. The Covid pandemic happened; restrictions were put in place, and two weeks of waiting turned into two years.

In the meantime, circumstances changed. Alexandria and I ended up moving and then became parents with the birth of our first child. Parenthood made months-long canoe journeys more complicated. I continued to do smaller expeditions for the Royal Canadian Geographical Society, as my livelihood depended on it. But shorter journeys weren't as remunerative, and in the time since I'd first seen the falcon, I often found my mind drifting back to it and musing on the idea of following it.

Alexandria thought I ought to attempt the journey; otherwise, she pointed out, I'd be haunted by regret that I never did. But as much as I felt the pull of adventure, I also felt that homesickness for my family would be the hardest part, something that was new to me, as I'd never been a parent on any previous long adventure. Alexandria, however, said that in the grand scheme of things three months or so was no great length of time, that I'd have a good story to tell our son when he was old enough, and that absence only makes the heart grow fonder. Ultimately I agreed with her wisdom; I never did like to leave a project unfinished.

With the melting of the snows and return of spring I determined to give the journey my best shot. I'd wanted to start right from our doorstep, and to that end we rented a little cottage in

Norfolk County at Long Point, not far from our old place in St. Williams. Long Point is a large marshy peninsula that juts far into Lake Erie, and just about the best birdwatching area in Canada.

From the cottage we searched the skies with our binoculars for any signs of migrating falcons. There were ducks, geese, and tundra swans by the hundreds, all heading north thousands of kilometres to the arctic lands. Then, one clear April evening, I spotted a peregrine falcon gliding across the lake—and the old feeling of wanderlust and adventure kindled inside me again. The time had come to pack my gear and load up my trusty red canoe. I resolved to set off the next morning.

Alexandria and Thomas, our little son who was just over a year old, wished me well, encouraging me. I hugged them both and told them I'd be back before they knew it.

2

LONG POINT

I T WAS A fine morning to be setting off on an adventure. The last of the snow and ice had melted away, the skies were clear, the winds light, and although there were no leaves on the trees quite yet, the day felt as if it would warm up nicely. The date was April 24. I wore a fleece sweater with a light jacket over it, my broad-brimmed explorer's hat, and khaki hiking pants with large side pockets—handy for stuffing in such every-day items as flint and steel for making fires, a compass, and a Swiss Army knife.

Extending almost forty kilometres into Lake Erie's often stormy waters, Long Point's immense size means that anyone looking at a map of Lake Erie will immediately notice it—for there's nothing else quite like it. The first several kilometres from the mainland are heavily developed with cottages and marinas, but beyond this lies what's been called the only true "wilderness" left in southern Ontario: a large, wild tract with no road access. This section has been kept free of development and largely off limits through a combination of a private hunting preserve owned since 1866 by the Long Point Company, as well as a federally protected National Wildlife Area, leaving the peninsula a rich oasis. Besides the vast numbers of birds of all kinds, the Point is home to a great diversity of turtles, snakes, frogs, and mammal species.

The cottage was about a kilometre from the nearest water access, so I'd strapped my canoe and gear onto a small collapsible cart and wheeled it down the road. The cart consisted of two wheels on an aluminum frame, which I'd found on sale at the local Canadian Tire. When I had everything balanced just right, it took almost all the weight, allowing me to push the sixty-pound canoe with another sixty pounds of gear and food rations loaded inside of it with ease. This was a relief, as I knew if I were to have any chance of actually reaching the Arctic, much would depend on the effectiveness of this cart. The dried food I kept stored inside a watertight plastic barrel, and my camping gear in a backpack. As I pushed the canoe along the road things were quiet and peaceful, with hardly a sound to be heard other than the birds singing and the neighbour blaring Metallica on their stereo system.

It took only ten minutes to wheel my canoe to the historic Old Cut Lighthouse, which is tucked away in just about the last place you'd expect to find a lighthouse. It's well inland from the tip of Long Point, near what had once been a channel or "cut" across the peninsula, allowing ships to take a shortcut rather than risk navigating the treacherous currents around the stormy Point. Most of the cut has long since filled in from Erie's infamous storms (hence the name "Old Cut"), but the lighthouse still stands and what remains of the cut is now a harbour.

Even with the lighthouse's construction Long Point remained deadly for mariners. Not for nothing, after all, has it been called the "graveyard of the Great Lakes." An estimated two hundred ships have been wrecked and lost in fierce storms around the Point—sending countless sailors to a watery grave. If local legend is to be believed, not all of these wrecks were purely the result of the weather. In the 1800s, some locals were said to occasionally douse the lighthouse's lanterns when a merchant ship was offshore, thereby letting it wreck on the Point's shoals—and afterward salvaging the valuables for themselves.

With the lighthouse long since decommissioned, it gradually became dilapidated and put up for sale, passing through several hands over the twentieth century. When in 1999 it was listed again, it seemed this piece of history might at last be torn down. But luckily for all who value nautical history, this time the lighthouse was purchased by Peter and Brigitte Westaway, who lovingly and meticulously restored it and transformed what had been the lighthouse keeper's living quarters into a charming cottage. Living in Norfolk County, I'd met them, and kind and generous as they are, they'd since helped support my expeditions. In fact, the position I held at the Royal Canadian Geographical Society, Westaway Explorer-in-Residence, had been named in their honour.

Peter and Brigitte met me outside their lighthouse. They asked if I needed breakfast or anything else before setting off, but I assured them I was well-fed (I had eaten half a bagel that morning) and eager to be underway while the winds were still light. Peter agreed this was prudent, as he was an old paddler himself and well appreciated the challenges of canoeing on the Great Lakes. So they wished me well and saw me off as I wheeled my canoe across the lighthouse lawn to a small channel of marshy water, which connects to Long Point Bay.

I shoved the canoe into the water, stepped in, and pushed off. It felt a little surreal to be setting out for the Arctic, and perhaps a bit daunting if I dwelt on all the obstacles I was likely to face—the fierce storms and huge waves that could sink even ocean-going ships, the difficulty of finding campsites in heavily populated areas, the challenge of navigating safely around hydroelectric dams and commercial shipping lanes, the powerful whitewater rapids and frigid water temperatures, the gruelling portages, and the polar bears that might make me an appetizer—but I tried to concentrate only on the task at hand. That's my general approach to any big undertaking, whether organizing the closet or canoeing to the Arctic: the key is to mentally break it up into a series of smaller tasks that can be chipped away at. Thus I tried not to think of myself as setting off on of 3,400-kilometre journey, but rather as embarking on a day's paddling, with the goal of doing the best I could that day and not worrying too much about the days to come.

My plan was to follow Lake Erie's shoreline all the way to the Niagara River, then head down it. This river has a notable waterfall on it, so I'd have to portage around it, but afterwards I'd be able to canoe the rest of the way to Lake Ontario. From there, it'd be only three thousand more kilometres until I reached the Arctic.

In any case, the peaceful surroundings put my mind at ease: on either bank of the marshy channel were cattails, cottonwoods, and oaks. Up ahead I noticed a beaver lodge and some painted turtles sunning themselves on a log. Little songbirds fluttered among the trees, singing and tweeting cheerfully, while a handsome kingfisher perched on a branch overlooking the water. Maybe it was just my imagination, but it seemed as if all of nature was particularly cheerful this morning, and I couldn't help but almost feel the wildlife were wishing me well on my journey. Even the oaks and cottonwoods, swaying in the breeze, seemed to be bidding me on my way.

As I neared the end of the channel, it widened and joined another marshy passageway. Along the bank were rickety old boathouses, rusted and falling apart. A little more paddling brought me into Long Point Bay's open expanse, where a howling wind greeted me. But the waves weren't large, so I decided to paddle straight across the shipwreck-filled bay rather than follow the shoreline.

Cruising along offshore, my repetitive paddle strokes soon put me in a reflective mood, and visions of the past seemed to swell up before me. There was a time when the countless inlets of the Great Lakes allowed illegal traders, smugglers, and even cutthroats to flourish. Of these unscrupulous characters, the most notorious was an ex–Royal Navy sailor named David Ramsey, who'd taken up life as a Great Lakes trader in the late 1700s and liked to frequent Long Point's waters. It wasn't long before he was mixed up in all sorts of trouble—he murdered at least half a dozen people, boasting about it later. Such a ruthless figure inspired no end of legends, including that Ramsey buried a hoard of ill-gotten gold on one of Long Point's sandy ridges. The gold Ramsey supposedly procured on one of his trading voyages to Fort Detroit—Detroit, in that day, being little more than a fur-trading post. Ramsey was said to have hidden the treasure with the intention of recovering it later. But he was unable to retrieve it before his death. Whatever the truth of the legend, many a fortune hunter has since searched in vain among the Point's sandy ridges.

Fortunately, not all early residents of the Point were quite so bloodthirsty. One of the most heroic was Abigail Becker, the "Angel of Long Point." With her husband Jeremiah, a trapper and fisherman, Abigail lived in a cabin amid Long Point's isolated dunes, where she raised their numerous children. When the gales of November and December wrecked ships off the Point, many sailors, half-drowned and hypothermic, would wash up. With her husband away on trapping trips and her children too young to be much help, more than once Abigail single-handedly rescued these half-dead sailors, sometimes risking her own life by wading out into the thundering surf to pull the unconscious sailors ashore. For her heroic efforts, Abigail became celebrated throughout the Great Lakes.

But if there was anything the locals around Long Point feared more than cutthroats or storms, it was witchcraft. In Canada's backwoods villages, fear of witches remained commonplace in the 1700s, with Long Point Bay the rumoured haunt of several. Their sworn enemy was Dr. John Troyer, a German witch hunter and exorcist, who in 1790 had built himself a sturdy cabin overlooking the bay. Troyer must have been resourceful—not only did he survive in the wild, but with little more than an axe, he felled the giant oaks and pines around his home and built himself a sloop for lake voyages. Troyer was famous for his reputedly vast knowledge of potions, magic charms, and wild plants. His advice was sought far and wide not only for sickness and injury, but for dealing with witchcraft. Troyer took the threat of witchcraft so seriously that at night he slept with a "witch trap" outside his cabin door for protection. (The trap, it seems, was actually an old bear trap with spring-loaded iron jaws that would slam shut if stepped on in the dark. One hopes he never forgot about it when letting the dog out.) But it was his so-called "exorcisms" that earned Dr. Troyer his widest renown. His skills were more than once called upon to expunge hauntings, break spells or curses, deal with cases of humans transforming into animals, and provide other dedicated services that are getting hard to find nowadays.

The wind drove me closer to shore, but on the bright side, this allowed me a better view of my old stomping grounds around the little village of St. Williams. Tracing my eye along the wooded shoreline, I sought out the former location of Dr. Troyer's homestead. The ravages of time over the past two and a half centuries have left little trace of it, but his weathered gravestone still stands there in a field.

Snow geese passed overhead as I drew another stroke of my paddle. Like the falcons, they too were headed north. Other migrating birds were also about: Canada geese, sandhill cranes, ducks, various plovers and terns. Any of these birds might provide food for a passing falcon—as falcons, unlike eagles, mostly prey on other birds for their main diet. For this reason peregrines were long called "duck hawks," since they especially like to prey on ducks. Their common name, peregrine, means wanderer, and reflects their migratory proclivities. I scanned in all directions from my canoe, but I didn't see any more peregrines. Falcons are fast flyers, though, and often difficult to spot. Some stay around Lake Erie all winter, while others come from farther south, sometimes as far as Central America. On their flight north, if they get hungry, Long Point provides a convenient pit stop for fast food.

In the mid-twentieth century, the number of falcons, along with bald eagles, declined dramatically owing to pesticide use, specifically DDT, which caused their eggshells to thin. Fortunately, with the banning of DDT, their populations have gradually recovered. Attempts have even been made to introduce falcons into urban landscapes, on the theory that skyscrapers are similar to the sheer cliffs they like to nest on and that urban pigeon populations provide ample prey. But to me at least, I felt there was something far more special about seeing falcons in their natural habitats.

An object moving underwater diverted my attention from the birds. As it surfaced, I was startled to see some prehistoric-looking creature. Then I realized that it was only an enormous algae-encrusted snapping turtle. The ancient turtle eyed me suspiciously before diving back down. Snapping turtles can live more than a century, and their jaws are thought to be powerful enough to bite clean through a human finger. As children, my brother and I used to collect snapping turtle eggs in the spring, put them in a terrarium under a heat lamp, wait for them to hatch, and then marvel at what looked like miniature dinosaurs, with their armoured shells and dragon-like tails. After they got too big, we'd let them go in the pond at the edge of the woods that surrounded our family home—and I like to think they're still there now.

After I rounded Turkey Point the wind died, leaving the lake calm and smooth. Sky and water seemed to merge imperceptibly on the horizon. Given that it was still April, the lake was practically deserted with hardly any boats about. I canoed by Turkey Point beach with its numerous cottages.

Rising above the cottages I could see a steep, wooded hill. In the late 1700s, Governor Simcoe, Upper Canada's first governor, had resolved to fortify this hilltop. But the vastness of the Canadian frontier that Simcoe had to defend from a potential American invasion—two thousand kilometres of Great Lakes shoreline—meant there weren't enough troops on hand to carry out these fortification plans. Not until 1814, the last year of the bloody war that erupted in 1812 with the American invasion, was a fort erected overlooking Turkey Point. Luckily for the Canadians, the forest itself proved a more effective defence than the fort—the American invaders who landed at Norfolk County, it was reported, became lost in the woods before retreating days later, though not before they'd burned a number of homes, farms, and mills. After the war, the fort fell into ruins, and today little trace of it is left. The site is now the Turkey Point Golf Course, with only a small cairn testifying to the fort's former existence.

As I continued paddling east the temperature climbed, the lake still smooth as glass. But I knew Lake Erie's fearsome and well-earned reputation among mariners and how fast it could turn squally. Of all the Great Lakes, Erie is the shallowest (sixty-two feet deep on average), which makes it dangerous. Huge waves, called "meteotsunamis" by meteorologists, can pick up quickly, with little warning. The lake's relative shallowness contributes to its volatility through what's been dubbed the bathtub effect: just as climbing into a full tub makes the water slosh back and forth against its sides, so too can the right wind conditions on Lake Erie produce sudden storm surges. These surges can cause the water to rise twelve feet or more, flooding coastal towns like Port Dover and unexpectedly sweeping people off piers and shorelines.

I alternated between paddling close to land and a few kilometres offshore whenever there was a bay to cut across. Paddling that far from land in a canoe, especially in April when water temperatures are frigid, can be slightly unsettling. But the calm conditions allowed me to make good progress, and I canoed steadily along, following the coastline. Much of it was wooded with the broad-leaved trees of the Carolinian forest. These include rare species found nowhere else in Canada—notably shagbark hickory (the nuts of which are edible), tulip trees (which grow over a hundred feet high), sassafras (the roots were long used to make a spicy beverage), and cucumber magnolia (Canada's only native magnolia). In places, little winding streams trickled into the lake through narrow ravines set amid high bluffs. Along the top of one, I watched a whitetail deer wander among the ash and maple trees, nibbling on the spring buds.

Cottages appeared here and there, often it seemed with Herculean efforts to prevent their lakeshores from eroding into Erie's waters—I was amazed by all manner of breakwalls that lakefront property owners had devised to try to stem the inevitable erosion. These ranged from crude piles of concrete slabs, tractor tires, and construction debris tossed into the lake, to elaborately designed steel and stone barriers and terraces that must have cost a princely sum to erect. In many places, though, I saw that these efforts to stem the lake's natural erosion caused by wave action had been in vain—boathouses, docks, backyard sheds, and in one place someone's unfortunately situated cottage itself, had either plunged over the cliffs into the lake or were on the verge of doing so.

In the afternoon I passed by several little hamlets— Normandale, Fishers Glen, Port Ryerse—and finally the larger town of Port Dover. Most of these communities were established in the late 1700s by Loyalist refugees who, finding themselves on the losing side of the American Revolution, fled to Canada's wilderness to rebuild their lives from scratch. But, being situated on Canada's south coast, they'd found themselves on the front lines of the War of 1812. By the time it was over, nearly all the Canadian villages and towns along the Great Lakes had been pillaged and burned by American armies and raiding parties. One Canadian farmer serving in the local militia had been shot seventeen times, but somehow managed to survive. The lake itself became a battleground, with huge warships prowling Erie's bays, inlets, and islands. The largest naval battle ever fought on freshwater played out on Erie's stormy surface in 1813, and more than one shipwreck from the war still lies on Erie's bottom.

The calm conditions enticed me to keep paddling after dark, with just enough moonlight to see by. Finally, at nine p.m., having canoed about forty kilometres, I found a secluded stretch of wooded shore to make camp on. I pitched my tent on a rocky beach, flipping my canoe over beside it. The stones weren't the softest mattress, but I was tired enough that they felt fine for one night.

3

WIND AND WAVES

I AWOKE BEFORE dawn to get an early start while the lake
was still calm. For breakfast I ate an apple and a granola bar,
then pushed off. Erie seemed almost strangely calm and quiet
in the predawn darkness, with hardly any lights from houses
to break up the view along the shore. But the vast slumbering
waters of the lake felt to me like some sleeping giant, one that
I knew would sooner or later wake up and show all its terrifying fury. In total I had almost two hundred kilometres to travel
along the lake before I could escape down the Niagara River.
So I figured it was best to get as far as I could before facing one
of Erie's gales.

As the sky lightened it revealed threatening grey clouds
gathering on the horizon. I kept paddling, surprised by how
wild the shoreline appeared. Most of Lake Erie is heavily developed with cottages or lakefront homes, but this stretch, it seemed
to me, was utterly deserted. The shore was mostly scrubby and
tangled forest, but I noticed amid the brambles, grapevines,

and cottonwoods several abandoned houses. They were dilapidated and evidently had been unoccupied for some time. In the faint light, drifting alone in my canoe, the sight of these decrepit houses poking out of the woods felt a little eerie.

Soon I became aware of a hum on the horizon, as of machinery, which grew steadily louder as I paddled on, though there was still no sign of anything on shore except bushes and trees. But I now realized where I was and why the houses had been boarded up. I'd reached Nanticoke, an industrial area where the Stelco steelworks and an oil refinery are located. The incessant drone from the factories keeps the shoreline here from development, and those decrepit houses were likely either abandoned for that reason or perhaps bought out by the steelworks as part of a planned future expansion. Ironically, if you could ignore the loud mechanical buzz and whirr of machinery, this stretch of Erie's shoreline was actually quite scenic and pleasing.

Ahead of me loomed a long pier or causeway extending into the lake. The causeway is part of the steelworks, allowing steel and other materials to be loaded offshore onto huge freighter ships for transport. Just now there weren't any ships about, and luckily, I didn't have to paddle all the way offshore to get around the causeway: it had an opening where canoes and small boats could slip under a bridge. A short distance after this was a second industrial port, this time for the oil refinery, where a massive freighter was moored. I sped by it as fast as I could paddle, my fifteen-foot canoe appearing as frail and fragile as an autumn leaf next to the huge, towering steel ship.

My progress improved when a westerly breeze sprang up, giving me a nice tailwind. I unfurled a small sail, shaped like an umbrella, to catch the wind and help drive me forward. Sailing a canoe can be a bit challenging, but the beauty of this little sail was that it didn't require a mast and could simply be lashed with a bit of string tied from the top of the sail to my seat. When the wind shifted, the sail would just flutter and fall back into the canoe. The wind was perfect now, allowing me to cruise nicely, paddling as I went to further increase my speed.

At times I was quite far from land, given that several peninsulas jutted into the lake and I had to round each of them. To do so I'd aim the canoe's bow at the farthest point, then steer for it across the intervening bay. The largest of these bays lay between Nanticoke and Peacock Point. Here I found myself a kilometre and a half offshore, flying along at a good pace under sail. On the distant shore I could see people in their backyards looking and pointing at me as I passed, almost as if the sight of someone sailing a canoe on Lake Erie in April, when the water temperature is frigid and hypothermia only a plunge away, was unusual.

The afternoon brought with it a heavy downpour. I pushed on, but to my consternation found that my rain jacket had soaked right through. The wet afternoon turned into an even wetter evening. It was grey and dismal, with the rain steady and temperatures dropping to a frosty five degrees Celsius. Around eight p.m., having covered about forty-four kilometres, chilled and soaking wet, I landed on a small driftwood-covered beach to make camp. I was on a stretch of secluded shoreline somewhere in Haldimand County, a rural district with lots of old farms. After I put up my tent in a sheltered clump of willows, a warm freeze-dried meal of pasta made me feel better. I crawled inside, exhausted but satisfied.

✳

THE NEXT DAY was very gusty, with sizable waves, more grey skies, and cold temperatures. Still, I managed to paddle onward, sailing between points whenever conditions favoured it. However, because the waves made me unwilling to canoe too far off land, every time I came to a peninsula jutting out into the lake, I'd have to turn sideways to the wind to get around it. This meant dropping sail and carefully riding over the waves as they came in.

When I reached Port Maitland, situated at the mouth of the Grand River, I had a five-kilometre bay to traverse. A light rain was falling, but the wind was just right, so I decided to sail across it. Just as I neared the entrance to the Grand River, off my starboard bow I saw a big commercial fishing vessel rapidly materialize. It was evidently returning to port after going out to set nets, probably for perch. At one time Lake Erie's rich waters supported a huge commercial fishing industry. But by the mid-twentieth century, overfishing and industrial pollution had caused the fishery to collapse. Today, a half-century on, the passage of stricter environmental laws has allowed the lakes to gradually recover, and although the fishery is only a shadow of its heyday, commercial fishing boats again operate.

Across the bay I came to Rock Point, a forested peninsula protected as a provincial park. I'd never been along this shore before and was surprised to find limestone rocks and crystal-clear water. Rising like a ghostly mirage out of the water in the distance stood an old lighthouse. This could only be Mohawk Island Lighthouse, which perches on a rocky isle nearly two kilometres offshore. Built in the mid-1840s, it's an impressive stone structure with a keeper's quarters attached to it, almost resembling a ruined medieval tower. The last lighthouse keeper to reside on the island was Richard Foster, a World War I veteran who was awarded the post in recognition of his war service. In 1932, Foster left the island in a small skiff with his twenty-five-year-old son, James, heading for the mainland. Alas, they never made it—their boat foundered among ice floes, and their bodies were later found washed up. Today the deserted island's only inhabitants are the gulls, terns, and cormorants that nest around the abandoned lighthouse.

By early afternoon the westerly winds had increased, and with the sail, I was flying along at some of the fastest speeds I'd ever reached in a canoe. But given the size of the waves, I only dared do this for short stretches when I was within the relative safety of a sheltered bay, meaning most of the time I was reduced to just paddling. By noon I'd rounded Mohawk Point, carefully avoiding the crashing surf off its tip. Rounding this headland provided me some relief from the waves, and I was again able to raise sail and whip along at a fast clip within another bay.

But after this bay I found myself in increasingly rough conditions. The wind was now really gusting. Given the waves, I thought it wise to switch solely to paddling. The key was to maintain balance and roll along with each incoming swell. This worked well until a larger wave caught me broadside, tossing a spray of cold water into the boat. Realizing the danger, I made a turn for shore and drove hard into a sandy beach.

I hauled my canoe up a safe distance, then looked around. It turned out that I'd landed at Long Beach Conservation Area in Wainfleet, a rural municipality in western Niagara. I pulled the fleece hood up under my jacket and waved my gloved hands around to warm up. The beach backed onto an overgrown hill; once I'd climbed it I could see just how angry Erie looked, with a bitterly cold wind whipping up whitecaps. The park was still closed for the season with just empty campsites and stacked rows of picnic tables.

The thought crossed my mind of making camp here early. But it was still only mid-afternoon. I paced up and down contemplating what to do. Just to the east was a large peninsula, Morgan's Point, extending several kilometres into the lake. On its far shore the lake would be partially sheltered from the fierce westerly winds. The waves ruled out paddling, but I still had my cart, stowed away in the front of the canoe. With it I could wheel my canoe and gear down the road to Morgan's Point, and with any luck, relaunch into the more sheltered waters there. On my past northern adventures I'd relied on a similar tactic when faced with large waves; portaging a short distance to the lee side of big peninsulas was often enough to allow me to continue paddling. Since it worked in the Arctic, I saw no reason why it shouldn't also work here. And looking on the bright side of things, after being cramped in a canoe, my legs could do with a stretch.

After hauling the canoe up the steep hill, I wheeled it across the campground to the road. The cart was now squeaking a bit, presumably from the rain and waves getting into its bearings. Along the road I passed old farms with grazing cows that stared curiously at me, though they said nothing. Beyond the farms I came to the far side of Morgan's Point, which forms part of a bay full of cottages. Luckily, as I'd suspected, the point was large enough to create a windbreak from the howling westerlies. So I unstrapped the canoe, carried it over some rocks down to the water, then repacked it. Although the waves were smaller, for a canoe they were still considerable.

The hardest part was the initial launch through the surf. The key is in the timing: first waiting for a break between waves and then pushing and paddling as fast as possible to get deep enough out. Once I'd managed this, I was able to cautiously continue eastward. The wind chill was below freezing, but my furious paddle strokes kept me warm.

Within a few hours I was battling even larger waves that threatened to spill over my canoe. In desperation I paddled as fast as I could to reach the safety of Port Colborne's harbour. The harbour—formed by a breakwall more than a kilometre long running parallel to the mainland—shields the town from Erie's massive storms. But while the breakwall protects Port Colborne, it has the opposite effect for small boats trying to pass along its outer side: the incoming waves ricochet off the wall, sloshing back out with great violence and creating a vortex of dual wave action, incoming and outgoing, a perfect nightmare for a canoeist. So it was with considerable relief that I reached the harbour, putting to shore without delay on the nearest beach.

Port Colborne is the southern terminus of the Welland Canal, which connects Lake Erie to Lake Ontario, allowing ships to bypass Niagara Falls. Fronting the western and inner parts of the harbour are nice old houses, while tucked in the eastern corner is a marina protected by a second, inner breakwall. But dominating the entire scene is the mighty ADM flour mill, a massive grey industrial building that looms high over the little city beside it.

My immediate problem was finding somewhere to camp. I'd landed on a narrow beach backed by a steel wall. It felt much too exposed to camp here, which in any case would be brazenly trespassing in full view. I felt if it came down to it, since I couldn't put up my tent, I'd just have to sleep in my canoe. In the meantime, I sat and rested against the wall. The inclement weather—the rain had picked up and the wind was still relentless—made this unpleasant. The thought of my nice snug tent became irresistible, and I decided I'd have to find somewhere more secluded to make a proper camp.

I examined my map to see if I could come up with any ideas. Until the wind slackened, I was trapped inside the harbour. But I noticed on the map that a small creek drained into the harbour's northwest corner. This creek led inland to a forest, which, given the circumstances, seemed appealing for a night's stay. I hauled my canoe back to the water's edge and shoved off, heading for the creek's mouth.

It took only a short paddle to reach the creek's outlet, but as soon as I did, my hopes were dashed. Access to the creek was shut off by a floodgate barrier beneath a bridge, and any thought of just camping on the near side of the outlet was ruled out by signs stating "No Camping," which I took to mean camping was prohibited.

It was getting dark, and I was running out of options. I shivered in the wind and rain as I glanced about, trying to think up some new plan. On the far side of the harbour lay the marina, grain elevators, and an overgrown industrial area

that looked semi-abandoned. But, given the gathering darkness, I was reluctant to paddle across the commercial shipping
lanes—where a giant freighter entering or exiting the canal
could run over my tiny canoe in the dark without ever so much
as noticing. The marina seemed to be my only choice.

It was about a kilometre from the creek's mouth to the
marina entrance and I wasted no time getting underway,
paddling hard in the twilight. Even inside the breakwall the
westerly wind remained fierce, and it helped drive me along
at a rapid pace. The light was growing fainter, making it hard
to see. My eyes were fixed on the twinkling marina lights
in the distance, trying to make out if there was anywhere I
might camp.

Then something loomed out of the water right in my
path—a submerged concrete dock. I swung my paddle forward
to stop myself from smashing into it. Furious backpaddling
counteracted the strong wind and my previous momentum,
and just in the nick of time I executed a tight turn to avoid the
flooded structure. The sharp turn drove the canoe into the shallows, bringing me to shore. Such a near miss suggested it might
be unwise to keep paddling in the dark. But I hadn't reached
the marina and all around me were houses.

A small beach ran along the shore. Camping here might
work, but of course I couldn't camp in someone's backyard
without permission. Just one house over from where I'd landed
I saw some canoes and kayaks stored beside a grove of trees.
This seemed encouraging. I walked along the beach, across the
backyard, and around to a side door. It was perhaps regret-
table that, not having washed for three days, I looked a bit

dishevelled. But there was nothing to be done; I'd just have to knock, introduce myself, and ask permission to camp on their beach for the night.

I gave the door a few loud raps and waited.

4

BREAKWATER

A FLOOD OF light from the door opening caused me to blink as my eyes adjusted. To my surprise, two young men appeared who didn't look much older than nineteen or twenty.

"Hello," I said.

"Hello," they said back.

I was about to say I was canoeing to the Arctic and looking for a place to camp, but then I thought that might make me seem crazy, so I kept things brief. "Sorry to bother you, but I've canoed a long way. I set off from Long Point three days ago, and this is as far as I can get tonight. It's too dark for me to go any farther and I have nowhere else to go. Could I camp on your beach for the night?"

"Oh," they said, looking surprised. "Probably that's no problem," one of them added. "I'll get my dad and ask. But come in while you wait."

"Thank you, but my boots are muddy and I'm all wet."

But they insisted I come in anyway, and since I couldn't refuse their hospitality, I stepped in the doorway and remained on the mat. In a few minutes three other people materialized. This it turned out was their parents Brad and Jillian, as well as their uncle Jeff. They were all very warm and friendly, offering me dinner, which of course I politely declined (I'd already eaten a couple power bars that evening) and explained that all I needed was a campsite. This was granted to me, along with anything else I might need—food, water, batteries, a hot shower. Such hospitality to a total stranger who'd just knocked on their door I found quite surprising and heartening. It seemed I could hardly have chosen a better place to land.

Other than the campsite, I declined all their kind offers, as I already felt bad for interrupting their evening, and generally, once I set off on an adventure, I prefer to avoid outside distractions or comforts, as I find it detracts from my mental routine. In the dark I set up my tent on the beach. It was a cold night with the temperature hovering around freezing. The rain alternated with wet snow. One of the sons, Daniel, came down and showed me an outlet where I could charge any electronics. But with the wet weather I thought it best not to. Brad also came down and again asked if I needed anything.

"Your beach is all I need," I said. "I'm already in your debt for it."

Brad assured me that it was nothing, and that they were happy to have me camp there. I learned that he was a recently retired geologist, and that we were familiar with some of the same remote northern locations. We talked about this for some time, but I was exhausted, and hoped to get underway before dawn to take advantage of whatever relative calm there might be. Brad said he'd be up to see me off.

Despite the cold, I slept quite well on the beach beneath the cottonwoods. The temperature dropped below freezing, turning the rain to snow. By four-thirty a.m. I was awake and packing up my snow-covered tent in the dark. My fingers grew numb as I took down the drenched tent and rolled it up tightly. Brad came down from the house, carrying with him a camera and a telephoto lens. He was, it turned out, a talented photographer and wanted to get a few photos of me setting off.

It was still dark as I pushed my canoe into the water, with a moderate onshore wind and a steady snowfall. I turned and thanked Brad and his family once more for their hospitality, feeling very fortunate that I'd happened upon their beach. Then I stepped into the canoe and set off. In the distance, gleaming faintly through the falling snow, were the lights of the flour mill. I started by heading toward it, then angled toward the shipping lane and the opening in the breakwall. Noisy seagulls were flying about.

The gap in the breakwall is about two hundred metres wide, with a traditional-looking lighthouse marking one side and a smaller, automated beacon atop a short tower marking the other. The commercial shipping lane runs through this small channel, allowing the big freighters to come and go from the Welland Canal—and to round the breakwall, I had no choice but to pass through it too. Such large ships inevitably have blind spots that would make it difficult to see a little canoe far below their decks. The freighters too, despite their size, move surprisingly fast. Even if a freighter managed to spot me, such massive ships can't turn on a dime or stop abruptly, so it likely wouldn't make any difference.

These cheerful thoughts were on my mind as I paddled through the snow toward the harbour's outlet. By the time I neared it the sky had lightened into a grey morning, with a chilling wind. My pace had been brisk since pushing off from Brad's place, but now that I was nearing the shipping lane, I let up—to make sure the coast was clear and to catch my breath for a final burst of energy. Glancing up the canal, I saw no sign of any oncoming ships, but the giant outline of the mill partly obstructed my view. Moored on the other side of the canal was a rusted old freighter that looked decommissioned.

With no ships in sight I swung my paddle through the frigid water toward the shipping lane. Hard strokes propelled me across the channel. A few more strokes and I was safely across, breathing a deep sigh of relief.

It took a moment before I became conscious of a more perilous situation. Although the lake had seemed calm from the beach, once I'd left the protection of the breakwall, I was surprised to find large swells. Port Colborne lies near Lake Erie's eastern end, meaning the prevailing winds have almost the entire expanse of the lake over which to gather force; even a relatively light wind is often enough to generate sizable swells. The danger I found myself in only slowly dawned on me. The breakwall, which I'd counted on as a possible refuge in the event of trouble, wasn't what I expected: it was a concrete, slippery sloped barrier washed by big rolling waves—a death trap.

Since the breakwall offered no refuge, the nearest place where I could now safely land was Nickel Beach, more than a kilometre and a half away. A lot can happen in a kilometre and a half in the best of times, but with the snow coming down thickly and the swells causing my stomach to feel a bit like it does on a roller coaster, the situation was uncomfortable. My instincts were to hug the breakwall and follow it back to land—but these instincts were wrong. The ricocheting effect of the waves hitting the concrete barrier then rushing back out made the water nearest the breakwall too rough, knocking my canoe around and threatening to throw me into the freezing water. I had to cautiously steer farther out into the lake's grey immensity.

When a swell would come I'd ride up with it, then sweep back down, paddling breathlessly in between. Riding up on yet another swell, from the crest of it I could see whitecaps breaking on the distant shore, which appeared hopelessly far away. Even on a warm summer's day it would have been unsettling to navigate such large swells so far from land, but on a snowy day in April it was terrifying. If I went into the water, the situation would be extremely dangerous. Given the frosty conditions, hypothermia would set in rapidly. If someone had chanced to be out on shore (unlikely in the bitter weather of early morning), I'd be frozen long before they spotted me through the falling snow. There was nothing to do but summon up all the ability I could muster to keep my canoe upright on the giant swells—just hoping that a larger one wouldn't swamp over the stern. Above all, I tried to keep my canoe straight and not allow it to turn into the oncoming swells.

Despite the cold and snow, my palms were sweaty and my heart was almost in my throat. To encourage myself, I tried to think of all the other times I'd paddled waves this large far from land—but I couldn't recall any. When all else fails, I find talking to my canoe helps. So I assured the canoe not to worry and that everything would be fine. The force of the swells was at least driving us toward the distant beach. After few more tense minutes, I could nearly breathe easy. I surfed a wave into shore, then leapt out into the shallows.

In the distance I saw an SUV drive up and a man emerge with a tripod and a camera. It was Brad, come to capture more photos of me. He parked down the beach and began walking in my direction. As I waited I turned to look back at the lake— and made up my mind that I never wished to repeat such a terrifying experience. When Brad came up I told him about the challenge of paddling around the breakwall and asked if swells like that were typical here. He said they were, and warned me about Point Abino, the biggest peninsula jutting into the whole eastern end of the lake. It was almost always rough out there, Brad said, and in a whole year there might be only a handful of days when conditions were calm enough to get out to Point Abino even in a motorboat. This didn't sound terribly encouraging. I asked if he knew what the wind forecast was for today. Gusts were rising to forty-five kilometres by mid-morning. For a canoeist, anything above twenty-five kilometres can be a serious challenge. However, my immediate concern was the next point on the lake, which I could see in the distance.

"Well," I said, looking out at the whitecaps, "I don't think I can round those points in these waves. I'll have to wait for the wind to die down. Perhaps this evening it'll be calm enough for me to continue."

Brad said he had to take off, but that he might come back later and bring me some Tim Hortons if I were still around. I said I may or may not be, depending on what the wind brought. I watched as Brad drove off back down the beach. The snow had turned to a drizzling rain.

Given the weather, it seemed the best thing I could do was find a spot to rest, saving my energy for a hard paddle should conditions improve later. The beach rose to some sand dunes and a forest. I hauled my canoe to the foot of a dune and then set off into the woods to see what I might find. A short distance in was a clearing that looked as if it'd been used before as a campsite. However, as I approached closer to examine it, I noticed dozens of discarded needles strewn all over the ground, and they weren't the kind my grandmother uses for her sewing projects.

The idea of resting here didn't seem as appealing anymore, and thinking of the long miles that lay ahead of me and the inevitable delays I'd be sure to encounter, I began to feel eager to push on while it was still possible. The wind forecast, after all, might only get worse, and I had no wish to be stranded here for days. The cold and rainy weather, too, was an extra motivation to keep moving.

So I fetched the cart and set it up. I wasn't sure I'd be able to wheel it over sand, but it turned out that by sticking close to the water, where the sand was wet and hardpacked, it rolled along nicely. After about a kilometre the beach grew smaller, with rocks on the left and surf reaching ever higher on the right. Finally, I came to a spot where the rocks blocked all passage by land while the lake itself was still too rough to paddle. But I'd noticed a path leading up a steep, sandy hill. Just on the other side of that hill, according to the map, was Lakeshore Road. If I could get through the woods to it, I could follow it past the stormy point and hopefully be able to resume paddling on its more sheltered eastern shore.

Leaving my canoe behind, I went ahead to scout things out. The trail wasn't marked, but it was well-worn, and I felt optimistic about dragging the canoe up it and through the forest. I'd have to take the backpack and barrel separately to lessen the load, but with a bit of effort it looked like I'd be able to get through. Still, it seemed prudent to make sure the trail led where I hoped it did. Not wanting to leave my canoe unattended for too long, I jogged off at a brisk pace, ducking under big oaks and beeches, then down the far side. Through the woods I could see the winding road ahead. As I scampered down the steep hill toward it, I suddenly came right up against a chain-link fence topped with barbed wire.

There was no gate or opening, but I followed the fence to see where it might lead. It came to a right angle, then turned up a driveway along a wooded neighbouring property with a house on it. Where the fence ran along this property there wasn't any barbed wire—so if I could carry my canoe and gear here, I might be able to toss them over it. Then all I'd have to do was climb the fence and resume portaging on the other side.

Just then three men emerged from behind the house along a narrow path leading to the driveway.

"Hello," I called.

Turning around, they looked surprised to see someone in the woods on the other side of the fence. I asked if one of them was the property owner. A man in a plaid jacket answered that it was his house. The other two looked like construction workers, and it seemed as if they were building a new shed or a deck in the backyard. I apologized for bothering them, but quickly explained that I was canoeing through Lake Erie all the way out to the Gulf of St. Lawrence and then heading north to Labrador, and asked if I could have permission to climb his fence to finish my portage.

The three of them stared at me for a moment. I expected to be told that this wasn't a public trail and to beat it. Then the owner said, "No problem at all. But there's no need to climb the fence. I'll let you use my staircase down to the beach. It'll be much easier."

After this generous offer, the owner introduced himself as Ed. He was curious about my journey and asked me quite a few questions about it. I appreciated his kindness and thanked him for it. Then I climbed down his high stairs to the beach far below and fetched my gear. It took four loads to bring everything up the narrow, winding staircase, which ran down the cliff overlooking the lake. Ed kindly insisted on giving me a hand with the canoe. I assured him this wasn't necessary, but in truth it would have been a challenge balancing the canoe over my head up the narrow staircase, so I was grateful for his help. When all the loads were up, I reassembled everything on the cart, thanked Ed profusely for his assistance, and then wheeled the assemblage down his steep driveway to the road.

Luckily it was a quiet road without much traffic. Winding through tall trees and old lakefront houses, I found it to be rather peaceful, at least compared to my experiences beyond the breakwall. The rain had let up somewhat, with just a sporadic sprinkle, though it was still cold. I soon came to a side road and turned right on it. This took me back to the lake, which still wasn't calm, with the icy wind kindling whitecaps. As much as I was reluctant to portage farther, after my experience paddling the giant swells in the snow, I felt a bit like a cat that had used up eight of its nine lives. So I decided to keep portaging until conditions improved.

Portaging can be wearisome, but I told myself that, on the bright side, at least I could explore a few places I'd never seen before. Just up from the beach were old, picturesque stone arches marking the entrance to an unpaved "fire lane," one of several narrow private roads that skirt along the wooded Lake Erie shore in these parts. I began pushing my canoe down it.

It took me through a beautiful old forest with a timeless feel, a place of ancient oaks, maples, and hickories, with grand old houses or cottages spaced out here and there through the woods. The first hints of spring greenery were just emerging from the forest floor. I followed this enchanting little lane for several kilometres; eventually it took me alongside an old farm and some tall rushes and thicker forest.

I heard a vehicle approaching; up ahead around a bend came an old Ford pickup truck in what seemed like excellent condition. Behind the wheel was a white-haired old gentleman who looked nearly eighty. I waved to be polite as I pushed the canoe along, and he waved back. Then he stopped and rolled down the window.

"I've lived on this road for thirty years," he said, smiling, "and this is the first time I've ever seen anyone push a canoe down it."

"Oh," I said. "It's a great cart. Makes it really easy to push, if you've been thinking of getting one."

"Where are you heading?"

"Just up there a way." I gestured vaguely.

He nodded cheerfully at this and wished me well, before driving off.

A little farther on I came to Pinecrest Road, which led me back to the lake. But the waves were still fierce, so after debating a bit, I decided there was nothing for it but to keep pushing my canoe a bit farther. Not long afterward a red truck passed me and slowed down. Behind the wheel was an older, grey-moustached man in a ball cap.

"What are you doing?" he asked.

"Portaging my canoe."

"Where?"

"Down the road."

"Where are you going?"

"Just up there," I said, with another casual gesture, "to where I can put into the lake."

"Where'd you come from?"

"Long Point."

"Long Point?!" he exclaimed.

"Yes."

"That's a rough lake out there," said the man.

I nodded.

"I worked on a tugboat, and I know how bad Erie gets. Storms pick up quick here."

I nodded again.

"Where are you heading?" he asked.

"The Niagara River," I replied.

"That's where you're stopping?"

"No, I'm going to Lake Ontario, then the St. Lawrence River, and then working my way north to Labrador and the Arctic."

He stared at me as if I were crazy. After a few seconds he slowly shook his head. I expected him to try to dissuade me, but instead he surprised me with his response. "All I can say," he said after a pause, "is there anything I can do to help you?"

This cheered me, and I thanked the driver, but said I already had everything I needed. He wished me well with real warmth, waved, then drove off. A short time later I was still pushing my canoe along when I heard another vehicle approaching. Turning to look, I was surprised to see the same moustached man who'd stopped earlier.

"Look," he said through the open window, "are you *sure* you don't need anything?"

I assured him I was well-equipped.

"I can bring you a hot meal, or anything else you might need. I admire what you're doing. Reminds me of what I wished I'd done when I was young."

"I appreciate your offer, but I've got plenty of food."

"It's awfully cold out. I live only a short distance from here. I can give you a ride. Get some hot food and shower, and if you want, I can drop you right back here afterwards."

"That's a very kind offer, but I'm keen to keep going," I explained. (The fact is, if you start stopping like this only four days into a 3,400-kilometre journey, you'll never make it.)

The man nodded as if he expected as much. "Well," he said, "good luck."

I thanked him, and he waved and drove off once more. He had in fact helped me—to receive such well wishes and kindness felt encouraging, like new wind in my sails.

Just up ahead I came to Centennial Park, which was deserted. By now it was late afternoon, and although the wind was still strong, the waves looked manageable, at least as far as Point Abino. So I relaunched my canoe, paddled hard to get through the surf, then continued along the shoreline. Luckily, it was mostly beaches, which made things easier since there wasn't a ricochet effect like with a breakwall.

However, as I neared Point Abino, the waves became rougher. Mindful of Brad's warning, I landed on the beach near where the point begins. Here, I'd have no choice but to portage again to get around the point's storm-tossed waters, where tragically, many mariners have drowned. During the great storm of 1913, which generated hurricane-force winds, an American ship stationed off Point Albino, *Buffalo* (LV-82), sank with the loss of all six crew members.

I loaded my canoe on the cart and then pushed it along the shoulder of a road leading inland. The Point itself is remarkably wild, with old-growth forest containing many rare and endangered species. There are no trails or roads across it, so I'd have to make quite a detour to reach its far side.

This took me a couple of hours to complete, and by the time I was pushing my canoe down Point Abino Road the sun was sinking below the horizon on another cold, grey evening. The atmosphere of this country road was very much to my taste.

There were swampy old forests with the haunting calls of owls echoing out of them, and I passed several abandoned houses, overgrown and surrounded by ancient, creaking trees. Why these houses were abandoned I had no idea, but they certainly did appear a bit spooky surrounded by swamp woods on a chill night with the sun going down.

Late in the evening I reached the eastern shore of Point Abino and the sheltered waters of Crystal Beach. This beautiful beach is surrounded by grand old lakefront homes—mostly, so the locals say, owned by wealthy Americans as summer retreats. In any case, I found the place utterly deserted, as it was still only April 28 and the season doesn't typically begin until the May long weekend. I would have asked permission, but there was no one to ask, with not a light on in sight. So I simply launched my canoe into the quiet waters of the sheltered bay, paddled halfway across, and had my pick of anywhere I liked on the beach. In the darkness I set up my tent and crawled inside, exhausted.

The next morning I was up before dawn in the bitter cold. Overnight the temperature had plunged to minus nine. The sand had frozen as hard as cement; to extract my tent pegs I had to yank with considerable force. I bundled up in extra layers, with warm gloves and the second, warmer jacket I'd packed. Then I launched my canoe into the lake, which thankfully was relatively calm. A crescent moon hung low on the horizon, which still remained visible even after the sun rose in a purplish-red glow. The beauty of the scene felt like something out of another time and place.

I was determined to reach the Niagara River this morning, and therefore paddled as hard as I could. The lake stayed mostly calm, but there were still whitecaps off the rocky points that I had to gingerly navigate, keeping a sharp eye out for hidden rocks. A few Bonaparte's gulls were drifting on the waves. As I zipped along about a kilometre from land, I saw a man with a camera on the distant shore taking photos of me. I wondered if it was Brad.

Five hours of hard paddling brought me to the end of Lake Erie, with the city of Buffalo, New York, on the horizon. I felt relieved to be bidding goodbye to Erie, and all things considered, counted myself as having got off lucky paddling its moody waters. But I couldn't breathe too easy: new challenges were waiting ahead. Already a strong, swift current was pulling my canoe along—I'd reached the mighty Niagara River.

5

NIAGARA RIVER

THE SUN GLISTENED off the rippling waters of the Niagara River as I entered into it. In the distance loomed the high span of the Peace Bridge, linking Canada to New York State. On the right shore were Buffalo's skyscrapers, while on the left were parkland and the gleaming cannons and battlements of historic Fort Erie, a stone fortress with a long, bloodsoaked history.

Built in 1764 by the British army, Fort Erie was originally a remote outpost, designed to assert control of the Great Lakes in a region that had only recently seen the end of fighting between the French and British empires. It remained a small post until the eruption of the War of 1812 made it a battleground. In the first year of the war the Americans launched a night attack below the fort, capturing two warships anchored there. Over the following two years, raids and counterraids, cannon fire, and attacks on ships became part of life along the river. The fighting reached a climax in the summer of 1814 when a large American invasion force captured the fort. This provoked a protracted counter siege, with British and Canadian troops attempting to retake it. As winter approached, the Americans—cut off and with their ranks decimated—stuffed the fort with gunpowder, blew it up, and retreated back to Buffalo. An uneasy peace treaty ended the war the following month.

Fort Erie, however, hadn't seen the last of its fighting days. It lay in crumbling ruins for another half century until in 1866 it was suddenly seized by a second invasion force from across the river. This was no official army, but rather a motley battalion of Irish rebels, called Fenians, who had conceived the somewhat fantastical plan of conquering parts of Canada, then holding it ransom in exchange for Ireland's independence from the British Empire. They seized the old ruined fort as a makeshift head-quarters, but were soon surrounded by Canadian militia. A brief but bloody battle followed nearby at Ridgeway, resulting in the defeat of the Fenians and their plans.

Today the fort has been restored and part of the original woods and battlefield surrounding it have been preserved. But much of the rest of the once blood-soaked grounds is now made up of neighbourhoods. The fort's manager, Travis, was a friend of mine. I thought I might see him as I drifted by, but the only one around was a lone fisherman casting on the limestone rocks below the fort. He told me he was after steelheads and salmon, but as of yet, hadn't met with much luck.

The swift current and my own strokes rapidly propelled me downstream toward the Peace Bridge. I'd heard that canoeing under the bridge is dangerous. And it's true that if you drive over it and happen to look over the side, you'll see swirling eddies and a menacing-looking concrete ice breaker. But some seventeen years earlier I'd walked along the path under the bridge, and I remembered thinking the current didn't look that bad. On the other hand, I hadn't seen it since, and there was a small part of me that hesitated to trust the hazy memory of my teenage judgment on so important a matter. To be safe, I intended to land on shore above the bridge, then hike ahead to scout things out.

But as I whipped along on the fast current, it became apparent that there was a slight flaw in this otherwise fine plan. I'd overlooked that downstream of the fort the riverbanks have been built up into stone walls. The walls meant I couldn't get out, and given the strong current, I couldn't turn back—I was trapped. With the river sucking me along, I now had no choice but to run the rapids under the bridge. I supressed my fears and told myself to trust my hazy teenage judgment after all.

The bridge was fast approaching, so I shifted to a kneeling position. This concentrates the weight lower in the canoe, making it more stable and giving the paddler greater control. Then I used my paddle to slow the canoe down—when entering rapids, there's a natural urge to just keep paddling, but paddling increases your speed, making it harder to react to unseen rocks or other hazards.

Even with my polarized sunglasses the glaring sun made it difficult to distinguish exactly what lay up ahead. I was sticking to the left shore, but it appeared there might be rocks, so I angled outward a little, though I wanted to remain on the near side of the bridge's first giant pillar, where the river was roaring by. Some rapids materialized before the bridge, but these

I paddled through without trouble. Once through them, I saw that the current under the bridge itself, while fast, wasn't rough, and my apprehensions evaporated.

As I zoomed under the huge span of the bridge, I noticed some people on shore above the stone wall taking photos. It was my friend Travis, the manager of Old Fort Erie, and two of his colleagues, and beside them with his camera was Brad. Below the bridge I managed to swing into shore, spinning my canoe upstream and grasping onto an iron ladder, where it was possible to brace myself in the current and talk to them. They warned me that downriver was a waterfall. I assured them I'd heard of it. More ominously, Brad said he'd heard the wind was bad down by Grand Island—where the river widens—and that apparently someone he knew had trouble there even in a motor-boat. I thanked them for the warning, and then, not fancying hanging onto a rail for much longer, shoved off and continued downriver.

The wind was gusting, but within the river's relatively nar-row confines and on its swift current, my progress remained rapid. A couple of kilometres down from the Peace Bridge is a rusty old train bridge that spans the waterway. I passed under it and kept going, until I approached Grand Island, which is part of the United States. Here the river is nearly two kilometres wide, and there were strong cross gusts that slowed my prog-ress. The wind was actually driving me into the Canadian shore, which in this section is somewhat marshy, with cattails, fallen trees, and cormorants. Wading in the shallows were also blue herons, attracted by the river's rich fish life. The current close to shore here is minimal, so that I'd have to either paddle far

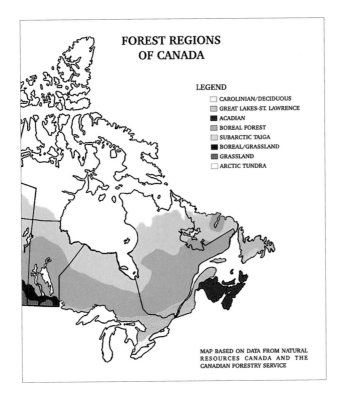

FOREST REGIONS OF CANADA

LEGEND
- CAROLINIAN/DECIDUOUS
- GREAT LAKES-ST. LAWRENCE
- ACADIAN
- BOREAL FOREST
- SUBARCTIC TAIGA
- BOREAL/GRASSLAND
- GRASSLAND
- ARCTIC TUNDRA

MAP BASED ON DATA FROM NATURAL RESOURCES CANADA AND THE CANADIAN FORESTRY SERVICE

Map of major forest regions or ecozones in central/eastern Canada. My journey spanned five distinct natural regions from the Carolinian forests of southernmost Ontario to the Arctic tundra.

Day 1, April 24: Pushing my canoe down the road at Long Point. "The cottage was about a kilometre from the nearest water access, so I'd strapped my canoe and gear onto a small collapsible cart and wheeled it down the road." (photo credit: Alexandria Shoalts)

Setting off for the Arctic on Lake Erie. The Old Cut Lighthouse is visible behind me.

Sandhill cranes stalking through Turkey Point marsh. Like peregrine falcons and other birds, the cranes migrate each spring to the Arctic.

Heading beyond the breakwall at Port Colborne on a brisk April morning. This photo was captured by Brad Wood on a telephoto lens from more than a kilometre away. (photo credit: Brad Wood)

Thinking out my next move on Nickel Beach in Port Colborne after rounding the breakwall. (photo credit: Brad Wood)

Paddling on Lake Erie with wind turbines in New York State behind me.
(photo credit: Brad Wood)

Canoeing through some rough water just before the Peace Bridge on the Niagara River.
(photo credit: Brad Wood)

Portaging my canoe around Niagara Falls early in the morning.

Making camp in the woods by the Burlington Skyway. The Skyway is the second bridge visible in the background. The nearer one is the lift bridge over the canal that leads into Hamilton Harbour.

Paddling through the Toronto Islands.

"I also spotted crouching along the shore a dexterous raccoon hunting for frogs or fish. Many times when paddling wild rivers I've observed raccoons out in daylight, balancing on rocks midstream hunting fish, and I always thought these wild raccoons differed a great deal from their urban counterparts."

Sunset over the Thousand Islands on the St. Lawrence River.

One of many freighters I encountered on the St. Lawrence and Great Lakes. Avoiding them proved a major concern.

Camping in a little clump of forest beside the Jacques Cartier Bridge in Montreal.

Paddling through the swamp labyrinth. "Even the muskrats, I noticed, when they needed a break from the water, climbed the trees—something I'd never seen before."

out to the centre of the river to take advantage of it or make do without current by hugging the shoreline. As it was, I thought it prudent to stay close to shore.

Another sixteen kilometres of paddling and I could hear a distant roar: *Niagara Falls.* The current had increased perceptibly, although the wind, luckily, had died away. My plan was to reach Navy Island, a thickly wooded, uninhabited island only four and a half kilometres from the brink of the Horseshoe Falls. I figured this lonely island would be the perfect spot to spend the night undisturbed.

Continuing close to the Canadian shore I spotted the island. It looked somewhat forbidding, a slice of forested wilderness with high banks in midstream. Nevertheless, I turned my canoe from the mainland and aimed toward it. The current, as one might guess, was strong and pushed my canoe downriver as I paddled across. It was an uneasy feeling knowing that just downstream was Niagara Falls—I could see a plume of mist rising from the drop. The swirls and eddies were everywhere in the middle of the river, and although I was paddling hard, the current was still sucking me in the falls' direction. If I broke a paddle, let it slip out of my grasp, or suffered some muscle spasm or cramp, things would be bad indeed. Something like this actually happened in 1960 when a motorboat near here experienced engine trouble. On board were three people. Terror-stricken, they were sucked inexorably toward the thundering brink. As they neared it, the boat overturned in the rapids and all three went into the surging water. Tourists on shore managed to pluck one of them to safety, but the other two—a man and a boy—plunged over the falls. The man drowned, but miraculously the boy survived.

The current drove me three hundred metres downriver of where I'd originally aimed, but I managed to land on the island's steep shoreline around its midway point. A high embankment cloaked in thorn bushes greeted me. I'd have to scale the thorny embankment to make camp, but first it seemed prudent to tie my canoe to a sturdy tree. Otherwise, if it slipped loose and got sucked over the falls, I'd be stranded. Afterward I scampered up the bank to explore the woods.

Isolated by the river's swift current and left undeveloped, the island felt like a sort of time capsule, or to my imagination, almost like some enchanted isle that offered a rare glimpse of what southern Ontario must have looked like centuries ago. There were grand old oak trees, shagbark hickories, creaking sugar maples, giant black walnuts, and towering dead ashes. Wandering alone among these ancient trees in the fading light, with the murmur of the river all around, my mind drifted over this storied place.

When rebellion swept Upper Canada in 1837, the island became the hideout of the rebel leader William Lyon Mackenzie. From the island, Mackenzie and his followers proclaimed the Republic of Canada, hoisting up a new flag for the country and denouncing the British monarchy. Skirmishes and battles followed in the closest thing Canada has ever had to a civil war. When Loyalist forces learned of the whereabouts of Mackenzie's secret hideout, they planned to attack and capture Mackenzie's ship, *The Caroline*. After a brief skirmish the ship was captured, towed to the middle of the river, and lit on fire. Then in a spectacular scene tourists would have loved, the current carried the burning ship over the falls.

Soon after, Mackenzie was forced to abandon the island and his rebellion collapsed.

With my fishing rod, I caught a rainbow trout just off the island's shore and had it for dinner over a fire, cooking it on a green stick. As I sat huddled next to the flickering firelight, watching the shadows dance among the big oaks encircling my campsite, visions of the past seemed to kindle up before me. Camped out alone on the island, I felt almost like a rebel of old.

※

I WOKE BEFORE dawn, tense with anticipation. My plan was to paddle across the river in the dark, land on the Canadian shore, and then, using the aluminum cart, push my canoe past the falls and whirlpool rapids before most tourists were astir. I didn't want to attract attention to myself if I could avoid it, as that would cause delays.

With the aid of a flashlight I dismantled my tent, then climbed through the woods and brambles back to the water's edge. Once the canoe was packed I shoved off into the dark, paddling hard to overcome the current sucking me in the falls' direction. It was a little nerve-racking, but I had excellent motivation not to allow myself to drift downstream. My fast strokes drove the canoe back across the river. It was still dark when I neared the mainland, but instead of landing, I pivoted the canoe. It seemed safe to go just a bit farther, which would shorten the lengthy portage.

I had to be cautious, as near the shore were submerged rocks that could tip me into the river if I slammed into one.

Meanwhile the roar of the falls grew louder and louder. Immediately above the falls is a one-kilometre stretch of some of the most violent rapids on earth, a furious vortex of surging water. But luckily, I didn't have to worry about them, since up from these dangerous rapids is the hydro intake, and if I missed my landing spot, I'd be sucked into these giant turbines long before even reaching the rapids.

When through the gloom I discerned the mouth of the Chippawa River—a small tributary joining the Niagara—I knew I'd reached the last safe place to get out. I canoed along-side the wooded shoreline, then jumped onto the rocks, pulling the canoe up securely. Just on the other side of the trees was the Niagara Parkway, which winds along the water, and on its far side were spacious houses. But this early in the morning the road was quiet, with no one around as I set up my cart in the dark. I took a little extra care in strapping the canoe on and loading the backpack, barrel, and some freshwater I was carrying just right. This was going to be a long portage after all, and I didn't want to have any unnecessary delays. In total, to safely bypass the hydro intake, the falls, as well as the Niagara Gorge and its famous whirlpool, I'd have to portage thirteen kilometres to Queenston.

I began by wheeling my canoe along a narrow walking path that follows the river. There was a time when portaging around the falls was a common occurrence, but it'd probably been two hundred years since someone had last done so. Prior to the con-struction of the first Welland Canal in the 1820s, anyone in a boat or canoe travelling from Lake Ontario to Lake Erie, or vice versa, had no choice but to bypass the falls and rapids on

NIAGARA RIVER | 53

foot. Originally this was done by a simple path through the giant old-growth forest that once towered alongside the river, bathed by the eternal mist of the falls, which creates a micro-climate of rich rainforest. The advent of the canal in the early 1800s, with its systems of locks, allowed for a much quicker, easier, and safer passage for boats travelling between the lakes. (If you're wondering why I didn't take the canal, it's for commercial shipping traffic and motorboats only—my little canoe would easily be run over by a freighter in its narrow confines.) Today, more than two and a half centuries later, the road is still called the Portage Road, but now it's used by motor vehicles rather than canoeists.

I'd gone about two kilometres along the trail, dawn breaking, when a police officer drove by. I hoped he wouldn't notice anything unusual, but he did, and pulled over. His vehicle indicated that he was Niagara Parks Police, which are Canada's second oldest police force, formed in 1887 by the provincial government of Ontario to police the Niagara Parks.

"What are you doing?" asked the officer through his window.

"Portaging around the falls."

He looked at me suspiciously. "You're not going to try putting into the rapids above the falls? Going over them?"

I half laughed at this, though it was true that past daredevils had attempted to paddle the falls, which had never ended well. "No," I said, "that's the exact opposite of what I'm trying to do. I'm on land because I don't want to go over the falls."

"Where are you heading?"

"I have to get to Queenston, where I can put back into the river below the gorge."

He seemed surprised. "Do you know how far that is?"

"Thirteen kilometres."

"That's a long way."

"Well, I'm heading to the Gulf of St. Lawrence so it doesn't seem that long to me."

"What? How are you going to get to Queenston from here?" he asked again.

"Isn't this path paved the whole way? That makes it easy. The cart takes most of the weight—all I have to do is push." I could see him debating in his mind, so I sensed that I'd better offer more of an explanation. "That's why I'm here early. I want to get this portage done as early as I can before anyone else is around."

"All right," he said, "I can see you have a plan. I'll get out of your way and let you get on with it. And I'll tell you what: I'll radio all the other units along the Parkway to let them know you're coming so no one else bothers you."

"Thank you," I said.

He waved, and then headed off toward the falls. I kept pushing, eager to make up for lost time. A narrow footbridge led me across part of the river adjacent to the Ontario Power Company Gate House. Luckily my canoe was just slender enough to squeeze onto the footbridge. I next passed Dufferin Park, where Canada geese and mergansers huddled in its sheltered waters, and over a second footbridge. Here I had my first good look at the raging rapids up close—I couldn't help but look on them with fear and awe. In 1990, an American kayaker, Jesse Sharp, attempted to paddle the rapids and then over the Horseshoe Falls. His body was never recovered, but his dented kayak washed up below the brink. Five years later another daredevil, Robert Overacker, came up with the novel idea of running the rapids on a Jet Ski and then deploying a parachute as he plunged over the falls. It sounded fine on paper, but when he soared over the brink, the parachute failed to open and he drowned.

Midstream in the violent water, stranded on some rocks, was an old iron boat—a scow that ran aground back in 1918. The terrifying incident occurred when the eighty-foot-long boat broke free of a tow rope and was sucked downstream into the rapids. On board were two men, clinging for dear life as the boat rushed toward the falls, tossing wildly in the roaring water. Luckily the boat caught on some rocks less than eight hundred metres from the brink. For seventeen harrowing hours the men were trapped, fearing that at any moment the powerful current might knock the boat loose. They were rescued when a grappling gun shot a rope out to them, allowing them to cross on an improvised harness. A century later, the rusted-out boat is still stuck in the rapids above the falls, just waiting for a day when a big storm knocks it over.

Still wheeling along the trail by the roar of the rapids, I passed a spectacular old limestone building that looked more like something out of Ancient Rome than Canada—this was the old power house building, a grand edifice from an earlier era. Today it's vacant and has been for years—a strange mouldering ruin just above the mighty falls. Not long after this was a third footbridge, which ran alongside the furious churning water. Only a stone's throw ahead I could see a huge plume of mist: the falls. As I was nearing it two more police vehicles pulled up.

My first thought was that the earlier officer hadn't radioed his colleagues after all.

"Hello," said the officer in the first car through her open window.

"Hello," I said back.

"We heard from another of our units that you're going around the falls."

"Yes."

"That's awesome. How are you going to get around Table Rock though?"

"Along this path," I said, slightly confused. Table Rock is the tourist centre situated beside the brink of the falls. It had once been an actual "table rock" that extended precariously over the brink, but the erosion caused by millions of gallons of water pouring over had long ago caused the overhanging rock to plunge into the abyss. But the spot has ever since been known as Table Rock.

"The trail is closed there due to construction," explained the officer.

"Oh," I said. "I guess I'll have to find some other way."

"Well," said the officer, "we don't want you going out on the road, so we'll just close it down for you in that section and let you pass through without having to worry about traffic."

"Oh wow, thanks," I replied, grateful for this unexpected help.

"All right," she replied, "we'll see you down there."

"Thank you!" I resumed pushing.

A few minutes later I was beside the brink of the Horseshoe Falls, marvelling at the raw power of millions of cubic metres of water hurtling over the edge with a thunderous roar. The sun was now fully up, the temperature climbing. Up ahead was the sidewalk construction that had closed the path. The police, in two vehicles, had their lights flashing on the road below the Table Rock building. I turned and pushed the canoe through a parking lot toward the street. Once I'd swung onto the road, one police vehicle drove ahead of me at a walking pace while the other followed behind, lights flashing.

Reflecting on the hundreds of portages I'd done in god-forsaken mosquito-infested swamps or windswept boulder fields in lonely corners of the Arctic, I couldn't help but laugh at the bizarre fact that I was portaging my canoe with my own police escort around one of the world's most famous landmarks. The only witnesses to this strange procession were some park landscapers and gardeners, a couple of maintenance staff, and a few of the arriving construction workers.

It took only a few minutes to get beyond the construction. After bypassing it I pushed the canoe back onto the path, waving goodbye to the officers. I was now on the narrow stone walkway immediately in front of the falls. Hundreds of feet below in the limestone canyon—eroded over the last twelve thousand years by the power of the falls—was the *Maid of the Mist* anchorage, or at least what used to be the *Maid of the Mist*. Huge numbers of noisy gulls squawked and flew above the turbulent water.

It was over this deep gorge in 1860 that two rival tightrope walkers, the Great Blondin and the Great Farini, went head-to-head in an era of no safety nets, competing to outdo each other over a summer of escalating stunts. Blondin was a classically trained French tightrope artist who'd had years of experience touring Europe. "Farini" was the stage name of a Canadian farm boy named William Hunt who'd taught himself tightrope walking in his family's hayloft and was just twenty-two when he showed up at the falls to challenge the world-famous Blondin. The high-flying stunts of these two rivals stunned crowds that numbered in the thousands, as both men did handstands, cartwheels, somersaults, crossed blindfolded, lowered themselves down to the raging waters and back up, and even carried volunteers across. Amazingly, though the bookmakers placed odds on both tumbling to their deaths, neither one did.

I passed a few tourists evidently from abroad as I pushed my canoe opposite the American Falls, which are shallower and rockier than the Horseshoe Falls. They looked at me rather curiously, but seemed to think that portaging canoes around the falls must be a normal Canadian occurrence, as I just casually nodded to them. A few vehicles drove along the Parkway, with some curious looks and a few honks. I escaped from their gazes by passing under the shadows of the Rainbow Bridge, which links Canada to the United States. After this I pushed by the Bird Kingdom, a tourist attraction, and then the Travelodge, where a guest standing on a balcony stared down at me.

"Long portage?" he shouted jokingly from above.

"I've had longer," I replied, which was true.

Up ahead was a steep incline, and I really had to exert myself to push the canoe up it. As I was pushing up the hill, a woman passed me coming down. "Going fishing?" she asked, smiling, apparently unable to imagine any other reason someone would wheel a canoe here.

I nodded. It seemed easier than trying to explain things.

I kept up a brisk pace, eager to get out of the main tourist area. On my right was the two-hundred-foot drop to the river while on my left sat bed-and-breakfasts, the occasional inn, and Victorian and Edwardian houses. At about the four-kilometre mark from the brink I passed an impressive stone church with a gothic tower. An inscription indicated that it had been built in 1865. After this I passed under a train bridge, and then the Whirlpool Rapids Bridge. Beyond this the river squeezes into an even narrower span and again becomes a churning cauldron of massive whitewater rapids. It'd taken me over an hour to reach this point, and I was keen to keep going before more people were about.

I passed more hotels and then the Whirlpool Aero Car, which spans the gorge on a high cable. It hadn't opened for the day yet, and other than a caretaker who paused from cleaning the windows to stare at me, no one was there. After this the river's course makes an abrupt turn, forming one of the most powerful whirlpools in the world. The force of the surging river here has cut away the limestone into a backwater, where the river races around before exiting back down the gorge on the far side. Surrounding the whirlpool are cliffs and a considerable forest. The sheer sides of the gorge, combined with the fearsome river current, have preserved this forest, leaving it a relic of the old-growth that once cloaked eastern North America with all sorts of fascinating trees, rare plants, endangered species, and strange rock formations. I was so intrigued by it that I had to resist the urge to detour into the woods and explore. But it seemed unwise to leave my canoe and gear unattended for long, so I kept portaging.

On the far side of the whirlpool an older jogger, who looked perhaps in her mid-sixties but in excellent shape, was coming up the path. Her jogging seemed so determined that I thought she might pass right by, but she veered toward me.

"What are you doing with that canoe?" she asked, panting.

"Portaging."

"Where?"

"Around the falls and back to Queenston," I explained.

She looked at me as if I were crazy. "You couldn't get anyone to drive you?"

"Well, this cart works great. It takes most of the weight, so all I have to do is push."

"You're going fishing?"

"Mostly just paddling."

"I jog this path every day and I've never seen anyone push a canoe along it."

"How strange."

She wished me all the best, and I her, then we went our respective ways.

Another three kilometres of pushing took me past the Niagara Glen Nature Reserve, then alongside the mighty Sir Adam Beck Generating Stations, which harness the raw power of the river for electricity. They were once the world's largest hydroelectric stations. These massive works I don't recommend walking alongside if you're afraid of heights. They tower far above the swirling river below.

Near the centre of these hydro dams on the opposite side of the narrow road is a Power Generation office. As I was pushing my canoe by it, a car pulled in and a young woman stepped out.

She smiled at me in a manner that suggested it was not every morning one saw an idiot pushing a canoe by the largest hydro-electric facility in the province. She seemed to supress a laugh, then disappeared into the building.

Up ahead an elderly couple were strolling up the narrow pathway and eagerly waved me down. But it turned out all they wanted was directions to the Butterfly Conservatory. I pointed them the right way. After that several more people passed me, including some cyclists, all expressing bafflement.

My spirits rose when in the distance I spotted the high span of the Queenston–Lewiston Bridge. This meant the portage was nearly over. The gorge here is nearly three hundred feet deep, its sheer limestone cliffs crowned by remnants of the ancient forest. At Queenston the gorge ends and the cliffs take a sharp turn inland, forming the Niagara Escarpment.

After passing under the bridge, I reached the famous battle-field of Queenston Heights. It was here that one of the most dramatic battles in North American history unfolded. At these narrow cliffs a badly outnumbered force of Canadian militia, British redcoats, and Six Nations Warriors, under the charis-matic leadership of the dashing General Isaac Brock, held back a vastly larger American invasion force in what was once called "Canada's Thermopylae." Fierce fighting ravaged the little vil-lage of Queenston, as homes burned and smoke filled the air. Thousands of American troops swarmed across the surging river, but the Canadians pinned them down from the cliffs above with a withering fire, and many of the Americans were swept away to their deaths by the fierce current. Others were on boats sunk by cannon fire. Brock and his loyal Canadian second-in-command,

John Macdonell, were both killed in the battle, which ended in a rout of the American forces.

After the war, a large stone monument was erected on the quiet battlefield overlooking the heights to hold the mortal remains of both Brock and MacDonnell. But in 1840 an Irish rebel blew it up, partly destroying it. The memory of Brock had by that point become legendary, and the outrage caused by the attack led to a massive grassroots campaign to raise money for a new and even larger monument. It's this impressive, classical monument—carved out of limestone quarried directly from the escarpment, and so unlike anything else in Canada—that towers high above the cliffs here today.

When I reached this ghost-haunted landscape, rich in legend and lore, I cut away from the Parkway and followed a trail inland through the forest. I knew the area well; this trail would wind down the steep side of the escarpment and take me into the village of Queenston, where I could reach the river and relaunch the canoe. But as I advanced down the trail, I spotted a gigantic old tree I'd never seen before—a cottonwood of enormous diameter—so of course I had to stop to take a closer look, along with a few photographs, before continuing.

I came out of the forest into the quiet streets of Queenston, which seemed to breathe history. On my left was an ivy-covered stone house that had once belonged to the rebel leader William Lyon Mackenzie. From this house in the 1820s he edited one of Canada's first newspapers. Outside its front doors stood an ancient honey locust tree, planted (it's said) by Mackenzie himself. And just down the road was the homestead of Laura Secord, the celebrated heroine of the war who undertook an epic trek through the wilderness to warn local forces of an impending American attack. Secord's husband, James, had served in the Canadian militia and been severely wounded at Queenston Heights.

My mind filled with reflections on these long-ago events, I pushed my canoe through the village down to the river's edge. A narrow road led through the woods to a small boat launch. The current was still strong, and just to the right were the lofty three-hundred-foot-high cliffs of the gorge, but I was eager to get back on the water. As I was repacking my canoe and edging into the swirling blue water, a few fishermen came to ask what I was doing. I knew if I said I was canoeing to the Arctic it might spark questions, so I instead I just said I was canoeing through Lake Ontario. This seemed to stir as much interest as anything, though, and it was another twenty minutes before I could shove off from shore.

I had to paddle hard not to be swept back upstream into the gorge, as strong eddies cause the current to reverse and run upstream near the river's edges. In order to catch the down-stream current, I had to paddle out to the river's centre.

From there, it was another three hours of paddling into the wind, passing steep wooded banks on either shore, until Lake Ontario loomed into view.

6

LAKE ONTARIO'S SOUTH SHORE

A s i paddled down the final stretch of the Niagara River
toward Lake Ontario, the high stone walls and battlements of a castle-like structure appeared on the horizon. This
could only be Fort Niagara, a three-hundred-year-old stronghold built in the days when the French kings still held sway
over a huge swath of North America. The French Empire in
Canada had been, above all, a water-based empire, with control
of the rivers of North America forming the central arteries of
French power. To that end, as far back as the 1600s the French
had built wooden forts at the mouth of the Niagara River to
control its travel and commerce. These early forts, however,
were always vulnerable to attack with fire, so in 1726 the French
authorities began to erect a far more formidable stone fortress
at this strategic site. This impressive citadel has ever since been
known as the "French Castle," and it was this structure I was
studying from my canoe as I bobbed up and down in the river's
swift current.

The castle saw action in the Seven Years' War (1756–1763) when it endured a nineteen-day siege by British and colonial forces, which ended with the garrison's surrender. Thereafter it became a British stronghold, remaining as such throughout the American Revolution. With the close of that conflict, the castle eventually changed hands again, becoming a United States army outpost—and, in 1812, a launching pad for the invasion of Canada. When forces from the fortress burned the Canadian town of Niagara-on-the-Lake to the ground in the bitter winter of 1813, cries arose for vengeance against the stronghold and those responsible. This led to one of the most daring actions of the war, when under the leadership of Canadian-born General Gordon Drummond, British troops stormed the castle in a surprise night assault, massacring by bayonet some eighty members of its garrison.

Not wishing to reinvade the United States, I swung my paddle through the water to steer my canoe out of the middle of the river, where the international boundary runs, toward the tree-lined Canadian shore. There, atop a small hill, stood a much more modest wooden fort: Fort George, first built back in the 1790s to defend Canada from an American invasion. During the War of 1812 it was attacked and burned in the fighting. Swinging in closer to shore, from the stern of my canoe I eyed another historic structure right on the water: Navy Hall, established in 1765 as a British naval base after the conquest of New France. Like the fort, it was destroyed in the War of 1812; the handsome stone structure I was looking at had been rebuilt after the war.

Canadians nowadays seldom think of their country as having been moulded and formed in war, but to a traveller, especially one by canoe, the reality is all too obvious. Half-ruined forts, overgrown battlefields, discarded ramparts, and one-time naval bases are everywhere to be found, silent reminders of numerous wars waged for over two centuries. Downriver from these historic structures I passed some stately lakefront homes, a lighthouse, and a marina. Then I bid farewell to the Niagara River and for the first time dipped my paddle into Lake Ontario. My plan was to canoe all the way around it to the St. Lawrence River. The shortest route would be to follow the American shoreline, but I planned to stay in Canadian waters, which meant taking a longer course, just over four hundred kilometres in total.

The lake was relatively calm, with a moderate breeze as I entered the wide-open expanse. On my left were the historic homes of Niagara-on-the-Lake, on my right the lake's blue immensity. Its waters were a rich azure, strikingly clear, with the occasional fish visible below. Partly obscured by trees were the weathered outlines of yet another old fort—Fort Mississauga. This forgotten fortification—built at the end of the War of 1812 to replace the destroyed Fort George—today lies hidden away at the back of a golf course.

Once I'd passed the town, I found the shoreline surprisingly wild, with rich forests, quiet coves, and deserted pebble beaches. There were sheltered lagoons full of tundra swans, mallards, mergansers, geese, and other birds. Bald eagles nested in several tall cottonwoods, and I was amazed by how long I went without sighting any houses or buildings. Long stretches of undeveloped shoreline on western Lake Ontario are increasingly rare and form crucial habitats for migratory birds heading to the Arctic. At one point I drew up beside a marsh and got out, hoping to gain a closer look at some of these birds—and to see if by chance I might spot a peregrine falcon, attracted by all the easy prey.

Peregrines have bluish-grey backs, with lighter chests spotted and flecked with black, and distinctive dark markings below their large eyes, making them easy to recognize up close. In flight, their spectacular breakneck hunting dives, during which they strike unsuspecting birds of all kinds with their talons, render them almost unmistakable. Besides these traits, their oversized wings for their relatively smallish bodies (about the size of a crow) and high-pitched shrieks are also telltale signs.

Given their superb hunting abilities, for at least three thousand years wild peregrines have been caught and trained for use in falconry; that is, sport hunting for their human captors. In the Middle Ages, when falconry was a popular sport among kings and nobles, the gift of a wild falcon was sometimes made on important occasions of state, and peregrines became a symbol associated with aristocracy. It was said medieval knights valued their falcons as much as their swords.

I searched the skies and trees in the marsh, but despite all the prey at hand, especially the ducks, no falcons were in sight. So I returned to my canoe, and pushed off.

After this wild stretch came orchards, wineries, and other farms, as well as scatterings of lakeshore homes. I pressed on into the evening as the wind died, making for ideal conditions. On the horizon a thin line of land appeared: the Port Weller east pier, which was built to shelter the entrance to the Welland Canal. Despite its name, it bears little resemblance to a traditional pier, and is in fact an earth-covered peninsula reaching far into the lake. The last kilometre of the peninsula is made up of trails, forest, and overgrown meadows, which I figured would make a suitable camping site. But the sun was rapidly sinking below the horizon, and I had to reach it before dark. To do so, I'd have to strike off from the mainland, cutting diagonally across from the shoreline to the peninsula, which would shave off the distance.

I was racing against the sunset, paddling as hard as I could, watching the red orb of the sun inch ever closer to the horizon, trying to calculate whether I could make it before darkness descended. There were a number of fishing boats roaring back to the pier's marina, which made things risky, since in the dark any of them might collide with me. I weighed whether digging out my flashlight and rigging it to my canoe was worth it. But the flashlight was buried inside the waterproof sack that held my sleeping bag, and unpacking it would be difficult. By the time I got it out and everything repacked it'd likely be dark. It seemed the best choice was to make the most of the dying light and just keep paddling.

Alas, I was still about two kilometres from the peninsula when the fading sun had all but touched the watery horizon. I knew I wouldn't make it now, and with no moon, darkness would soon smother everything. I'd have to abandon my plan of reaching it and turn for the near shore. But that shore was either high banks with nowhere to camp below them, or else houses. Exhausted, I headed for it. It was pitch dark by the time I reached it. I was reluctant to test my luck and ask for permission to camp in someone's backyard the way I had in Port Colborne, as that had been a stormy night, and this was a calm one, where it seemed less probable of finding success.

There was nothing to do but keep going. I paddled wearily along until at last I reached the start of the long tree-covered peninsula running into the lake. I turned to follow it into the darkness, looking for anywhere to camp. When I reached a small marina protected by a breakwall, I could hear voices and see the glow of a bonfire at what looked like a trailer park. I paddled in to take a closer look, but it seemed too boisterous a place for someone in need of deep sleep. So on I went, hoping to find a more secluded spot.

It was after nine p.m. and I'd been travelling since four that morning. I'd hoped to reach the forests up ahead, but by now I was nearly drained of energy, so when I happened upon a little cove at the very end of the trailer park, I could resist no longer and went ashore. Jumping out, I saw no one, and I decided to make camp quickly.

It took four trips to haul all my gear and canoe up from the cove to the grass above, where I assembled everything under a poplar tree. I'd just begun putting up my tent when I heard someone approaching: a man was shuffling in my direction. He appeared to have come from the bonfire party. At first I thought he might not notice me in the dark. But as he neared it was obvious he'd see me, so I waved and called out hello.

He nodded at me.

"Sorry to bother you. I've been canoeing and was wondering if I could camp here for the night?"

"Oh sure," he said, sounding a bit tipsy. He didn't seem to think it was strange that someone had come ashore alone in the dark.

"Thank you."

He nodded again, and without another word shuffled off to the last trailer.

I finished making camp, then crawled into my tent. It was a cold night, with a frost that settled over everything. I woke up shivering several times, and had to rub my arms and legs to warm up. I had my jacket on and the hood zipped up, but even with three layers on I was still cold.

When I crawled out of my tent into the frosty morning, I expected to be gone before anyone saw me. But to my surprise, the man I'd spoken with the night before emerged from the trailer. He seemed to have sobered up, and asked me how I'd made out.

"Oh great," I said.

"Warm enough?"

"My clothes are super warm," I said, shivering uncontrollably.

"You're going fishing?"

I nodded. Since I'd slept in until five, I felt it was best to dispense with too much conversation, and telling someone you're canoeing to the Arctic isn't always the best means of going about that. So I just left it at fishing, which was technically accurate, as I did have a fishing rod and would undoubtedly use it a few more times before reaching the Arctic.

"Good luck." He waved.

"Thanks!"

The winds were relatively light as I launched my canoe into the lake, making good progress to the tip of the pier, where the big freighters enter and exit the Welland Canal. Unlike at Port Colborne, crossing the shipping lane here was a simple matter: the skies were clear, there were no big swells, and no perilous breakwalls. I zipped across quickly, rounded a lighthouse at the end of it, then paddled back to the mainland.

It was sunny but cold, though now I didn't mind it so much; paddling kept me warm, and at least it was dry. I next had to round the pier at Port Dalhousie, which seemed remarkably busy with walkers for a brisk morning in April. But glancing at my watch I saw it was a Saturday, and so the popularity of the pier was less a mystery.

Steady paddling soon brought me once more to wooded bluffs, farms, and orchards. The farmland in this area is considered among the richest in Canada, with excellent soil and a relatively moderate climate, so that it has long been famed for its fruit orchards, notably peaches and cherries. But in recent years, much of this farmland has disappeared due to development pressures, becoming highways, strip malls and subdivisions.

By midday I'd passed Jordan Harbour and Vineland, where pink cherry blossoms in the orchards swayed in the breeze. I could also spot wineries along the shore, but in many places steep bluffs prevented me from seeing much beyond them. What I did see were migrating birds: terns, ducks, gulls, cormorants. I landed at a few pebbly coves to stretch my legs, sip water, and eat a few granola bars. But the biting wind cut short any breaks and spurred me to keep canoeing.

By evening I'd reached Grimsby, until recently a small community best known for its peach orchards and historic homes, including the 234-year-old Nelles Manor, one of the oldest houses in Ontario. From the water the view of Grimsby was actually remarkably beautiful. Apart from shoreline bluffs, most of the land I'd passed so far was generally flat. But towering high above Grimsby is an almost mountain-like landscape, with multiple hills rising back from the water like the humps of an immense dragon. This is the Niagara Escarpment, which at Grimsby surges up dramatically and includes a pair of twin peaks. From a canoe, bobbing in the water, I could certainly appreciate why early settlers called the Escarpment the "mountain," an appellation that still carries on in certain place names, like Mountain Road. Drawing another stroke of my paddle through the clear waters, I felt lucky that I was able to experience this vista while it's still possible. The last few years had left this once rural community almost unrecognizable, as much of the orchards have been bulldozed, the forests cleared, and the farms paved over to make room for massive high rises, condos, and housing developments. In the near future, it seems, the planned construction of more high rises will entirely block the view.

By evening I'd glided into a sheltered cove at Fifty Point Conservation Area on the outskirts of Grimsby. It protects a remnant of the once rich forests that formerly cloaked the area and provides vital habitat for migratory birds, including falcons. I set up my tent on the edge of the woods in a secluded spot overlooking the lake. No one else was around, and other than a few terns, I had the half-moon beach all to myself. I cooked one of my freeze-dried pasta meals and filled up my thermos with hot green tea for the morning.

7

HEAD OF THE LAKE

THE WEATHER SHIFTED overnight: the temperature edged upward, bringing with it stronger winds. From inside my tent I could hear waves lapping against the shore, and when I crawled out at five a.m. the wind was blowing steadily. I packed my canoe carefully, balancing the weight just right for maximum stability. Luckily, the sheltered cove made launching easy.

I had to steer carefully to round Fifty Point. The shoreline, once I'd passed the entrance to a small marina, was almost all artificial, consisting of either steel breakwalls or else heaps of boulders. This made paddling more difficult, since it caused the waves to roll back after crashing into the barriers, hitting my canoe from both directions. A light rain had begun to fall and the winds were increasing. It was an east wind, generating big waves that crashed like thunder. The steel walls and wave-washed boulders left few safe landing places, and if I swamped here, there was scant refuge to be found on the exposed rocks.

Given the deteriorating conditions, I decided it'd be best to land at the first safe place I could find. This turned out to be a strip of beach between breakwalls, right behind someone's house. It wasn't a big target though; the beach was small, and protruding in the water just off from it was a concrete boulder, surf pounding into it.

I had to navigate carefully, reading the waves, and timing my dash to the shore just right between the surf. I hovered offshore in the rain and waves, lining up my canoe with the narrow gap I needed to hit. Then, after a big wave thundered into shore, I saw my chance and paddled hard. It was a wild ride as the waves caught me from behind and my canoe surged ahead. I zigzagged through the narrow opening to the beach, soaking my boots as I jumped into the surf to pull the canoe ashore. But I was happy just to have landed safely. Then I noticed a sign hammered into the ground: "Private Property, No Trespassing."

Fortunately, right next to the beach was a small creek draining through a culvert, evidently municipal property. Beside it were some landscaping rocks; these I climbed, tossing my backpack, barrel, and canoe above them onto a grassy laneway that ran between houses. The rain was coming down harder now, the waves growing into massive whitecaps. I clearly couldn't resume paddling in these conditions. But since I couldn't remain here either, I figured I'd set up my cart and wheel the canoe down the road until the wind died enough for me to relaunch. Given the wind direction and the shape of the lake—I was pinned down on the south shore near Stoney Creek—it seemed possible that if I simply portaged the canoe ahead a few kilometres toward the inner bay, the waves there wouldn't be as bad. So I lifted the canoe onto the aluminum cart, strapped it tightly, tossed in my soaking backpack and barrel, and set off.

After pushing my canoe through the neighbourhood I came to a small forest sandwiched between new high-rise condos. It seemed a sad sight, a last remnant of a once mighty woodland. Still, I noticed it was a sanctuary for birds and other wildlife. Judging by how rich it looked, it must have really been something in its day. On its far side I could see that the waves on the lake were still massive. There was nothing for it but to portage a little farther and see if conditions might improve. I left the newer builds and passed into an older neighbourhood.

Then, a little farther along, I came to Confederation Park and the start of the Hamilton Beach trail. It turned out to be a quiet little gem of a trail, wooded and remarkably secluded, though the cold, rainy weather may have had something to do with that. Right beside it was a relatively large forest with nice pines that seemed a bird paradise, with black-capped chickadees, white- and red-breasted nuthatches, hairy and downy woodpeckers, robins, cardinals, blue jays, and others. These urban forests are important on many levels, for wildlife and people alike, and stand as vivid reminders of what once was.

I pushed my canoe along, pausing at some interesting interpretative signs I wouldn't have seen from the water (reminding myself as I did so that there's an upside to just about everything, even portaging.) Some of the signs outlined the importance of the lakeshore here for migratory birds, which gave me a new appreciation for the area, while others discussed local history.

Just offshore here during the War of 1812, two marauding American warships, the USS *Scourge* and USS *Hamilton*, ran into serious trouble—and not from the Canadian ships trying to sink them. The danger came from the lake itself. In August 1813 a ferocious gale sank both warships, taking eighty-four sailors down into the depths. The ghostly wrecks were discovered in the twentieth century, well-preserved by the cold waters. It was a stark reminder that if the lake's storms could sink 112-foot-warships, they could easily sink my canoe, and the huge whitecaps currently pounding the shore were offering a pretty good indication of that.

A legendary naval action also occurred here, just a month after the sinking of the ships. On September 28, 1813, an American squadron, numbering some ten warships, attacked a smaller six-ship British squadron off York's harbour. The badly outnumbered British and Canadians, after a sharp battle, raced here to Burlington Bay with the American fleet in hot pursuit. The bay sits tucked behind a massive sandbar (the very one I was now portaging along), where the Americans wouldn't dare follow. On the high bluffs overlooking the water, the locals had built powerful shore batteries, well-armed with cannons, which could destroy any ships. The British fleet managed to deftly navigate through the narrow channel, and so live to fight another day.

The trail took me below the Burlington Skyway, which connects Lake Ontario's south and north shores. While from a vehicle it seems as if the skyway runs over water, there's actually a thin strip of land beneath it. A narrow canal transects this strip, allowing ships access to Hamilton Harbour. The trail led me to the canal, with a lighthouse marking its entrance. Due to the canal's walls, there was no way down to the water, and even if it hadn't been stormy, it'd be too dangerous given Hamilton Harbour's busy freighter traffic. The rain had turned heavy, and I was soaked right through, despite my rain jacket and rain pants. The trail next veered under the small lift bridge that spans the canal, where I halted to escape the downpour. I had to shake my hands to warm up.

A pedestrian staircase led up to the bridge itself and to a footpath across it, with the trail continuing on the far side. In order to get up the stairway I'd have to unstrap my canoe and carry it over my head, then return for the cart, backpack, and barrel, taking each of these across one at a time: four trips in total. Then, once I'd reached the other side, I could repack everything. I was slightly apprehensive, however, about leaving my canoe and gear unattended while moving the other loads. But the stormy weather made setting back out onto the lake impossible, and as for staying put here until the weather improved, there was nowhere on this side of the canal where I could camp.

It seemed the best thing to do was compress my loads so there'd be less to carry and no loose items. I began putting my camera, water bottle, thermos, rain boots (I'd switched into my hiking ones), and fishing rod either into my backpack or clipped to the outside of it. As I was doing this, I heard footsteps and turned around to see a couple walking along the trail toward me. I tried to act natural, but they asked what I was doing.

"Well," I said, "I'm heading to the Arctic."

"What?"

"I'm heading through Lake Ontario to the St. Lawrence River, and from there to Labrador and eventually north to the Arctic."

The two of them stared at me. Just at that moment, a second couple happened along. They too asked what I was doing with a canoe under a bridge. Before I could answer, the other two did for me. Now there was a general murmur of surprise and offers of assistance.

"Well, I just need to get everything across the bridge," I began. "If you'd be nice enough to watch my canoe while I carry my gear over, I'll be in your debt." But before I'd even finished speaking, they'd already picked up my gear and started carrying it. I tried to say that this wasn't necessary, but they wouldn't hear of it, and so I grabbed onto the other end of my canoe, and with one of them, began carrying it toward the stairway. The others had grabbed my backpack, barrel, and the cart. This surprise help from perfect strangers proved a blessing, as it otherwise would have meant a lengthy delay to make the four trips across. As we walked we became properly acquainted; their names were Carla, Stuart, Tom, and Eileen.

When we reached the far side of the bridge and the footpath, they all asked what else they could do to help me. "Well," I said, "you've already helped me more than I could have hoped. But I don't know this area well, and with the waves this big, I don't think I'll be able to paddle again until morning. Do you know anywhere I might camp for the night?"

"You can follow this trail down to Spencer Smith Park in Burlington," Tom explained. "But it's busy there, and after that it's downtown Burlington. So if you have to camp, you'd be better off somewhere around here."

"There's a small bit of forest near where the canal goes into the lake," Stuart added. "I don't think anyone would bother you there."

I thanked them once more for all their help. When we parted ways, Tom and Eileen asked if I'd object to their bringing me something from Tim Hortons. I had no objection at all.

In the meantime, I took shelter under some oaks overlooking Burlington Beach. It was only mid-afternoon, so I was reluctant to make camp, although given the grey skies and howling winds, it seemed unlikely that the waves would calm down enough to relaunch anytime soon. A short time later I was heartened by the sight of Tom and Eileen pulling up in their vehicle. They handed me an extra-large green tea and two cookies. I thanked them for it, and they wished me well with a sincerity that put an extra spring in my step.

With the rain still coming down steadily, I was eager to find a forest to shelter in. I retraced my steps back down the path toward the canal, pushing my canoe toward the clump of woods that Stuart had suggested as a possible camping site. A narrow, unofficial pathway veered off into this scrubby forest of wild grapevines, cottonwoods, and bushes. The pathway led me into a clearing with a firepit, broken glass, part of a barbecue, a discarded fire extinguisher, a rickety wood bench, some busted furniture, and a bench seat from a vehicle propped in front of some masonry, creating a fireplace between two cottonwoods. My first impression was that I'd stumbled upon some local kids' hideout, but a closer inspection led me to conclude that this was actually a homeless encampment.

No one was around at present, so I left my canoe and explored the surrounding woods. There were some rock piles and concrete slabs overgrown with wild grapevines, where I saw a few eastern cottontails—Ontario's only native rabbit species—disappear into crevices. I decided to wait and see if anyone might come along. The rainy afternoon and evening passed away without anyone showing up. My only company were three squirrels, some robins, and a few red-winged blackbirds. If not for the steady roar of traffic crossing the Burlington Skyway high above, I thought this little patch of forest would be quite peaceful.

It seemed the cold, wet weather might have driven any denizens of this homeless encampment elsewhere. But I couldn't be sure, and not wanting to intrude on someone else's camping place without permission, as the sun was going down I shifted over to a more secluded spot, at the very tip of land in the shelter of some cottonwoods right beside the rocky shoreline. I put my tent on a level patch of sandy, leaf-covered ground just as darkness fell. Then I crawled inside and changed into my dry clothes.

From my tent I listened to the surf pounding the nearby rocks, tossing spray into the air. With all the wet weather, I'd had little chance to use my small solar panel to charge my phone, and it was nearly dead. I'd eventually reach a place with no service. But I figured I'd send Alexandria a text to let her know where I was camping. I had no doubt she'd send me some encouraging words. A few minutes later I received this message: "Hopefully someone doesn't rob and knife you in the night."

8

GTA

B EFORE DAWN THE next morning I got out my flashlight and began packing up the tent. At some point during
the night I'd heard the waves die; now only gentle swells were
rolling in. I shoved off and paddled through them in the dark,
letting the lights of the cityscape guide me. When I reached
the north shore at Burlington, I turned and followed along it.
I paddled hard, as I knew it'd be a long way before I'd likely find
anywhere that I could camp again.

I was expecting the Burlington, Oakville, and Mississauga
shoreline to consist mainly of high-rise condos and commercial
properties, but I found that most of it was in fact made up of big
lakefront houses, including a few enormous Downton Abbey–
like estates that astonished me with their size and ornateness.
Interspersed with these expensive homes were city parks, marinas, and a few industrial areas. The lake seemed practically
deserted apart from the occasional passing freighter in the far
distance. It was a strange feeling to be paddling along a vast

urban landscape home to millions, but to have what felt like virtually the huge empty lake to myself. However, it was only May 2; come summer I knew these waters would be swarming with boats.

Near Oakville I had to avoid an almost kilometre-long Petro-Canada pier, and then detour around another pier at the Mississauga Cement Plant. A third pier followed shortly after this, which seemed to be connected to a factory that produces oils and lubricants. None of these industrial piers had any openings where a canoe could pass underneath, forcing me to paddle far offshore to round them, just hoping as I did so that a giant freighter wouldn't run me over. At one of them a huge freighter was unloading what looked like oil, or maybe balsamic vinegar—some dark liquid, in any case, was shooting out of a trough attached to the ship into a giant steel container.

By evening, gigantic inhuman-looking skyscrapers loomed into view—I'd reached the outskirts of Toronto. Since the early twentieth century the city's rapid growth has devoured thousands of acres of wetlands, forests, and farms around the sprawling metropolis, with the population increasing tenfold. These dramatic changes include Yonge Street's evolution from a muddy farmers' lane, with pigs and cattle on their way to market and wolves and black bears lurking just behind the wooden storefronts, to the gridlocked traffic of today.

The wind had been rising, creating strong headwinds slowing my progress. I battled against them, until near the mouth of the Humber River, I came upon some inner laneway, which was evidently used by rowers. I cut into it, which helped shelter me from the choppy waters. One thing I immediately noticed about paddling here, in sharp contrast to everywhere else I'd been so far, was the immense amount of litter visible in the water and along the shoreline—an unfortunate byproduct of a city home to millions.

I was racing along, knowing that I had to reach the Toronto Islands before dark. These islands, a chain of thirteen, were the only wild place I could think of as a campsite. I'd never been there, but I had few other options. By the time I reached Ontario Place, a former amusement park spread across three artificial islands and connected to the mainland by footbridges, it was nearly dark.

I was paddling at a furious rate, worried that I'd find myself stranded in this busy city after sundown. The Toronto Islands were still several kilometres ahead of me. I'd taken the inner channel along Ontario Place to escape the wind, but now I realized I'd made a mistake: what I'd thought from a satellite image was a final footbridge was actually a solid causeway linking this last bit of parkland to the mainland. That meant I couldn't paddle under it as I had with the other bridges: I'd have to portage. The sidewalks up ahead were crowded; this was Toronto after all. Fortunately, it was only a narrow footpath I had to cross to get to the water on the other side, and I was determined to do it in record time.

There was a photographer taking what looked like engagement photos of a young couple in the park by the water. They were in the only good landing place, and paddling furiously, I skidded my canoe right up to the marshy shore beside them, then jumped out.

"Sorry to bother you," I said. "I'll be gone quickly."

The photographer just nodded politely and didn't seem too perturbed. It occurred to me that in a city of millions, they were probably used to interruptions.

In any case I pulled up the canoe and took everything out of it, set up the cart, then quickly strapped the canoe onto it. Tossing my packs and paddles back into the canoe, at a run I began pushing. I had to build up speed to get over a curb, across a pedestrian walkway, and then along a narrow laneway down to the water on the other side. It was only a matter of minutes, and the passersby seemed to assume that I was just really eager to go fishing.

Rapidly I unstrapped the canoe, lifted it gently over the concrete to the water below, and had to delicately repack everything as quickly as I could before it drifted off. Then I stepped in and took up my paddle with all the energy I could muster. Darkness was coming on fast and I had to race ahead, not knowing what I might find in Toronto's harbour. On my left was a marina, on my right Billy Bishop airport, which sits on one of the Toronto Islands and is connected to the mainland by passenger ferries (and an underground tunnel).

Having a passenger ferry run over me in the dark was something it seemed best to avoid. But there was just a bit of twilight left, and since I didn't have any lights on my canoe, it was imperative that I make camp before dark. I had taken up a racing position, kneeling and paddling like mad down a concrete-walled channel. Immediately ahead the airport ferry zoomed across the channel with surprising speed. A sign posted in capital letters stated something to the effect that pleasure boats were prohibited, but it was getting too dark to read and anyway I was already committed. Juggling all these urban hazards made me long for a simpler time when all I had to worry about was polar bears.

I saw my chance when the ferry zoomed past again; once it was gone, with a final burst of my remaining energy, I paddled as hard as I could, zipping through the channel, then rounding a corner by some warehouses. The sun had disappeared beyond the horizon, but now I took this as something of a relief. Accustomed to wilderness travel, there was something a little uncomfortable about paddling under the gaze of so many people.

But with the darkness, I was now invisible, and I had little to fear so long as I kept close to the shore along the airport, where none of the larger boats or other ferries that ply the Toronto waters could go. However, I could hear some airplanes taking off, and I wasn't entirely certain whether I was violating some policy by coming too close to the runway, or possibly even triggering some sensor. I turned this over in my mind as I paddled along, and reassured myself that such fears were groundless, as there could be no reason why a canoe in the water here would be of any interference to the planes. The lights from a second ferry terminal loomed into view on the island ahead, though it seemed the last ferry had already docked for the night.

Behind me were the massive glittering lights of downtown Toronto's numerous skyscrapers; glancing back at them over my shoulder, it stirred a strange contrast to think there were millions of people jammed in that little area of asphalt, steel, glass, and concrete, while I was alone among the western islands. The quiet, forested islands felt refreshingly wild. The artificial glow from the city was enough to illuminate the dark outline of the trees, allowing me to navigate through the island channels.

Some of the Toronto Islands have a small number of houses and others have parks and recreational facilities, but a few of the heavily forested ones are uninhabited. I found one of the wilder of these deserted islands and pulled my canoe ashore in thick woods. It had been fifteen hours since I'd set off from the Burlington Skyway that morning, and I'd covered sixty-two kilometres. Exhausted, I found a place beneath an oak tree to spread out for the night.

✳

I WAS UP well before dawn, but even in the woods the artificial glow from Toronto made it easy to see. My breakfast was some almonds and a few granola bars, after which I was back on the water. I was in the middle of the sheltered island chain, weaving through tranquil channels just as the dawn light came up. I was pleasantly surprised by these islands; although only a kilometre offshore from Toronto, they seemed a world away—a quiet little oasis with beavers, woodpeckers, and bays full of mallards, pintails, swans, and geese.

These islands were the reason for the city's existence. The shelter they provide from the lake's powerful storms forms the only large natural harbour in eastern Lake Ontario with easy access—the extensive sandbars at Hamilton Harbour historically made it too treacherous for shipping. As a result, French traders chose Toronto as a site for a small fur-trading post in 1750, where ships could safely unload cargoes. With the British conquest of New France in the Seven Years' War, the post was abandoned. But the shelter of the islands remained a strategic asset, leading the British to begin settling the Toronto shore in earnest in the 1780s.

By the War of 1812 the settlement had become the provincial capital, and in 1813 an American invasion fleet attacked it. After an amphibious assault and fierce landing battle, the British abandoned their defence of the capital as hopeless, leaving the Canadian militia on their own. Realizing the battle was lost, the order was given to ignite Fort York's powder magazine, causing a tremendous explosion that killed or wounded hundreds of invading Americans, including their commander, the explorer Zebulon Pike, who was crushed by falling debris. In revenge, the surviving Americans looted and burned much of the town, including the provincial legislative assembly.

I passed under a footbridge and alongside a park featuring a little demonstration farm for children to explore. On another island stood a weathered church and a grand but time-worn edifice with tall columns in front—this, it turned out, was the Royal Canadian Yacht Club building. Established in 1852, it's reputed to be one of the world's oldest yacht clubs. After rounding the clubhouse, I paddled toward the end of the island chain; ferries were once more busily moving about the inner harbour.

On I went through the eastern channel, passing by Toronto's port. Now that I'd left the shelter of the inner islands, I discovered a fierce easterly wind, exhausting to paddle against. Guarding the eastern approach to Toronto Harbour is Tommy Thompson Park, a large artificial peninsula made up of construction debris dumped into the lake and since transformed into much-needed greenspace for the city. The peninsula is just a slender spit of land, and given the gusting wind, I figured I could cut across it and save myself some paddling.

I landed at a narrow spot. There was a steep, rocky embankment to climb—too rocky for the cart—but I quickly carried my four loads across, including the canoe, to reach the shore on the far side, facing out toward the lake. The waves were sizable, but with determined effort I'd be able to keep going. I launched the canoe and followed the shoreline back toward the mainland, passing by dump trucks and backhoes shovelling more construction debris into the water.

But even with the shortcut paddling into stiff winds was rapidly draining my energy. By the time I reached the Beaches, a two-and-a-half-kilometre stretch of sandy shore on Toronto's east side, I had to rest. Despite the cold and winds, the beach was busy with walkers and dogs, though no one, aside from me, was in the water. I dug some more nuts and granola bars out of my barrel to muster the strength to keep paddling. While I was along this beach I was recognized by a passerby who'd read my books. He asked me what I was doing; I briefly explained and we chatted for a few minutes before I shoved off again into the gusting wind.

In between frantic paddle bursts I admired a beautiful and graceful old utility building overlooking the water. This, it turned out, was the R.C. Harris Water Treatment Plant, a 1930s-era Art Deco–style building that I can say with confidence is the nicest water treatment facility I've ever seen. Beyond the plant is a remarkably wild shoreline with high, forest-crowned bluffs that tower over the water. At the base of these bluffs lies a bit of shoreline with trees, driftwood, and quiet coves.

There wasn't a soul in sight, and I was amazed at how deserted it seemed. But the high eroded bluffs prevent any easy access, and other than an occasional steep trail winding down from above, there's no way to reach these places other than by water. This went on for a long way, quiet little cove after cove, with abundant birds and rich forests, so that I almost had to remind myself that I was still within Toronto. I could barely believe that so much greenspace could exist right here within the city limits, directly below Scarborough. But what kept the shoreline so wild were the high, eroded bluffs.

By late afternoon I'd reached a spot where the cliffs rose even higher: the famous Scarborough Bluffs, a city park and popular lookout spot. I'd never been here before, and I found it a strange landscape, eerie and almost a little otherworldly, though the solitude and dreary weather (it had begun to rain) likely had something to do with it. I was a little apprehensive about paddling beneath these towering, constantly eroding cliffs, when it seemed that at any moment part of them might collapse in a landslide. But the fierce winds made it difficult to canoe farther offshore. Exhausted, I paddled into a little cove at the foot of the cliffs, where a trail wound down and I could see a few people milling about. As I landed they disappeared up the pathway, evidently eager to reach the parking lot before the rain turned any heavier. I too was eager to find some sheltered spot for the night. But a quick search revealed nowhere suitable—the ground was either muddy and marshy, or else steep slopes. Plus, I didn't like the idea of camping somewhere this well-trodden, even if the weather had temporarily driven everyone away.

So, wearily, I climbed back into my canoe and shoved off to paddle out of the cove and search for somewhere else to camp. I passed the entrance to a marina, and briefly looked around but saw nothing promising, so I pushed on into the wind and rain. Just a little farther was another beach, Bluffer's Beach, which backs onto a forest. With the rain coming down harder now, I used my remaining strength to reach the end of this beach and land onshore. It looked deserted, and the thick woods and bluffs behind seemed encouraging. In any case, the winds made paddling any farther impractical, and it'd be dark in another hour. I hauled my canoe up the beach and made camp on the edge of the woods.

Crawling into a tent and changing into dry clothing felt heavenly, and when with my little stove I boiled a cup of herbal tea, I felt as if I had just about everything I could ask for. Outside a storm raged, with lashing rain, screaming winds, and cold temperatures, but in my tent I was warm and snug.

When morning dawned the wind was still gusting, though it had now shifted direction so that it was coming from the south, creating sizable whitecaps. They were too big to paddle, which meant for the time being I was stuck onshore. Later in the morning I took advantage of a break in the rain to spread my wet clothing onto the canoe to dry. I also dragged the canoe back toward the waterline and loaded everything into it so that I'd be ready to depart as soon as the wind slackened.

In the meantime I rested on the beach. I was again amazed at how secluded it was, considering I was still within Toronto's city limits. Some red-winged blackbirds called from out of the phragmite bushes behind me, but other than the birds and the sound of the surf, there wasn't much to be heard. In the far distance occasional dog walkers appeared, but few ventured all the way down the beach to where I was sitting. Only a handful did throughout the morning, and they all proved friendly. One told me about how drugs had nearly ruined his life, particularly fentanyl, and advised me that it was best to go easy on the stuff. Another individual who was walking a sharp-eyed border collie, chatted with me about how he'd once attempted to ride a bicycle from Vancouver to South America. A woman who walked by told me she edited a local community news blog, and that she always walked the beach here. I remarked to each of these passersby how surprised I was to find so much protected and secluded greenspace along the Scarborough lakeshore. They all told me proudly that this was what they loved about the area.

The waves remained formidable all morning, and it wasn't until the afternoon that I decided to take my chances and push on. Once I steered through the pounding surf, things weren't too bad, and I was able to make decent progress. I passed more forests that I was surprised to see, then cut across a large bay toward the huge Pickering Nuclear Generating Station. Finally, a long way off, I made camp on a secluded little beach backed by rich woods, with a beautiful half-moon rising in the darkened sky.

9

BAY OF QUINTE

THE NEXT DAY the winds were favourable and I continued east. After passing some ugly urban sprawl devouring
the countryside near Bowmanville, I camped on a rocky shore
beneath some forested bluffs. But after this the wind shifted
easterly again, spawning powerful headwinds that it took all
my strength to overcome.

At Port Hope, concrete breakwalls running out into the lake
at the Ganaraska River's mouth presented a challenge. So far
these human-made structures were proving the hardest part of
my journey. Big waves were smashing into their vertical sides,
then ricocheting back out, hitting me from both directions. The
waves knocked my canoe about as I struggled to get around
them without capsizing. It took an intense mental and physical effort—staying calm while paddling hard but carefully—to
make it through. By the time I reached the safety of the shore,
I had to jump out just to breathe a sign of relief and drink some
water. Once I'd caught my breath, I relaunched and continued.

A few kilometres outside Port Hope I landed and made camp on a lonely stretch of wooded shore. Now that I'd passed Toronto, the shoreline had become wilder, and there weren't any houses or buildings in sight. But not far inland lay train tracks running parallel to the lake. I thought the trains might keep me up at night, but I was wrong—what kept me up was the even louder roaring of the wind. The gusts were so strong that they shook and rumbled my tent, causing a terrible racket with the taut outer rainfly. The result was a restless night, as the roar regularly stirred me from my sleep, and I had to keep going out into the cold to drive the stakes back into the sand. I couldn't help but smile a little at the irony—I'd slept so peacefully several nights on solid rocks, and now, camped on soft sand, I was unable to enjoy it due to the wind's ceaseless roaring.

When morning dawned, I glanced outside my tent to see huge whitecaps smashing into the beach. These waves were the largest I'd seen so far and made it easy to picture how Lake Ontario has claimed hundreds of ships. One of the most tragic of these shipwrecks happened not far east of where I was now camped. In October 1804, the government schooner HMS *Speedy*, built six years earlier at Kingston Harbour, vanished overnight in a fierce storm with no survivors. Only a few pieces of wreckage ever washed up. In a pre-industrial era when populations were but a tiny fraction of today's, the loss of an entire ship would have been devastating to Upper Canada's small, tight-knit society. On board were some of the colony's most prominent figures, including the solicitor general, along with six handwritten copies of Upper Canada's constitution.

Still, I considered myself lucky to be windbound in this wild stretch and not somewhere more populated. The surrounding forest provided ample firewood, meaning I could cook a lunch of freeze-dried rice and vegetables and make some tea. And at least it was sunny, allowing me to make the most of the delay by drying some things and resting comfortably by a campfire, which I'd sheltered by digging a small pit. In the shallows near shore the water was a brilliant sky blue, which abruptly became dark blue where deeper water began, looking almost Caribbean-like.

Not until four p.m. did the wind slacken enough for me to depart. By evening it had faded to a near calm, and I pushed on eastward well after dark. I had little choice, as I found the lakeshore was made up of high, eroded cliffs with nowhere to camp beneath them. Finally, near ten o'clock, with no other options, in the moonlight I came upon a gravel shore. The moon provided enough silver light for me to pitch the tent and unpack my things.

This central section of Lake Ontario from roughly Bowmanville's outskirts through to Presqu'ile I found remarkably quiet. Parts of the lakeshore reminded me of Lake Superior, with its enchantingly blue water, smooth pebble beaches crisscrossed by driftwood logs, and dense cedar forests. There weren't any other boats around and I even went a whole day without encountering anyone at all. Not even a road hugged the coast here, so that it was possible to feel, in the immensity of the lake and quietness of it all, that I was alone in the world.

And yet there wasn't any real reason to feel lonely, since there were birds and wildlife to keep me company. I saw kingfishers, bank swallows, robins, common terns, Bonaparte's gulls, herring gulls, green-winged teals, mergansers, eagles, tundra swans, geese—yet still no falcons. But I knew they were out there somewhere, making their own journeys north. The thought of it drove me on. Wandering along the deserted shorelines were also red foxes, coyotes, and the occasional deer.

The apprehensions I'd faced over the last two weeks travelling by canoe on the vastness of two stormy Great Lakes were nearly at an end. Ahead of me lay the sheltered waters of the Bay of Quinte, which meant for the remaining distance on Lake Ontario I'd be relatively protected. The end of the lake at Kingston was still a hundred and thirty kilometres by water, but, if you glance at a map of the lake, you'll see a giant upside-down-triangle-shaped peninsula jutting into its eastern end, which is Prince Edward County. On the inner, sheltered side of this huge peninsula is the Bay of Quinte, a zigzagging passage of waters famous for its scenery and fishing. For centuries, travellers had taken advantage of its sheltered waters by portaging across a narrow bit of forest—known as the Carrying Place—in order to avoid the infamously stormy waters on the open lake. Such was the bay's value for navigation that in 1882 construction began on the eight-kilometre-long Murray Canal, which eliminated the need for a portage by connecting the two bodies of water. Today the canal is no longer used by commercial shipping traffic, which was perfect for me, as it meant I could paddle straight through it to the Bay of Quinte.

All I had to do first was get around Presqu'ile Point, a narrow, sandy peninsula. It was a calm day as I paddled toward this huge stretch of sandy white beach. The water was remarkably clear, and the rare calm weather and balmy conditions left me in a dreamy mood. Paddling along absent-mindedly toward the beach, my reverie was suddenly interrupted by a crack.

Glancing down, I saw with horror that my ultra-light carbon-fibre paddle had snapped right in the middle. I'd distractedly pried with it off the gunwale to finish a stroke, something routinely done with wooden paddles but best avoided with carbon-fibre ones. I'd started the journey relying on my traditional paddle carved from the wood of a wild cherry tree. I still had that paddle with me, but I'd been experimenting with this second, modern paddle. It'd been a gift to me from a high school teacher in London, Ontario, who'd designed and built it himself as part of a start-up company specializing in racing paddles. At first, enamoured as I was with traditional paddles, I'd accepted it with some skepticism. But over the past five hundred kilometres I'd grown highly appreciative of it—it was incredibly light, and the short, bent-shaft design maximized the efficiency of each stroke. Indeed, the paddle was as light as a feather, so that when I now switched back to my cherry paddle, it felt like a hunk of lumber in my hands. There wasn't any way to easily repair the damage to the carbon-fibre paddle—duct-taping it would never work—and thinking of the long miles that lay ahead of me, I texted the teacher-turned-inventor, Chris, to ask if it might be possible for him to mail a replacement to an address along the St. Lawrence River. Fortunately, he generously offered to send me his own personal paddle, one that he'd made and raced with.

I quickly portaged straight across the narrow Presqu'ile Point, which saved me several hours of paddling all the way around it. On the far shore I launched my canoe in a marshy channel where swans were nesting among the cattails. Beyond Presqu'ile the scenery was beautiful, with high forested hills interspersed with old farms rising back from the lakeshore. A short paddle took me to the entrance of the historic Murray Canal.

The canal banks were lined with ancient stone blocks, while beyond were forests of cottonwoods, cedars, sugar maples, and a vast number of dead ash trees—killed by the emerald ash borer, an invasive beetle accidentally introduced to North America in 2002 with devastating consequences. In just twenty years, these rapacious beetles have killed millions of ash trees. But all those dead ash trees were, at the moment at least, providing an unrivalled buffet for woodpeckers, which feed on insects in dead trees. The pecking of dozens of woodpeckers filled the air, and amid the din I heard the distinct laughing call of a giant pileated woodpecker echoing out of the woods. As I proceeded along the banks I passed a few people fishing. In a couple of hours, I'd completed my transit of the canal and reached the Bay of Quinte.

I made camp for the night on a little uninhabited island several kilometres offshore in the middle of the bay. Large wild grapevines flourished on the island and there were some Canada geese on it. However, the best camping site on the island, beneath the spreading branches of a great oak, was already occupied—by a nesting swan. Everywhere else on the island was rather tangled with grapevines and thick shrubbery. But I hadn't the heart to scare a swan from a nest, so I made do with what I could find on the island's opposite shore. The sun was just setting as I pitched my tent in a thicket beside some boulders in the overgrown

woods. The rocks at least made for nice tables and chairs, allowing me to sit comfortably while boiling water on my miniature
camp stove. After a satisfying dinner of freeze-dried lasagna,
I crawled into my tent.

When morning dawned, I discovered that there were only
a few granola bars and almonds left for my breakfast. It'd been
fifteen days since I set off from Long Point, and I was running
low on rations. Luckily just up ahead on the lakeshore was the
small town of Trenton, which had a grocery store only a stone's
throw from the water. I could hide my canoe in the woods there,
then make a dash to the store to replenish my supplies.

An hour's paddle brought me to the lakeshore beneath the
grocery store. Some weeping willows, bushes, and cattails easily
served to conceal my canoe. I then sprinted up into the parking
lot behind the store, where shipping crates were piled up, and
headed for the entrance. In less than thirty minutes I'd loaded
up on apples, granola bars, nuts, jerky, dried pasta, instant rice,
and a few perishables like yogurt and grapes. A short time later,
I was back on the lake paddling, snacking as I did so on some of
the rare delicacies I'd acquired. I'd been living off only a meal a
day for the last couple of weeks, so it felt wonderful to suddenly
have an abundance of food.

As I canoed along I passed several fishing boats with people
on board trolling. The Bay of Quinte's sheltered waters attract
anglers year-round. Just as I polished off my yogurt I heard a
roaring engine overhead and looked up to see a military aircraft—a Canadian Forces Hercules—landing at CFB Trenton,
Canada's largest air force base. Established in 1931, many of the
Allied pilots who trained here would go on to fight the German

Luftwaffe in World War II. A little farther on I passed under a very high bridge, linking the small city of Belleville to Prince Edward County.

That night, having paddled most of the day along the mainland shore, I made camp in the only place I could find: a field partially overgrown with scrubby apple trees. There weren't any houses in sight, and the whole area felt strangely deserted. It was only after I'd pitched my tent that I realized I was in a cow pasture. This made me slightly uneasy, as I knew some farms kept bulls among the cows. I pictured an angry bull stampeding into my tent in the night. But I reassured myself that this wasn't, on balance, any riskier than all the time I'd spent sleeping on the arctic tundra with muskoxen stomping about. Their horns are similar to a bull's, and I knew from past experience that they can be surprisingly aggressive when they stumble upon a tent in the dark. But here at least I had some apple trees that I could climb to escape, whereas in the Arctic there aren't any trees.

Fortunately, the night passed peacefully without any bulls trampling me. I was gone before dawn, and just as the sun was rising I passed under another high bridge, the Quinte Skyway, which links the community of Deseronto to Prince Edward County. After the bridge I took a sharp turn south, following a zigzagging bay back toward the main body of Lake Ontario. Here the scenery was even more beautiful, with wonderful wooded hills overlooking the water. As I cruised in closer to shore to gain a better look, I saw that the forests were made up of old-growth sugar maples, red oaks, and other ancient trees. Cottages and homes were thinly scattered among the hills, as well as the occasional farm. These areas, like other parts of southern Ontario, were largely first settled and farmed in the late 1780s by refugees from the American Revolution. This included members of the once mighty Six Nations Iroquois Confederacy, a centuries-old alliance of six First Nations—the Seneca, Oneida, Cayuga, Onondaga, Mohawk, and the Tuscarora, who were the last to join. But the American Revolution split the Confederacy, with most of the Seneca, Cayuga, Onondaga, and Mohawk fighting on the British side, while the Oneida and Tuscarora took up arms with the rebels. When the British were defeated, the tribes that had fought with them lost their traditional homelands that had now fallen under the control of the United States. Like the other Loyalists, they fled to Canada to rebuild, with many settling on the Bay of Quinte.

On fallen trees reaching out over the water lay half a dozen northern map turtles happily sunning themselves. These striking turtles have colourful patterns on their shells that resemble a map, hence the name. I also spotted crouching along the shore a dexterous raccoon hunting for frogs or fish. Raccoons, I think, suffer from something of a public relations problem on account of their city cousins, which most people associate with raids on trash cans and gardens. But the majority of raccoons aren't actually urban dwellers, but still very much creatures of the wild, and in my experience, rather hard workers when it comes to their hunting and fishing. Many times when paddling wild rivers I've observed raccoons out in daylight, balancing on rocks midstream hunting fish, and I always thought these wild raccoons differed a great deal from their urban counterparts.

Off Glenora I encountered a small passenger ferry shuttling cars between the mainland and Prince Edward County.

Just above this historic little village rises a steep hill that locals rather generously once named the "mountain." It's a geographical curiosity owing to a deep lake that sits on its summit. Legends have clustered about this "lake on the mountain" for centuries, including that it's bottomless and has no source. I found it added a nice colour to things as I paddled in the shadow of the hills.

I pushed on for another fifteen kilometres, passing more farms and two-century-old homesteads that I felt more than likely had some ghost stories associated with them. By now the sun was dipping below the horizon and I was eagerly scanning the shore for a possible spot to spend the night. It was mostly all farms, so I landed at one and hiked up a hill to a farmhouse to ask permission to camp. It seemed to be a horse farm, as I noticed quite a few horses in pasture, as well as some adjoining cornfields. I met an older couple outside the house on their driveway, who, unfortunately, I seemed to spook at first by my sudden appearance in the fading light. But after my apologies and explanation, they were as friendly as anyone I'd encountered, and kindly granted me permission to set up my tent. After thanking them, I made camp in the dark by a swampy stream flowing into the lake.

10

THOUSAND ISLANDS

M Y JOURNEY THROUGH Lake Ontario was nearly complete. The next morning, bright and early, I paddled past Amherst Island and watched Lake Ontario narrow toward its outlet—the St. Lawrence River, which drains all the Great Lakes into the Atlantic Ocean. Situated at this strategic crossroads is the city of Kingston, which, like most Canadian cities, had begun as a fur-trading post. It'd been founded in the age of empires as a French outpost back in 1673.

Despite my resupply just two days earlier, I was feeling ravenous, and I'd already eaten through much of my restocked provisions. The map tantalizingly indicated that there was a Subway located on Kingston's outskirts, just inland from the river, and as I paddled, stroke after stroke, images of a foot-long sandwich with fresh toppings haunted my dreams. I couldn't resist, so I resolved I'd find some place to hide my canoe and make a dash to the Subway.

But what the map hadn't indicated was that near the Subway, the shoreline was all limestone cliffs. Approaching in my canoe, I saw that there'd be no easy way to get up to the road where the Subway stood. Still, I reminded myself that mere cliffs shouldn't prevent someone from enjoying a Subway sandwich. I steered closer to shore, inspecting the rocky cliffs for any possible landing site. Luck was with me: hidden beneath overhanging willows and cedars I found a little cove. There were some waves, but I was quick to drive my canoe ashore and jump out, then haul it up before the swells smashed it against the rocks. It took every ounce of my strength— spurred on by thoughts of fresh crunchy peppers—to heave the loaded canoe up the steep embankment into the cove. The eroded ground here was still steep enough that the canoe could slide back into the water, or be knocked loose by a wave from a passing freighter. So with rope I lashed the canoe to one of the stouter willows. One thing I didn't have to worry about was anyone stumbling upon it in my absence—the cliffs would see to that. Now all I had to do was scale the cliffs to my mouth-watering lunch.

This proved a little more challenging than I'd anticipated. I dug into the steep slope with my boots, pulling at roots or whatever else I could grab to edge my way up. I was wearing my rubber paddling boots (my hiking boots were stashed away), which weren't the best for climbing. There was also broken glass that forced me to be careful where I grasped. But my appetite drove me on, and huffing and puffing, I eventually managed to haul myself to the top.

Once up, I dashed through the bushes along the road's shoulder toward the Subway. When I burst in, the young clerk supressed a laugh at my obvious eagerness. I ordered a twelve-inch cold cut on multigrain, with two cookies, a bag of chips, and an iced tea. Then, my coveted prize in hand, I ran back like a bandit to the cove beneath the cliffs to enjoy my lunch in the company of my canoe. It was every bit as delicious as I dreamed it would be.

With my gnawing hunger satisfied, I relaunched my canoe and resumed paddling toward Kingston proper, wondering what other marvels this historic city might hold in store. It's long been known as the "Limestone City" for its many stone buildings. I'd already seen some of that limestone in the form of the cliffs I'd scaled. For more than three centuries, quarries have extracted the stone here for construction. Along the shore, I passed a number of nice houses, interspersed with forests and parkland. But my first view of the city's famous limestone archi-tecture wasn't necessarily the most hospitable—it was Kingston Penitentiary. This grand old prison is among the oldest in North America, and certainly among the most visually impres-sive—it was built in 1833–34 out of solid limestone blocks hewn from the local quarries. The prison remained in operation for nearly two centuries, housing some of the country's most notor-ious criminals. When it closed in 2013, it was the oldest prison in the world in continuous use, which I suppose is a testament to the sturdiness of the original construction. From my position on the water, bobbing in my canoe, it certainly did seem like an ominous-looking fortress.

A little farther along I spotted poking through the trees the towers and spires of Queen's University, founded in 1841. Nearby, guarding the waterfront, stood a castle tower. This is one of four waterfront towers built almost two centuries ago to guard Kingston. Known as "Martello Towers" after the medieval Corsican fortress on which they were modelled, these impressive bastions were designed to counter oncoming enemy ships with cannon fire. Their design allowed a small number of defenders to hold off a much larger attacking force. The ones at Kingston had been built in the 1840s, following renewed fears of another American invasion. Fortunately, the crisis this time was averted peacefully, though certainly over the centuries Kingston has seen a lot of blood spilled. The French Fort Frontenac was attacked in 1688 by Mohawk warriors from the south, who were the enemies of France's fur trade allies, the Wendat and other northern tribes. The French managed to hold on to Frontenac until 1758, when, after a brief siege, the fort's badly outnumbered garrison surrendered to the British.

After this I passed by the historic downtown with its stately limestone buildings, including the grand city hall, the high dome of which was visible from the water. I next cut across the mouth of the Cataraqui River, which drains into the St. Lawrence from the north. On the west bank, just beyond where downtown Kingston sits, are the crumbled three-and-a-half-century-old ruins of Fort Frontenac. The original masonry has been excavated by archaeologists, and parts of the bastion walls sit exposed to view, alongside later fortifications.

From my canoe I scanned the horizon, taking in numerous historical monuments and castle-like structures. Across the water from Fort Frontenac is the Royal Military College, established in 1874 to instruct Canada's military officers. I could see on its bucolic grounds an imposing limestone arch; etched into it are the names of fallen graduates killed serving on missions since the 1800s. A ferry zoomed across the harbour in front of me, heading toward Wolfe Island, a large island with farms and a permanent population numbering several thousand.

Across a second bay from the college, commanding the high ground, loomed the battlements of a second fortress—a star-shaped, thick-walled construction known as Fort Henry. This strategic high point, which overlooks the entrance to Kingston Harbour, had been fortified in the War of 1812 to guard against American attack. The fort standing today was built in the 1830s at a time of renewed threats of American invasion, which remained a concern in Canada for almost a century and a half. I paddled closer toward the wooded shore for a better look at things, noticing as I did so a second Martello tower on the water's edge.

The sun was sinking, and I had to find somewhere to camp. Glancing behind, I had my last look at Lake Ontario's wide expanse. Ahead of me lay the Thousand Islands of the St. Lawrence River, bathed in the golden light of the setting sun, which made them seem like some enchanted dreamscape. Despite the name, there are actually more than eighteen hundred islands in this chain that stretches downriver from Kingston. With that many islands ahead of me, I figured I ought to have an easy time finding campsites. The islands are roughly split between Canada and the United States, with the international boundary running through them. Many of the islands are studded with cottages, and the larger ones have permanent populations.

There were two forested islands, both uninhabited, just off from Fort Henry. So I put to shore on the larger of the two and pitched my tent in the woods. One thing immediately apparent about these islands was the dramatic change in rock formation—in sharp contrast to the white limestone cliffs beside Kingston, the rocks here were pinkish-red granite, part of a southern extension of the Canadian Shield. The Shield is by far the largest geological formation in Canada, covering almost half the country, all the way from the St. Lawrence River to the Northwest Territories, making up the iconic Group of Seven landscape.

The following days paddling through these bewitching islands full of natural beauty and charm proved a welcome break from the challenges of navigating two Great Lakes. I could relax and paddle downstream with the current, which was quite swift in those places where it squeezed between rocky islands. The water, too, was uncommonly clear; I frequently saw bass and pike swimming below. On some of the wilder islands I glimpsed deer wandering among the pine and oak forests. Loons drifted on the current, as did many ducks, swans, and geese, while eagles soared overhead. The cottages ranged from rustic cabins on the smallest rock outcrops to huge ornate mansions.

In this natural labyrinth of coves, bays, and islets, I had to pay careful attention to my map, as it was quite easy to get turned around. At Ivy Lea I canoed under the high span of the Thousand Islands Bridge, towering as it does far above the river.

Several giant freighters also passed me. The wake from these massive ships was considerable on the narrow confines of the river, knocking me around in my canoe on their waves as they steamed by.

These maze-like islands were once the hunting grounds of the infamous Bill Johnston, the "Pirate of the Thousand Islands." A Canadian by upbringing, Johnston had begun his career as a smuggler, transporting rum and other goods across the river by moonlight. Like most pirates though, his loyalties were flexible: when, during the War of 1812, he was accused of acting as an American spy (an offence punishable by death), Johnston openly turned pirate and preyed on Canadian merchant ships. But it wasn't until decades after the war that he reached the height of his notoriety. In the Rebellion of 1837, Johnston pledged his support to William Lyon Mackenzie, who in turn proclaimed him the "Admiral of the Eastern Navy." Johnston's piracy reached its apogee when he and his motley crew captured under darkness the passenger ship *Sir Robert Peel* and burned it to ashes. Despite the outrage from the attack and a price on his head, the wily old pirate managed to evade his pursuers for years by hiding out among the islands. He escaped Canadian justice by later settling down in the United States, where, given his folk hero status, juries refused to convict him.

I canoed by small communities scattered along the shore, most of them, like others in Ontario, founded in the late 1700s by American Revolution refugees. This includes Gananoque, Rockport, and Mallorytown Landing. It was a warm night, with clear skies and enough moonlight to see by, so I kept paddling well after dark, before finally making camp in a secluded park.

The next morning I was off again before dawn, passing Brockville then Prescott and admiring from my canoe the amazing number of old stone houses that have withstood the ravages of time in these Loyalist-era towns. Many of these houses were two centuries old or more, and some had even survived the depredations of the War of 1812. They gave a strong historic flair to the area. At Prescott another fort stood guarding the shore— Fort Wellington, which had been constructed during the war, then strengthened and rebuilt in subsequent years. The stronghold itself was never attacked, but its garrison fought in several battles. In the winter of 1813, a Canadian regiment stationed at the fort, the Glengarry Light Infantry, launched a raid across the frozen river on the American settlements in revenge for earlier attacks on the Canadian shore.

Downstream from the fort an old stone windmill towered like a castle turret above the surrounding trees. I landed on the rocky shore beneath it and climbed the forested bank to take a closer look. A short trail wound through the woods up to the weathered structure. The forest felt strangely quiet and deserted, with hardly a bird to be heard. The famous Battle of the Windmill had been fought here in 1838. After the uprising led by the William Lyon Mackenzie had been crushed, Mackenzie and other rebel leaders fled to the United States. There they recruited any soldier-of-fortune, adventurer, or bandit to join their cause with the promise of just rewards should they help invade Canada and overthrow the government. These would-be revolutionaries formed secret societies known as "Hunters' Lodges," and in November 1838 planned to strike across the St. Lawrence at Prescott. The expedition was placed under the command of a colourful Scandinavian adventurer named Nils von Schultz.

Under cover of darkness the invasion force crossed the river, landing outside Prescott. But rather than the welcome they anticipated as liberators, most of the local Canadians, with bitter memories of the last time invaders had come from the south, took up arms against them. Von Schultz and his band seized the windmill as a stronghold while a fierce battle raged around it. After days of fighting, cut off and surrounded, the desperate band had no choice but to surrender. Von Schultz and the other ringleaders were executed, while many of the rest were deported to a bleak penal colony on the far side of the world, Australia. About fifty of the invaders killed in the fighting were buried in a mass grave beside the windmill. Their restless ghosts, it's said, still haunt the site.

The wind was rising, so I turned back through the woods to fetch my canoe. Just a short distance downriver two enormous structures loomed into view. The first was the port of Johnstown, whose concrete grain elevator towered so high it made the trees below look like mere shrubs. The port is nearly a kilometre long, and I had no choice but to paddle alongside it. This made me quite nervous as it would put me in the path of any docking freighter, which could crush my canoe like a fly against the port's concrete walls. I paddled fast to get by the monstrous concrete building, which looked vaguely sinister with all its dirty broken windows, before any ships arrived.

Once safely beyond the port I drifted under the second enormous structure: a huge suspension bridge with twin towers linking Canada to the United States. It was in these waters that the Battle of the Thousand Islands was fought. In the middle of the river lies Chimney Island, which the French had turned into a formidable stronghold complete with a fort, cannons, and natural cliffs. When a British fleet sailed down from Lake Ontario in 1760 and attacked the island, the French, despite being badly outnumbered, put up a fierce defence—sinking two of the attacking ships and running a third aground under heavy fire. Fighting raged for days until, out of ammunition and with most of their garrison dead or wounded, the defenders finally surrendered.

On the far side of the bridge was a busy campground full of trailers. A kind of canal or side channel with cottages overlooking it allowed me to bypass the river's main shipping lane until I reached the little riverside village of Cardinal. The river curves here, which prevented me from seeing ahead. Along the riverbank was a large industrial plant or factory, and immediately out from it there seemed to be some turbulent water, possibly even rapids. A big freighter had just steamed through the narrow shipping channel at fast speed, and I was slightly wary of blindly canoeing around the river bend into water I didn't have any familiarity with—especially with the added hazard of boats motoring around. On the other hand, I'd never heard of any dangerous water here, and I was reluctant to delay. In any case, the extensive industrial works and fencing on shore precluded any possibility of landing and scouting ahead.

So I proceeded cautiously, assuring myself that there was nothing to worry about. I paddled round the bend and found the current increasing steadily until big rolling waves materialized.

The size of these surprised me, but I paddled straight through them, swooping up and down wildly, which spit me out into calmer water at the bottom. There were many fishing boats here—I counted ten in all—with anglers on board casting. The opening of the season and the nice weather had evidently brought them to this spot, where the swift current presumably makes for excellent pickerel fishing. After weaving through all the motorboats, I continued on my way.

Running alongside the St. Lawrence was a small canal connected to the river, with a few openings along its bushy banks where I could slip in and take advantage of its sheltered waters. I did so, and found myself in a narrow channel, with trees on either side. This went on for several kilometres, taking me past farms and forests, and just as the sun set and the moon came up, an abandoned stone farmhouse in the woods. Spruces and pines had grown up all around it; only its gabled roof and stone chimneys were peeking out. Surely, I thought, drawing a stroke of my paddle through the moon's reflection, if someone wished to make a horror movie, they could hardly find a better place.

Which reminded me that I needed to make camp. The shore was wild and secluded here, with scrubby, tangled woods and overgrown banks. I pushed on in the moonlight, weaving into a sort of lagoon, where I found a quiet place to set up my tent. By now I was thoroughly exhausted and ravenously hungry—this had been my longest ever day paddling, seventeen hours. In the moonlight I cooked some dried pasta and ate a few granola bars, then crawled into my sleeping bag and fell fast asleep.

✳

AT DAWN THE next morning, to get out of the lagoon, I had to perform a short portage across the Iroquois Boat Launch. This allowed me to bypass the Iroquois dam, which controls water levels on the St. Lawrence. The freighter ships have a system of locks that lets them bypass the river's dams, but locks aren't for canoes, and in any case, it was faster for me to just do the short portage.

A few hours' steady paddling brought me to the little village of Morrisburg. I knew it well, as it's my mother's hometown. Drifting on the current, I recognized a sheltered bay where my brother and I had fished as children twenty-five years earlier. I was pleased to see it unchanged, and that the village was still the same place I remembered. A little farther along was where I used to swim, hunting for golf balls, which I'd collect and resell to my uncle. He drove a hard bargain, but we'd finally settled on a price of a quarter a ball. I steered closer to the shore to see if anyone in the decades since had taken up my old hustle. It looked as if no one had, as I counted a veritable jackpot— some three dozen balls lying unclaimed on the rocky bottom.

Downstream of Morrisburg the river becomes remarkably wild, with miles of forested shoreline and islands without any houses or buildings. I saw deer and coyotes wandering the banks, and blue herons and waterfowl abounded in the shallows. The current was swift, with ripples and small rapids in places among the islands, which provide sanctuary for nesting birds. Fish, too, were clearly abundant; I spooked enormous schools of carp that must have numbered in the hundreds.

A few strokes more and a large stone obelisk standing atop a hill loomed into view. This monument commemorates the Battle of Crysler's Farm, when in November 1813 a small force of British and Canadian troops defeated a vastly larger American invasion army. A short way past the obelisk stands the Dickinson Lighthouse, build in 1865, and back from it, I could just make out Upper Canada Village through the trees, an attraction that recreates life here in the early 1800s. Beside it is the three-thousand-hectare Upper Canada Migratory Bird Sanctuary, which made me excited, as it was first large bird sanctuary I'd come across since setting off from Long Point. These pockets of preserved wildlands in southernmost Canada form crucial networks linking bird migration routes stretching all the way from the Arctic down to the Great Lakes and beyond. Paddling in closer to wooded Morrison Island, I was just in time for the spring migration. I spotted eagles, terns, gulls, loons, cormorants, various ducks, geese, and kingfishers, only a few of the more than one hundred and fifty species that have been observed here.

Ahead lay more wild islands, many of them created by the deliberate flooding of the river in the 1950s, which transformed the landscape. Before that time, only smaller draught boats could make it through this section of the St. Lawrence due to rapids. But in the mid-twentieth century the Canadian and American governments agreed on a plan to dam and flood the river, which would allow much larger ocean-going ships to travel all the way up the St. Lawrence. The damming deepened and greatly widened the river, resulting in "lost villages" that were entirely flooded. Nine villages in total, plus one inhabited island, were lost—the former village sites now lie at the bottom of the river.

Gliding over these flooded one-time towns was a bit of a strange feeling; the river is mostly quiet and wooded in this section, which makes it easy to imagine a forgotten, ghost-town landscape. Absent-mindedly I passed alongside a large, heavily wooded island known as Croil Island, without realizing that it's within American waters. I'd inadvertently crossed into New York State, paddling all the way around the island. No one, luckily, was around to notice my invasion of American waters, and I happily escaped back to the Canadian shore undetected.

Once safely back in Canada, I could see off my canoe's bow a long chain of about a dozen forested islands. These are the Woodlands Islands, which have parks and campgrounds, while the scenic Long Sault Parkway links them all together. The last of the chain is Moulinette, and here you will find the home of my aunt and uncle. Their house was my immediate destination. Alexandria had mailed them some fresh clothes and rations for me, and Chris, the paddle maker, had shipped his replacement paddle there.

I paddled hard across a big open stretch of river, zeroing in on my relatives' backyard. Standing there I saw a crowd of people had gathered—it seemed as if the whole island had come to greet me. But it was only my cousins and their children, along with my aunts, uncles, and grandmother. They welcomed me ashore with fresh food and pizza, asking how I'd fared.

After lunch and getting caught up on family news, I pitched my tent in the backyard, just above their beach. (My aunt and uncle had offered me a bed in the house, but I explained that my tent felt like a five-star hotel to me, and that I slept as well in it as I ever did in any bed. Plus their lawn was as soft and level as anyone could wish.)

A storm blew in that afternoon, with fierce winds and lashing rain that cut short the family get-together, but blew out just as quickly. I sorted through my gear, leaving behind some items I could do without, while adding some new batteries for my flashlight as well as the much-needed food and fresh clothes.

After a sumptuous breakfast the following morning of cereal, yogurt, apples, tea, and a bagel, I felt ready and eager for anything. My aunt had wished me well before leaving early for work, while my uncle saw me off on the riverbank. At seven in the morning I shoved my canoe in the water, waved, then jumped in and paddled off.

LA BELLE PROVINCE

I T WAS AN overcast day, with rain threatening. But despite the grey skies, several lofty mountains were visible on the horizon, which one doesn't often associate with southern Ontario. However, I was paddling only thirty-five kilometres north of the Adirondack Mountains across the border in New York State. These high peaks, which have twice hosted the Winter Olympics, are easily visible from eastern Ontario.

A short distance downstream a menacing-looking hydro-electric dam spanning the river loomed into sight: the Moses-Saunders Power Dam, which besides generating electricity, also controls water levels. With the wisdom that only comes from years of canoeing experience, I perceived almost at once that it was crucial not to get sucked into these hydro turbines. I'd have to land on shore and portage around them.

Still, I intended to get as close as possible to the large dam, to cut down on the length of the portage. However, it seemed that as a safety precaution, the authorities had fenced off the steep embankment along the shore for several kilometres, thereby preventing anyone from accidentally falling in or doing something stupid like canoeing here. I had to land immediately above it at Guindon Park, a thickly forested area on the outskirts of Cornwall.

The morning was mild, though I felt the odd raindrop from the skies above. After heaving my canoe ashore, I set up my two-wheeled cart and strapped the canoe and gear onto it. There was a path winding through the forest that I could follow; after a distance of about seven kilometres, it would take me beyond the dam. But I soon realized I had my work cut out for me: the kind-heartedness of my aunts had led all three of them to equip me with care packages, so that I was loaded down with apples, peanut butter and jam sandwiches, oranges, cookies, and much more packed food than I'd ever had before. Besides this I had several water jugs. All this extra weight was making it harder to push my canoe. Panting and sweating, I had to remove my jacket.

The forest I was passing through was very swampy, looking like something out of the Deep South, with stands of silver maples and cottonwoods rising out of black water and hickories and hawthorns growing on little dry clumps. It wasn't long before something bit me in the back. As might be guessed, the stagnant swamp water makes excellent mosquito breeding ground. It was still only mid-May, but as if by dark magic, the sudden warm spell had released these little winged pests, with dense clouds of them materializing to torment me. I'd switched at my aunt and uncle's into a new long-sleeved shirt in anticipation of warmer weather. But to my horror I now learned that it wasn't thick enough to protect against mosquitoes: they cut right through it. Pushing the heavily loaded canoe required two hands, leaving me unable to swat them away; it felt as if fifty or more of them were feeding on my back with impunity. This was maddening, but to swat them off I'd have to stop, and standing still only attracted more mosquitoes. It seemed there was no choice but to just grind my teeth and bear it the best I could, exerting all my energy to push as fast as possible.

Finally, I crossed a short causeway toward the generating station and the dam. A sign indicated that the main trail was closed due to construction, which forced me to find a side trail through the woods back to the river. After snacking on an apple, I launched my canoe out into the swirling waters below the hydro dam.

The water here was the fastest I'd seen anywhere on the St. Lawrence, driving me downriver at a rapid pace. Ahead loomed a bridge connecting the mainland to an island midstream. I aimed for its left side, the current speeding me under it. In contrast to the Peace Bridge's currents, which have a fearsome reputation but are mostly harmless, under this bridge were genuine hazards. Immediately beyond the bridge's supporting pillars were concrete towers rising straight out of the river— why they were there, I had no idea. But the force of the surging current diverting around the bridge's pillars and then hitting these towers caused the water to rush back, generating a furious eddy between the pillars. Clenching my paddle tighter, I steered my canoe around this seething vortex, visualizing as I did so the disaster that would follow if I accidentally hit one of the pillars or became trapped in the current between them.

Later I learned the story behind these mysterious towers. It turns out that the low bridge I'd canoed under had replaced an older skyway bridge demolished in 2015. When the skyway bridge was dismantled, its concrete support pillars were left up, generating the dangerous currents I'd seen. Replacing the bridge reportedly cost seventy-five million dollars, so perhaps for budget reasons the old pillars were never removed.

After avoiding the hazards under the bridge, I encountered more rough water up ahead. On my left was Lamoureux Park and the city of Cornwall (founded in 1784), with quite a few pedestrians taking advantage of the warm weather, and casting curious glances in my direction as I raced downstream through some minor rapids. I paddled by St. Lawrence College, before leaving the city behind and entering a wide section where the current slackened. Here many islands were scattered about, with forests and farms set back from the river. This part of the St. Lawrence is known as Lake St. Francis, since it's wide enough to resemble more of a lake than a river.

The rain that had been threatening all day finally caught up with me. The sky darkened ominously and thunder rumbled. This was followed by the heaviest rain I'd ever seen—an absolute torrential downpour that turned the entire river into millions of white ripples. My synthetic rain gear—pants and jacket—was no match for such a downpour and quickly soaked right through. I couldn't have been any wetter if I'd simply jumped overboard.

It was difficult to see much through the heavy rain, but I was trying to keep an eye on the lightning, which so far didn't seem too close—a few bolts struck the far shore. But with lightning, one doesn't like to be too cavalier, and in any case the heavy rain was rapidly filling up my canoe. I had a small bailer—a plastic drink container cut in half—but no amount of bailing could displace this much rain. So I paddled as fast as I could for shore. Alas, it was almost all steel breakwalls or rocky boulder piles, which prevented any landing. Finally, I reached a Catholic church's spacious grounds, where I managed to jump onto a steep, rocky embankment and partially haul up my flooded canoe.

When it seemed the thunder had moved off a safe distance, I bailed out the canoe and resumed paddling. The rain was still coming down steadily, but not as hard as before. The shore was filled with nice houses, and through back windows I could see people inside sitting down for dinner, which made me hungry. At one house an older couple were sitting outside on their back porch under an awning, watching the storm, and called to me.

"Do you need help?" they shouted.

I shook my head, and with a wave of thanks, kept paddling along.

On the south shore opposite from me was the Lake Saint-François National Wildlife Area, which protects a large stretch of wetlands and forests crucial for thousands of migrating waterfowl. It's also home to one of the most secretive and little-known birds: the mysterious yellow rail. This quail-like, yellowish-brown bird only lives deep in inaccessible marshes, and so is hardly ever seen by humans.

For the first time, the river's south shore was no longer the United States. Just past Cornwall the international border ceases to follow the river and instead makes a straight line east, running like that all the way to the mountains of New Hampshire. The result is that both sides of the St. Lawrence here, and the rest of the way downriver, are Canadian soil. Although the border might seem arbitrary, it's not—it's the product of centuries of warfare, as the numerous forts, battlefields, and towers I'd already passed testified. Here, the boundary largely reflects the physical geography of the mountain barrier, which naturally played a major role in military campaigns. Just as mountain barriers have formed natural boundaries in Asia and Europe, so too is the case here. It roughly reflects the ancient dividing line between the French and British colonies, which was inherited by Canada and the United States.

The rain lifted and a perfect rainbow formed. I paddled on briskly, as it was evening now, and drenched and chilled as I was, I was eager to find somewhere to camp. Plenty of wild, uninhabited islands lay about me, but most were too marshy for a campsite. I rounded Cameron's Point, pausing just long enough to enjoy the sight of a blue heron stalking through the water. Along this shore were several conservation areas and parks—still closed for the season—but just as the sun sank below the horizon I managed to find myself a secluded spot beneath some big silver maples in the marshy woods. The ground was damp and spongy, especially with the heavy rain, but by spreading out my tinfoil emergency blanket inside the tent, I was able to keep my sleeping bag dry. The feeling of getting out of wet clothes into dry ones was as wonderful as anything, and I stretched out contentedly, listening to Canada geese honk from somewhere in the marsh.

＊

I WOKE TO a very foggy morning, such that when I unzipped my tent, I couldn't see the river. The fog had swallowed everything up. I broke camp as quickly as I could manage in the dim light, trying my best not to misplace any vital piece of gear. Navigating through the fog was challenging, so as a precaution, I kept close to the shore. Blasts from ships' horns echoed eerily out of the mist, and I caught a fleeting glimpse of one of these steel giants before it vanished again like a ghost ship.

The fog only gradually lifted, and as it did, I was surprised to see a lone fisherman standing in a small boat, checking some traps tethered to long stakes in the shallows. It looked like he was trapping minnows, presumably for bait. I would have asked, but he seemed absorbed in his task, so I pushed on. After a few more hours of steady paddling I bid farewell to Ontario and crossed into Quebec.

By mid-morning the last of the fog had lifted and a hesitant sun was peeking through the clouds. I spread my wet clothes out in the canoe to catch whatever feeble rays they might. But they'd barely dried when thunder rumbled again and rain started. Flashes of lightning forced me to shore in a hurry. The shore wasn't particularly hospitable—I'd landed right beneath a busy road on a narrow strip of land. Everything nearby was commercial or residential properties. I was on the outskirts of Les Coteaux, a small municipality in westernmost Quebec.

With the storm intensifying, I hauled my canoe—flooded again from the downpour—onto the shore, then pulling up my hood, I huddled against a grassy embankment. I studied the skies and the wind direction, and tried to find some clue that perhaps better weather might be coming—but there wasn't any. Grey clouds extended in all directions as far as the eye could see. Given the thunder and the approaching darkness—it was already evening—I felt I might be stuck spending the night here. It wouldn't be possible to set up the tent on the narrow shore beneath the highway. I'd have to sleep in the open under a tree.

Just as I was contemplating this dismal prospect, a voice speaking in French attracted my attention. I turned and saw a young man in a hoodie standing above the embankment on the side of the road. He waved and asked me in French what I was doing and if I needed help. My French was limited; I'd taken a few university courses, but that was fifteen years ago. I answered the best I could, saying I was fine, and apologizing for my limited language skills.

"Oh, no problem," the young man responded in English. "Do you have anywhere to go?"

"No." I shook my head. "I'll just wait here until the storm passes, and then push on."

"You live around here?"

"No. I've been canoeing for twenty-four days. I started on Lake Erie, and I'm heading downriver."

He looked surprised. "How far are you going?"

"To the saltwater at least."

He seemed even more surprised. "I live near here, you're welcome to come camp at my place if you like."

"Oh," I said, "that's very nice of you. How far is your house?"

"Over there," he said, gesturing across the road and down an intersection toward a residential area.

"Oh, that's a bit far for me. I like to stay by the water, so that I can be ready to leave when conditions improve. But thank you. That's very kind of you."

"Okay," he said, smiling and nodding. Then he waved and wished me good luck, before jogging off to escape the rain. It was really quite encouraging to think that in almost nine hundred kilometres of paddling, everyone I'd met had been incredibly kind and eager to help me. It just goes to show that if you're ever feeling cynical about the state of the world, some old-fashioned travel might be the cure.

When a break in the thunderclouds came, I took advantage of it to relaunch. I paddled as fast as I could, eager to find somewhere to camp. There was a municipal quay running far into the water that I had to round, and then a small, exposed island, which didn't look very hospitable. I kept racing ahead, knowing that more storm cells might blow in. Beyond the quay the shore was entirely developed, with numerous houses. I was fast running out of options. Ahead was a small trailer park nestled beside the entrance to an old canal.

I could see some forested islands a bit farther along, but with the storm and high winds generating sizable waves across the wide-open expanse of river, the chances of reaching them before nightfall weren't good. So, shivering in the cold and rain, I landed at the trailer park. As far as I could tell it was still closed for the season. There were trailers parked in designated spots, but no sign of people. I decided to go investigate anyway. Perhaps if an attendant was around, I could ask permission to spend the night.

A quick search revealed no one, and with the wild weather, it didn't seem likely anyone would show up. The forecast was calling for seventy-kilometre-an-hour gusts and severe thunderstorms. But as I was walking back to my canoe I noticed a lone trailer with a light on. Someone, apparently, was here after all. Unsure what to do, I went back to the water to take another look at the sky. There were still thunderclouds, and the gusting wind was driving them northeast toward my position. The rain picked up, coming down heavy and drenching me, while the temperature had slipped to four degrees. My socks had soaked right through, and I was as wet as could be.

I was stuck here. Shivering, I went and stood under a willow. I decided that the best thing to do might be to go knock on that trailer's door and ask whoever was inside whether they thought anyone would object to me setting up a tent. I'd hesitated to do so, because I didn't want to be a nuisance—but the stormy weather at last overcame my hesitations.

I walked up to the trailer and let myself into a screened porch attached to it to rap on the door. I did so sheepishly, then stepped back to wait. A short time later, the door opened and an old lady peered out.

"Bonjour," I said.

"Bonjour." She nodded back, looking curiously at my soaking wet figure.

"I'm sorry," I said, speaking in French. "My name is Adam. My French isn't very good. Do you speak English?"

"No." She shook her head.

"Oh," I said, trying to rack my brain to remember more words to explain myself. "I've canoed a long way . . . I was wondering if it's possible to get permission to camp here?"

She looked me up and down, then after a pause, said in French, "That's no problem. You can camp here."

"Thank you," I replied. "I'll go get my things and put my tent there,"—I pointed to the only patch of grass in the immediate vicinity that hadn't become a puddle—"if that's okay?"

"Sure." She nodded.

I hurried off to fetch my canoe and gear and carry it to my designated spot. The old lady watched me from the shelter of the screened-in enclosure. When I'd finished moving everything, she motioned for me to come near.

"You look very wet," she said. "Come in and sit down out of the rain." She pointed to a chair on the porch.

I explained that I wouldn't wish to get her porch wet, but she wouldn't hear of it and gestured again to the chair. So I opened the door and sat down, while she disappeared into the trailer. A moment later she re-emerged with a steaming pot. I tried to say this wasn't necessary, but she insisted. It was hot French onion soup, which did seem more appealing than the granola bar I'd planned on having for dinner. Before I'd even finished the soup, my host brought out cheese and crackers.

"What's your name?" I asked, feeling bad that we hadn't had a proper introduction.

"Muriel," she said, gesturing at me to eat the cheese.

It may have been my famished state, but the cheese tasted like the best thing I'd ever eaten. As I was devouring it, Muriel and I communicated the best we could given my limited French. She told me that she stayed here at the campground from May through October, but that no one else had arrived yet for the season. For the last thirty-five years she'd spent her summers here. She was happy to have my company, she said, as it was quite lonely otherwise. She'd grown up on a farm nearby, and said that her father (if I understood correctly) made cheese like what I was eating. It was a light white variety, almost sweet to the taste, and seemed more delicious than any cheese I'd ever had. When she saw how much I enjoyed it, she gave me a block of it to take on my journey, and some crackers too. I thanked her with all my heart.

It felt good to get warm and dry in my tent, as I kept snacking on the cheese Muriel had given me. The rain let up in the night, but when dawn broke the wind was still strong and the skies remained grey and threatening. This motivated me to get moving before the wind turned any worse. It was unfortunate that I had to break camp without saying goodbye to Muriel. But she'd told me the night before not to delay on her account. I knew the day would be an arduous one, given that downstream was Grande Isle, a huge island with a series of hydro dams, locks, and rapids around it that would necessitate several lengthy portages.

The fierce wind gave me quite a battle just getting out of the small harbour. But once I'd managed it, my course turned so that the wind was now coming mostly from behind, which was less of a concern. Immediately ahead was a train bridge, then a second bridge followed by a chain of forested islands, and finally the first of three dams I'd have to bypass.

After paddling under the second bridge, I pushed on to a small park adjacent to the first dam. It was still cold, windy, and rainy, so once I landed I wasted little time in packing my canoe, setting up the cart, and pushing off down a sidewalk to bypass the dam. This took me through the small community of Coteau-du-Lac, where I admired an eighteenth-century stone mill that sat perched beside a small river flowing into the St. Lawrence. This aged edifice had apparently been used as a defensive bastion in the long-running wars that plagued New France, when attacks by both English settlers from the south and their Mohawk allies were commonplace. Just before this mill I'd seen the earthworks and loopholed walls of another old fort, Fort Coteau-du-Lac. After the British conquest of Canada, the new rulers had built the first locks in North America here to bypass the river's treacherous rapids, and this fortress to guard them.

Beyond the fort I headed back to the riverbank to relaunch. Having bypassed the first dams and rapids, I could paddle for another twelve kilometres downstream before hitting the next set. That is, if I managed to get there. I'd thought that, having made it through the Great Lakes, I'd no longer be at the mercy of the wind. But this proved wishful thinking: as I'd soon learn, I could be as much at the wind's mercy on the wide stretches of river as on a lake. A southwesterly was howling as I stood shivering from the cold and the rain, repacking my canoe. But the waves weren't large, and for the most part I'd have a tailwind, so without another thought, I embarked.

At first the wind helped speed me along. But ahead the river curved like a crescent moon, causing the wind to hit me broadside, with big waves threatening to spill over the gunwales. The intense gusts were so strong that I could barely steer—with the change in wind direction I was now too light on the stern end, making the canoe careen wildly. Only with the most determined strokes could I right the canoe and prevent it from flipping or slamming into the rocky shore.

When I finally rounded the bay, I took advantage of a lull to land in a forested cove at the mouth of a stream to catch my breath. Among the forest were wild cherries with pink blossoms and crooked overgrown apple trees, which at some point in the distant past must have belonged to an orchard that had since gone wild. Through their branches I spotted an old stone manor. I studied it from the woods while munching on an apple to recover my strength. It looked to be from the early 1800s.

Then I turned my attention to repacking the canoe in a way that would compensate for the shifting wind gusts. Normally, I kept it a little more heavily loaded in the bow, since I was often battling headwinds and weight concentrated in the front makes these easier to manage. But now I shifted some of my water jugs and loose items to behind my seat. With more weight behind me, the stern would catch the wind less and make it easier to steer.

If anything, the screaming winds had only increased since I'd come ashore, and the whitecaps were larger than I could have thought possible on a river. The forecast had again called for seventy-kilometre-an-hour winds (which normally rules out canoeing, but when journeying to the Arctic one mustn't be too squeamish). Ten kilometres downriver was another hydro dam—if I could just get there, the wind wouldn't matter since I'd have to spend the rest of the day on shore anyway, portaging around this second series of hydro installations.

I studied the map to see if I could come up with some strategy. My hopes rose when I noticed the historic canal running parallel to the river—if I could get there, its narrow stone walls would shelter me from the gusts. Pulling up a satellite image of the area on my phone, I saw what looked like a small creek joining the river about a kilometre and a half downstream of me. This creek, it seemed, drained a small pond right beside the canal—it could be my ticket into it. But running alongside the river was a busy highway, with breakwalls that would prevent any landing. Inspecting the satellite image as minutely as I could, it appeared the creek flowed through a culvert under the highway. If I could overcome the wind just long enough to reach the culvert, I could try to squeeze through it to the sheltered canal. But I had to be sure—if I blindly paddled into the culvert only to discover that it led to some dangerous hydro installation or had a grate across it, that would be bad.

The problem was that there was no way to tell from a satellite image. With the clock ticking and the weather only growing worse, I decided I'd just have to risk it. If at the last second I saw anything that looked hazardous, I'd pull out.

My plans made, I took up my paddle, shoved the canoe into the water, and hopped in. Hard paddling drove me out of the cove into the wind and lapping waves. It was a battle to keep the canoe from crashing into the rocky shores. I was on my knees, paddling with everything I had. The readjusted weight made steering easier, but with the howling gusts, it was still all I could do just to keep careening toward the culvert. Then, when I was opposite it, I saw my chance and spun the canoe into the opening.

12

MONTREAL

M Y CANOE SQUEEZED into the culvert; the ceiling was high enough that happily my head didn't smash into it. It was dark inside, but I could see light at the far end. There was no grate blocking the exit and no deadly-looking hydro installations. With relief I paddled the rest of the way through.

The culvert spit me out into a wooded pond on the other side, which, sheltered from the winds, was refreshingly tranquil. I paddled slowly to take in my surroundings. The weedy pond was several hundred metres long, with clear signs of beavers. A few more strokes revealed an unexpected sight— through a light rain I marvelled at the ruins of some castle-like chateau overlooking the pond's far shore, wondering what it could be. Paddling closer, it seemed to be some kind of old hydro pump house from an era when public works buildings were still made in an ornate style. The windows had been boarded shut; it looked as if it hadn't been in use for at least half a century.

Landing on a steep embankment, with a bit of huffing and puffing, I hauled my loaded canoe up the muddy slope toward the ruins to investigate. Beneath the chateau were arched aqueducts, which evidently had once controlled the water's flow. Immediately behind the chateau was the historic Soulanges Canal, which had been dug in the 1890s to replace even older canals. It had, in turn, been closed in 1958, when a much larger canal opened on the river's opposite shore to allow ocean-going freighters to bypass the dams and rapids.

The whole area appeared remarkably quiet. The fact that the canal was abandoned was perfect for me, as it meant I wouldn't have to worry about any ship traffic. I could portage my things to it, then paddle down its length, sheltered from the fierce winds, until I'd bypassed the hydro dams.

It took four hours to navigate through it on account of having to unpack and portage around the canal's derelict wooden locks, which were gradually rotting away. I was excited to see that the abandoned canal had become something of a wildlife oasis. In the rich woods that surrounded it I spotted numerous birds, among them a striking orange and black one perched on a sumac, which could only be a Baltimore oriole—the first I'd seen on my journey. Red squirrels chattered among the spruces, and I caught glimpses of wild turkeys and rabbits darting among the leafy undergrowth. By evening, I'd reached the canal's end at Lake Saint-Louis, another part of the St. Lawrence wide enough to be considered a lake. Nearby was Pointe-des-Cascades Nature Park, which preserves a large forest and several wild islands.

A heavy rain greeted me as I left the canal and paddled toward the woods at Pointe-des-Cascades. I was again drenched, but I took heart that the forest would offer shelter. I landed in a quiet cove beside some boulders, then portaged my stuff into the woods. In another hour the rain had passed, and though it was bitterly cold and still quite windy, I was able to use my little stove to boil water for tea and eat some of my remaining sandwiches. Then, chilled but content, I crawled into my tent.

✳

MAY 18 DAWNED very cold, but the wind had slackened and there wasn't any rain. I crawled outside my tent at four-thirty a.m. into the frosty air and began packing. As the bird flies the great city of Montreal was only twenty kilometres away, but to reach it I'd have to paddle thirty-five. The reason for this was twofold. First, I had to avoid the busy commercial shipping lanes where the big freighters roared along the southeastern shore, which would mean having to take the long way around the opposite side. Second, before I'd even finished packing the wind had already begun rising. At more than ten kilometres wide, Lake Saint-Louis is one of the widest points of the upper St. Lawrence, meaning there was no way to cut straight across it in a canoe—at least not safely.

From my campsite at Pointe-des-Cascades I crossed first to Perrot Island. It sits right at the mouth of where the Ottawa River joins the St. Lawrence and is a mix of farms, forests, and suburban communities. As I was paddling around this large island—battling what had turned into stiff headwinds— I admired several grand old churches as well as traditional New France–style houses with steep gabled roofs. To a traveller, it's hard not to appreciate how in Quebec, even the houses often have a unique style that reflects the province's rich heritage. Toward the eastern end of Perrot Island curiosity induced me to land on shore to inspect an ancient stone windmill overlooking the water. It turned out that it was over three centuries old—built in 1707–08. Near it stood a similarly aged stone farmhouse amid woods that made it easy to imagine stepping back in time.

After a granola bar and a sip of green tea from my thermos to warm up, I was back on the water paddling. A straight line from the windmill to Montreal Island was more than six and a half kilometres, but the bitter wind had grown so fierce that I didn't dare attempt such a long open-water crossing. I had to turn inland toward a bay, and once more battle fierce headwinds to reach a narrower point where it would be safe to cross. I managed this at a small archipelago of heavily wooded islands—Madore, Daoust, Dowker, and Caron—which allowed me to island hop across to the Montreal shoreline.

Montreal is itself an island in the St. Lawrence River, and one with a rich history. After the French explorer Jacques Cartier crossed the Atlantic in 1535, he ventured up a great river—which he called the "River of Canada"—until he reached an island with a mountain crowned with three distinct summits. He named this alluring-looking mountain "Mount Royal," which eventually became "Montreal." Fierce rapids around the island prevented Cartier from travelling any farther. Cartier hoped the river might flow straight to China, but this, it turned out, was not quite accurate. In the island's old-growth forests Cartier and his crew encountered a palisaded Iroquoian village, supported by farms producing corn, squash, and beans. Although language barriers prevented easy communications, the villagers informed Cartier that there were rich cities just to the west. Such tales whetted Cartier's avarice, but unwilling to leave the safety of his ship, in the end he never ventured any farther than the island he'd named "Mount Royal."

Not for almost a hundred years would any explorer make it past this mythical-seeming island with its three-peaked mountain and raging rapids. It was the extraordinary sailor Samuel de Champlain who finally did in 1611. Champlain succeeded by doing what Cartier would not—forgoing the safety of his ship at Mount Royal and instead travelling as the locals did: by birchbark canoe. However, these locals, it turned out, weren't the same people Cartier had encountered. The Iroquoian villagers had since been driven out and replaced by their traditional enemies, the more northern tribes of Wendat and Algonquins, who now had their own villages on the island. Champlain forged an alliance with these peoples—bound in blood—that was to have momentous consequences. The alliance committed Champlain and his French colonists to abetting the northern tribes in their long-running wars with the mighty Iroquois Confederacy to the south, which nearly spelled the doom of New France. A century of brutal warfare followed, with up to ten percent of the colony's population perishing in the wars.

Although Champlain had built a trading post on the island, not until the swashbuckling adventurer Paul de Chomedey de Maisonneuve arrived in 1642 did the French succeed in establishing a permanent village. It was this village that grew into Montreal—though it was more than once nearly wiped out in raids by the Iroquois Confederacy. When in 1701 the Iroquois

Wars finally ended, the island's fate still remained contentious. After a series of bloody battles, in 1760 a British army captured Montreal. With the British conquest came Scottish and English traders who made Montreal their new headquarters to capitalize on its strategic position in the fur trade. But the British faced their own challenge to ruling the island when an American army in 1775 captured the city and put it under occupation. For a brief time the Stars and Stripes flew over Montreal, until the Americans were driven out just a few years later. On their departure they attempted to burn the city as a parting gift, but luckily for the inhabitants, they failed.

The island was too heavily defended to ever be seriously threatened in the War of 1812, and it thereafter became Canada's largest and most economically important city—a status it would hold until the mid-twentieth century. For a time Montreal was even Canada's capital, replacing Quebec City, which had been the capital for over two hundred years, until a violent Tory mob attacked the parliament buildings in Montreal and burned them to the ground in 1849. Afterward, the Canadian capital eventually shifted to an obscure backwater known as Ottawa.

All these thoughts and more were on my mind as I completed my crossing and turned along the island of Montreal's shore. The pivot east meant the wind was now at my back, driving me along at a fast pace. On the distant horizon, I could see the skyscrapers of downtown Montreal, none of which rose higher than the green peaks of Mount Royal. I'd read that a longstanding bylaw decreed that no skyscraper could be built higher than the city's mountain namesake, in order to preserve its eminence. Bobbing up and down on the waves and taking in the view from my canoe, I had to agree with the wisdom of this old law. I felt there was something charming about Montreal's skyline that crowded Toronto's lacked.

Another contrast between the two old rivals that I noted was the far greater amount of greenspace surrounding Montreal. Several bird sanctuaries lie just outside the city, on islands in Lake Saint-Louis and along its shore—which excited me more than anything, as it meant the possibility of spotting migrating arctic species. There'd likely be northbound snow geese and Canada geese (a fair number of which actually nest on the arctic tundra), as well as many ducks, and if I kept a sharp eye out, perhaps even peregrine falcons.

As I neared the city proper, I canoed by more vestiges of the island's history, including grand stone buildings, historic churches, and another old windmill at Pointe-Claire built in 1710. Six kilometres past the windmill I came alongside a trio of small islands, the largest of which, Dorval, is inhabited and connected by a passenger ferry to Montreal. The winds, however, were gusting around fifty kilometres an hour. This forced me to stay close to shore, exerting all the energy I could muster to keep the canoe on course.

Complicating matters was that just up ahead were the Lachine Rapids, a five-kilometre stretch of deadly whitewater that has claimed many drowning victims. It was these large rapids with their huge standing waves and precipitous drops that had blocked Cartier's passage. Champlain himself had wisely portaged around the rapids, though two of his scouts drowned attempting to paddle them. It wasn't until the construction of the Lachine Canal in the 1820s that ships were able to navigate around the rapids. Today that canal, like many others along the St. Lawrence, is no longer in commercial use, having been replaced with a much larger, deeper canal capable of allowing the passage of huge ocean-going ships. At Montreal, this shipping lane separates from the main river just before the city and runs along the south shore. I, of course, couldn't take it due to the locks and hazards posed by the freighters.

When I reached the Lachine lighthouse, I was sweating from the all-consuming effort to make headway and soaked from a wave splashing over. Large waves were smashing into the lighthouse pier and ricocheting back out, hammering me from both directions. Two fishermen on the pier had front-row seats to my finest canoeing efforts—every paddling trick I'd ever learned combined with sheer determination was needed to force my canoe around the lighthouse without capsizing. Once I'd managed it I breathed a sign of relief, but there was no relief ahead—a long, narrow pier loomed, and the combination of strong river currents with wind-generated waves around it looked almost impossible. I let up for an instant to try to make an assessment, but that instant let the overpowering gusts drive me into the harbour near the Lachine Canal. Exhausted, I landed at a concrete boat launch behind some warehouse-looking buildings.

I hadn't originally noticed anyone behind the warehouses, but it turned out there were two men working on a boat that had been lifted up on shore. I soon made their acquaintances, and they turned out to be as friendly and helpful as anyone I'd met. They expressed considerable astonishment on learning that I'd canoed from Lake Erie. The taller and more talkative of the two, who introduced himself as Frank, warned me against paddling toward the rapids. He said that the prior October a fishing boat had been swept into them, and that a fire department vessel, in attempting a rescue, had itself capsized with one of the fire-fighters drowning.

My original plan had been to paddle under the Honoré Mercier Bridge to the head of the rapids, then land on shore and portage around them. But the ferocious gusts complicated this—the wind was gusting sideways across the current, creating additional whitecaps. Frank suggested that I could avoid the lengthy portage around the rapids by taking the historic Lachine Canal. This sounded sensible, except that I'd been under the impression that the canal was intersected by causeways that would necessitate portages around each one, and more critically, it didn't appear there was any straightforward access from the canal back to the river at Montreal's Old Port. But the locals informed me that this shouldn't be any trouble, as there was a marina that I could access there.

In any case, the fierce gusts left little choice. After thanking the two and receiving their hearty well-wishes, I pushed off again, heading for the canal's entrance. A short paddle brought me to a historic lock that had to be bypassed first. (These locks are still operational in the summer months, but this early in the year they weren't open yet.) To reach the canal, there was a busy roadway I'd have to cross. It was evening rush hour, with traffic whirling past. With my fifteen-foot canoe on the cart, the prospect of a long enough lull to make it safely across seemed doubtful. But it turned out I had nothing to worry about—a truck driver, seeing me, held up traffic by stopping his truck and motioning me to cross. The kindness of Canadians when they see someone with a canoe is really a wonderful thing. I waved in thanks and was soon back in the water on the opposite side.

The wind was still fierce, but the canal's high concrete walls effectively sheltered me, and I zipped along at a fast pace. There were several more historic locks and a few causeways that I had to bypass on foot before I could reach the canal's end at Montreal's Old Port. The final portage to reach the port proved to be a much longer and more difficult one. Originally, the canal had connected directly to the St. Lawrence River, but in the decades since its closing, it had been filled in and heavily built over near its original terminus. This meant nearly a kilometre-and-a-half-long portage through the busy city to reach the river.

Montreal seemed a very active city, with literally thousands of walkers, joggers, cyclists, and other pedestrians along the narrow trail that led toward the port. I tried to push my canoe through the crowds as fast as I could, as I knew I had to reach the river before nightfall. I received lots of curious looks and a few thumbs-up gestures, but the speed at which I pushed precluded conversations. The exception was when I reached an intersection, and a photographer began snapping shots of me. I rested for a moment and he chatted with me. He said he was a street photographer, and that in twenty years of taking portraits he'd never seen anyone portage a canoe through the city. I confessed it was a first for me too.

It was evening now, and I was eager to find some way back to the water before dark. This was critical, since I couldn't paddle the river after nightfall given the heavy shipping traffic at the city's port. But Montreal's Old Port was made up of high concrete walls towering over the river, and I couldn't see stairs or any other obvious way back down. It was very busy on the terraces along the walls, such that I found myself longing for the solitude of the river. At last, sweating from having pushed the canoe through the city, I spotted the marina below the walls. It turned out that it was only a seasonal marina, with floating docks attached to the concrete walls and a temporary ramp leading down to it from above.

I heaved my canoe up a curb, then quickly pushed it toward the long rampway. The ramp made a sharp right-angle turn, forcing me to readjust the canoe to squeeze through. But the canoe was too wide, and despite all my efforts, it wouldn't budge through the gate. The last thing I wanted to do in such a busy place—with daylight rapidly running out—was unload everything and have to take things individually down the long rampway.

Among the swarm of people moving about the walkway stood a young man leaning against the rail, munching on an overloaded pita, while keeping an eye on me. When he finished his pita he silently came over, made a friendly wave, and grabbed the end of my canoe. Such unprompted kindness was encouraging, but even with the two of us pushing, we couldn't wedge it through.

"If we can just lift it a little and turn it slightly, I think it might squeeze through," I said, indicating as I did so with my hands what I had in mind. My helper apparently didn't understand English, and I couldn't think of the right words in French to explain. But he seemed to intuitively grasp what I had in mind, and we went at it. I felt bad for him, as he couldn't have realized beforehand how heavy my canoe was with all the food, water, and gear stored inside it along with the cart—altogether it weighed nearly two hundred pounds. But he was a spry fellow, and with a bit of hard effort we at last managed to get it through. I thanked him profusely, but he just nodded that he would assist me the remainder of the way.

Together we got the canoe down the rampway, then had to lift and force it through a second gateway at the bottom on the floating docks. Some large luxury yachts were moored here, but the drop from the dock edge to the waterline was still too high for me to launch the canoe. There were docks lower to the water for smaller craft farther along the wall—but access to this area was blocked off by a locked gate. A posted sign indicated it was for club members only. My anonymous helper, meanwhile, was indicating with sign language that he thought we could toss the canoe over the side and then he could hand me all the gear from above. But given the height of the drop, I thought it best to exhaust all other possibilities before attempting such a gamble.

I pressed a buzzer by the locked gate and heard a voice answer on the other end.

"Sorry to bother you," I said into the buzzer, "but I've canoed a long way and I need access to the docks. Would you be able to let me through?"

"No problem. Just wait a moment," came the reply.

Through the locked gate I saw a young woman step out of a gatehouse and walk down the dock toward where my helper and I were standing. She unlocked the gate.

"Thank you," I said.

"Where are you going to paddle?" she asked.

"Downriver." I gestured casually.

"Downriver?" She looked alarmed.

"Yeah, under the bridge and out to the saltwater."

"That's dangerous!"

"How so?"

"Under the bridge, the current is very dangerous. I don't know the word in English . . ." She made a circular motion with her hand.

"Oh, a whirlpool?" I offered.

"Yes!"

"That's no big deal."

"No, no, no, very, very dangerous."

"I didn't see any whitewater on the satellite image there."

"You can't judge by that," she said, shaking her head.

"It can't be that bad."

"*It's very bad*. People drown under the bridge. When we see any small boat going that way, we immediately call 911 and the coast guard," she said.

I found this puzzling, since as far as I knew, all the dangerous whitewater was upstream. "But," I said, "how can that be when this is a marina. These boats must go downriver?"

"Yes but they're big boats, not a canoe, people don't canoe here."

"Well it can't be that bad if these boats go through it."

"You have to know the exact currents it's safe to go through," she said. "You can walk up to the top there and look at the current under the bridge."

"You'll watch my stuff for me?"

She and my pita-eating friend, who'd been silently listening to the conservation, both indicated they would.

I was pretty convinced that, much like the Peace Bridge on the Niagara River, there wasn't anything to fear here and the dangers were overblown. My real concern was the setting sun; I was desperate to escape from the city before it was too dark to paddle. So I raced ahead on foot as fast as I could, running up the rampway, then along the high concrete pier overlooking the river. Nearly two kilometres away in the distance was the Jacques Cartier Bridge with its supposedly deadly currents. From where I was standing it didn't look very threatening. I ran ahead to a high clock tower, but mindful of the fast-dwindling daylight, I stopped at the tower still more than a kilometre from the bridge. I was too far away to see it very clearly, but what I did see didn't look any worse than many stretches of water I'd already paddled. So I turned round and ran back as fast as I could through the crowds to my canoe.

"It doesn't look that bad," I said, catching my breath as I got back.

The young marina attendant shook her head in dismay. "This is not a good idea."

The friendly fellow who'd helped me was still standing by my canoe, guarding it. When he saw that I'd made up my mind, he gave me a thumbs-up, and I nodded and thanked him. It seemed he also didn't speak French, as he never said anything in any language. I regretted that I never learned his name, but he shuffled off up the rampway, to watch from above.

"Look," said the attendant, "I want to be clear that I think this is very, very bad and I'm not responsible for what happens. My shift is over and I'm leaving, but another employee is coming here and she can unlock the gate and let you back out if you change your mind."

"Thanks, but I'll be fine."

She shook her head, and as she did so, her shift replacement arrived. It was another young woman in her teens. They spoke rapidly in French to each other. I couldn't make out what they were saying other than the word "stupide." Then the first attendant headed up the rampway to the streets above and I was left on the floating docks with the newcomer.

"Is it really true that you call the coast guard whenever you see someone going under the bridge?"

"Yes," she said. But she seemed less inclined to dissuade me, and even volunteered to help wheel my canoe along the narrow floating plastic dock to a low point where I could easily set it in the water.

"Thank you," I said, zipping up my life jacket.

"Good luck," she replied.

I stepped into the canoe and shoved off. It'd be dark soon, so there wasn't a moment to lose. I paddled hard from the marina, then turned left around the quay into the river's main channel. The swirling current propelled me toward the high span of the Jacques Cartier Bridge.

13

"RIVER OF CANADA"

T HERE WERE A lot of eyes looking down at me from along the crowded pier and on nearby Parc de Dieppe, which is a narrow peninsula extending into the river. If I'd miscalculated, there'd be plenty of witnesses to testify to my foolishness. But so far I saw nothing alarming—the swirling water had a good, strong current, but it was of the kind that paddlers enjoy rather than anything dangerous. It was true there were back eddies where the current reversed, but these were easily avoided.

My only real fear was the large vessels, especially the big freighters constantly docking and departing from Montreal's extensive port. But the freighters were downstream of the Jacques Cartier Bridge, and only smaller vessels such as passenger ferries, coast guard ships, and pleasure yachts could travel upstream of it, which posed less of a concern. Still, I aimed for the river's right, away from the busy docks, to avoid any collisions. The bridge was supported by a massive stone and concrete pillar rising out of the river, with the current foaming around it. But it wasn't by any means difficult, and I canoed through almost casually, marvelling at how such an easy stretch of river could inspire so much misplaced fear. But I assume it's because most people—even most Canadians—don't have much paddling experience, and misjudge how sturdy a canoe actually is (perhaps based on hazy recollections of some long-ago summer camp experience). In reality, even a novice canoeist could handle the Jacques Cartier Bridge.

The current was so slight that I even spun my canoe around to hover below the bridge pillar, in order to scout the shore for a camping site. I was still within Montreal, but the sun had nearly set and the busy freighter traffic downstream precluded any possibility of canoeing in the dark. The bridge connects Montreal to St. Helen's Island and from there to the mainland. St. Helen's is full of walking trails, recreational facilities, a marina, and an amusement park. Under ordinary circumstances I wouldn't dream of camping somewhere like it, but compared to the crowded city I'd just passed through, it seemed quiet.

A clump of forest sat below the bridge along the shore, so I landed my canoe in some marshy grass beside it. It looked deserted, and when I climbed the wooded bank, I saw the area was fenced off with barbed wire. This was perfect, as it meant I didn't have to worry about anyone disturbing me in the night. With the sun going down, I fetched my canoe, hauled it up, and after tossing aside some loose sheet metal and construction debris, made myself a comfortable camp in the bushes and sumacs. It was surprisingly peaceful as I boiled up a pot of water on my little camp stove, while sitting on my overturned canoe and looking out at the lights of the historic city across the river.

I slept well in that sheltered nook, and was gone again in the grey dawn light. Although I hadn't feared the river's current, I *did* fear the freighter traffic. Montreal is, after all, one of Canada's largest and busiest commercial ports. Its elaborate port complex covers almost ten kilometres of shoreline, making it far larger than anything I'd encountered on the Great Lakes. Canoeing along St. Helen's Island, I could see the port's vast complex of concrete docks, warehouses, factories, and piles of shipping containers on the opposite shore. Given how busy things were, paddling on that side of the river was out of the question. But eventually I'd have to cross back to it—since that was the shore I needed to be on to actually turn north to the Arctic. This meant I had no choice but to cut straight across the busy shipping lanes used by the freighters. The thought of it gave me some anxiety.

When I reached the end of the island I zipped across the lane that leads into and out of the deep-water canal, the one that allows the giant freighters to bypass Montreal's rapids. A massive freighter had just steamed out of it, so I took the opportunity to paddle as hard as I could to the safety of the eastern shore. Here I could breathe easy for a time at least; paddling along the old suburb of Longueil. As I did so, I took the time to carefully study the busy port on the opposite shore, to learn whatever I could about the comings and goings of the freighters, in the hopes that it might improve my odds of safely crossing the main shipping lanes.

It was clear, as I'd suspected earlier on the Great Lakes, that from high above on the freighter's decks and bridges, they'd never be able to spot a tiny canoe below them, as I'd be fully in their blind spots. The largest of these freighters are a thousand feet long. Moreover, I was amazed to see just how heavily loaded they were—cranes were swinging vast numbers of shipping containers onto their decks at the port, stacking them five or six high. Other freighters were loaded with stacks of what looked like huge pipes, right up to the bridge. If anything, this would increase their blind spots. If I hadn't crossed to this side and instead paddled along the busy port, one of these freighters would surely have crushed my canoe like a fly against the concrete walls when it docked.

Tugboats were hovering about the freighters, looking like toys next to them, and coast guard ships were steaming around them too, inspecting them, it seemed. But despite my best efforts, I couldn't discern any means of figuring out the schedules of when the ships came and went. Some of them seemed to depart and arrive without any aid from the tugs at all, so that didn't prove a reliable prediction method. I was further amazed by the speed of these freighters—here in the St. Lawrence, they seemed to power along at much faster speeds than in the narrow canals. This wasn't encouraging, as even if the coast was clear when I attempted to cross, every few minutes another freighter seemed to appear out of nowhere.

I came upon a long, marshy, uninhabited island off the eastern shore known as Green Island. I swung alongside it, pausing just long enough to admire the fact that there was this much protected wildlife habitat near a major city. Ahead were more islands—and these, too, were mostly protected greens-pace. I steered for Charron Island, passed a ferry terminal, and then glided beside another long, swampy island, with posted signs indicating it was also protected wildlife habitat. These islands form a chain of five that are preserved as part of Îles-de-Boucherville Park, though the largest has farms on it too. The quietness of the islands I found a strange contrast to the teeming city just across the water.

From the last of the Boucherville islands I cut across the open water to a second swampy uninhabited island, Grande-Île. By now I'd bypassed the industrial docks on the opposite shore, so it was safe to be on that side again—that is, if I could get there. This location seemed to be my best chance to pull it off. The islands scattered through the river made the channel narrower, meaning less distance for me to cross, allowing me to muster up all my stamina to do it as fast as possible. The islands, too, provided shelter from the wind, so that I didn't have to worry as much about it slowing me down.

The freighter traffic, however, was incredibly busy—it seemed that each time I'd psyched myself up to begin racing across, some new ship would suddenly materialize on the horizon, forcing me to wait. Unlike with the canals, on the river the shipping lanes are wide enough to allow freighters to pass each other. This meant I could be hit from either direction. All told, to get safely across I had to canoe about seven hundred metres.

At last, I saw my chance: the coast was clear, and with my ultra-light racing paddle, I began canoeing across. I held back a little of my energy, so that if a ship were to suddenly appear, I'd have enough strength to turn back before it was too late. Within a few minutes I'd almost reached the point of no return, when I was as near to the far shore as the one I'd embarked from. It was at that moment that I glanced to my left and in disbelief saw a gigantic freighter loaded sky-high with shipping containers bearing down on me. "Oh *hell*," I exclaimed. "If we turn back now,"—I was speaking to the canoe—"we'll never make it. There's so much traffic. We've just got to go for it."

The canoe agreed, so I paddled furiously to race across before the ship reached us. But it seemed I'd underestimated the effect of the current and the wind, as despite my rapid strokes we seemed to barely edge forward while the ship loomed ever closer. It was a behemoth freighter, one of the biggest I'd ever seen—and it was rapidly gaining on me. On bended knee I was paddling like a madman, swinging the paddle with crazed effort until my lungs felt as if they'd burst. Seconds felt like minutes as the trees on the opposite shore only painstaking grew closer. I dared not look to my left at the oncoming freighter, concentrating every ounce on paddling.

At last I let out a huge gasp for air: I'd escaped the shipping lane. I turned back to watch the freighter—it was mercifully not as near as I'd feared. But its monstrous size had made it seem closer when I'd been directly in its path. It was nearly a thousand feet long. Painted on its side was the name "Hapag-Lloyd," which is one of the world's largest shipping companies. Their annual revenues reportedly exceed twenty-six billion dollars. Its deck was stacked at least five shipping crates high, which is probably necessary to earn twenty-six billion a year.

To steady my nerves, I ate a granola bar. Then I kept paddling. It was a relief to think I wouldn't have to cross the river again. For the next while the paddling would be easy, as I left Montreal behind and cruised alongside wild islands where ducks and blue herons nested. Foxes and white-tailed deer stared at me curiously as I drifted by. Meanwhile on the mainland, rising above the trees at villages or towns I passed, were Old World–style stone cathedrals or churches.

Rain developed in the afternoon, soaking me, but it soon tapered off. I pushed on late, making it some sixty-five kilometres downriver. Along the way I passed another National Wildlife Area, and then the Île Saint-Ours Bird Sanctuary. Both protect marshy, low-lying islands that provide habitat for thousands of migrating birds. The seasonal flooding of these islands allows marsh plants to flourish, which in turn attracts waterfowl, especially dabbling ducks—that is, ducks that feed primarily by tipping upside down, feet in the air and head underwater, rather than diving. These include northern pintails, wigeons, and gadwalls, whose largest nesting site in Quebec is right here on these protected islands.

But the same swampy conditions that made the shores attractive for waterfowl made finding anywhere to camp difficult. There wasn't much dry land readily available, so I ended up settling for a marsh on the mainland under some weeping willows. The ground was a bit spongy; in the dark I selected the driest spot I could find. But when a freighter steamed by, the wake it generated swept right through the marsh. Luckily, I hadn't pitched my tent yet, and I now put in the extra effort to haul everything a bit farther inland, so no ship's wake might soak me in the night.

✳

WHEN I BROKE camp the next morning before dawn, I could see in the dark above the far shore a huge fiery red glow: it looked like the Eye of Sauron, but in reality it was the blast furnaces at Sorel-Tracy. A massive industrial complex is situated at this spot, where freighters transport iron ore for processing. I canoed by on the opposite shore, then disappeared into a vast labyrinth of bucolic islands that spread across the river. Known variously as the Sorel Islands or the Archipelago of Lac Saint-Pierre, in total there are over a hundred islands here, all of them low-lying and most uninhabited, although the larger ones contain a few farms and villages. Taking one of the western channels through the islands, I found the landscape refreshingly beautiful, with old oaks and maples lining the riverbanks, along with occasional country homes, farms, and rich forests. But the farther I went into the islands, the swampier they became, until the farms and houses disappeared and I found myself in a landscape that looked more like a Louisiana swamp than Canada. The forests were so flooded that I could weave right through the trees in my canoe. Silver maples, cottonwoods, and willows predominated, which unlike other species can grow straight out of the water.

Scattered thinly through the swamp stood the odd cabin built on high stilts out of the water. But eventually even these disappeared, leaving nothing at all to break up the swampy labyrinth. This went on for miles, to the point where I began to think I might have to lash my canoe to a tree and spend the night sleeping in it. Even the muskrats, I noticed, when they needed a break from the water, climbed the trees—something I'd never seen before. Blue herons nested in the topmost branches, and echoing out of the swamp's depths could be heard the hammering of woodpeckers and the call of red-winged blackbirds.

It was an overcast day, and I could no longer make out the river's opposite bank. I'd reached a wide section of the St. Lawrence known as Lac Saint-Pierre, which is more than thirteen kilometres across. Everything seemed deserted: as far as I could see was nothing but swamp, not a house or building in sight. It was one of the strangest landscapes I'd ever encountered. Then, in the afternoon, strong headwinds developed, making canoeing almost impossible. Frantic strokes were needed just to inch the canoe forward, and if I rested even for a moment, the overpowering wind would drive me back upriver. There was nowhere to land and stretch my legs or even eat anything, as try as I may, I couldn't find even a square inch of dry ground. I had to hold onto a tree growing out of the swampy water just to rest and munch a granola bar. The fierce winds made me want to call it a day, but every time I plunged deeper into the swamp to search for dry land, none was to be found.

I pushed on, exhausted, until I finally stumbled upon a drier area full of green ferns beneath towering cottonwoods. I set my tent in the driest patch I could find. A white-breasted nuthatch came and kept me company, chirping and hopping up and down a cottonwood, as I made some tea and cooked a freeze-dried meal. But before I could enjoy it, thunder rumbled and rain began. So I ate inside my tent, listening to a storm rage all around me and hoping that a cottonwood wouldn't fall and crush me or lightning strike my metal tent pole.

Despite the storm, I managed to stay snug and comfortable on my little patch of ground. There's something undeniably a little uncanny about giant swamps. When I drifted off, a nightmare disturbed my sleep, and I sat up in my sleeping bag, alarmed. I'd dreamed that a big wave had swept into my tent and flooded the forest.

The storm passed in the night, but when I woke it was to find that a second storm had blown in. Since paddling in lightning seemed unwise, it forced me to stay holed up in my tent. It wasn't until mid-morning that the skies cleared and I was able to get underway. I'd hadn't seen a soul in twenty-four hours and was beginning to feel as if I'd passed through some portal into a strange world where nothing but swamp existed. Finally, after a few more kilometres, I at last spotted some sign of human life—a cabin on stilts appeared, and then gradually, other scattered cottages and buildings. The shoreline, too, slowly returned to normal. I was now somewhere on the outskirts of Trois-Rivières.

The day was unseasonably hot and humid, and the only clouds were well behind me on the distant horizon. But a tailwind was bringing them in my direction. The closer they came, the more alarming they looked—they weren't like any normal clouds, but more like orange-hued mountains stacked one atop another. One didn't need to be a meteorologist to tell there was something threatening about them. The wet weather had left my phone's battery dead, but in the canoe I plugged it into my small solar panel to charge it enough to look up the forecast. Environment Canada, it turned out, had issued a special weather alert calling for tornadoes heading right in my direction. Years of experience had convinced me that tornado canoeing is best avoided, so I determined almost at once that I'd have to find somewhere to ride out the storm.

Ahead was a sandy beach with a roadway running behind it. I landed here and heaved my canoe up on shore. The storm clouds were still several hours off, buying me time to find somewhere to camp. The beach itself was much too exposed, but twisting through its far end was a little creek that flowed under an old stone bridge. I contemplated paddling under the bridge, then waiting out the tornado beneath it. But if the storm lasted a long time, or caused the water to surge, this might not be very comfortable.

Downriver was the city of Trois-Rivières, and I didn't have much confidence about finding somewhere to camp there. Another option was to follow the creek farther inland; it led to an historic 1700s-era manor. But the manor was in a forest, and camping near trees in a tornado also seemed ill-advised. I debated what to do. If I continued downriver, it was impossible to say what I might find. But if I stayed here there wasn't much shelter. When in doubt, push on, I told myself. So I jumped back in the canoe and set off, paddling as swiftly as I could, scouting the shore as I went.

Luck it seemed was with me, as only a kilometre and a half downriver I came upon some sort of summer camp. It was surrounded by forest, but there appeared to be a decent-sized clearing where I could pitch my tent without having to worry too much about trees crashing into it. I landed on the beachy shore, glanced over my shoulder at the menacing-looking sky on the horizon, then climbed through the forest to the clearing above. There were some cabins in the distance with someone who looked like a caretaker outside them.

He spotted me and I waved.

"Hello," I said, speaking in French, "I'm sorry to bother you. My French isn't very good. Do you speak English?"

"No."

"Oh." I really had to rack my brain to exhaust my entire French vocabulary. I made out, as best as I could, that I'd canoed from Ontario and that I still had a ways to go, and that there was a big storm coming. I pointed to the distant sky, but the woods obscured the view, and the weather didn't actually seem that threatening where we stood. I didn't know the word for tornado, but I had my phone and showed him the radar image. Then he understood completely, and enthusiastically offered to help me however he could. His name was Marc and he was the caretaker for the camp, which if I understood correctly was a retreat for the Roman Catholic Church. No one other than himself was here at present, and he had to leave soon. I pointed out the grassy clearing and asked if I could set up my tent there. Marc assured me that it was no problem. He also showed me where I could replenish my water supply, and asked about my journey. He then expressed some concern about the wisdom of camping in a tent during a tornado. With a kindness that warmed the heart, Marc said he would leave one of the cabins unlocked, and urged me to take shelter in it if the storm became too intense.

Marc then departed and I was left alone. I returned to the riverbank to study the sky; the wind was bringing the massive orange-hued clouds on the horizon ever closer. But oddly enough, where I was it was still hot and sunny, and with a surfeit of time on my hands, I decided to do something I hadn't done in a month—bathe. The riverbank was sandy, so I swam out, feeling wonderfully refreshed, though the St. Lawrence in May is rather chilly, so my swim was brief. In any case, the storm was coming, and I needed to prepare.

I selected the safest spot I could in the centre of the clearing, though it wasn't encouraging when I eyeballed the length of the oaks on the forest edge and saw that if one fell it'd still easily crush my tent. But oaks are sturdy trees and I hoped for the best. Then I carefully set up my tent, angling it toward the wind. I staked it down with four guy lines, driving the pegs deep into the hard ground to secure them. My backpack I put inside for a little extra weight. Then the question was what to do with my canoe. I'd read of expeditions that had lost their canoes in the night when they were carried away by fierce gales. As a precaution against such a calamity, in arctic storms I'd often tied my canoe down or loaded it with rocks. But all things considered, conditions didn't seem that bad, so I decided just to flip it over in a little depression beside some oaks in the woods. Then I crawled into my tent to wait for the storm.

14

TROIS-RIVIÈRES

I ATE A FREEZE-DRIED dinner of lasagna in my tent, stretching out comfortably on my sleeping bag. The tent's door I left unzipped so I could keep an eye on things, but I began to think that perhaps all the talk of tornadoes had been overblown. No sooner had the thought occurred than the sky darkened, the wind increased sharply, and rain rattled. Suddenly an alarm went off—it was my phone lying beside me. It sounded like an Amber Alert, and I wondered if a child had gone missing. But instead it was something I'd never seen before—an imminent Tornado Warning for my location. With commendable directness, it left little to the imagination, stating: "This is a dangerous and potentially life-threatening situation." It advised to take cover immediately.

I decided it might be wise to take Marc up on his offer. The cabin he'd left unlocked was about two hundred metres through the woods. Tossing on my jacket, I dashed outside into the rain and wind. The trees were swaying and the angry sky seemed suffocated in a sea of clouds. Through the forest I headed toward the cabin. Its veranda had a view of the wide St. Lawrence. With terrifying suddenness the storm struck—purplish lightning bolts hit the shore, while the wind almost instantly kindled ferocious whitecaps on the river. In front of the cabins were two portable gazebos, which I'd noted when I'd first come ashore as places of possible refuge if I wasn't able to set up my tent. Now I watched as the wind lifted the first of these gazebos into the air and smashed it against the cabin nearest me. The second gazebo was thrown into a maple tree. Meanwhile branches fell to the ground and the eavestroughs were ripped off the cabin where I stood. Marc had left a light on inside, but within seconds it cut out as the power was lost. I stepped into the cabin just as hail pelted its windows. I'd seen many storms in my adventurous career, but I'd never encountered anything like this—the river looked like no river I'd ever seen but more like a frothing sea of impossibly large waves. I shuddered at the thought of trying to canoe in something like that. As I watched the storm wreak havoc on the camp, I resigned myself to the fact that my tent was destroyed and my canoe swept away.

I told myself there was no use crying over spilt milk—that I'd just have to find replacements and continue. The storm passed quickly, and as soon as it'd dissipated, I ran from the cabin back through the rain to salvage whatever I could of my gear. When I arrived in the clearing I could barely believe my eyes—there was my tent staked down exactly as I'd left it, without so much as a rip or tear, and my canoe perfectly fine wedged right by the oaks. I was so overjoyed to see them unharmed that I almost felt like hugging them. None of my gear it turned out had been damaged (though sadly the same wasn't true for the summer camp).

The tornado, if that's what it was (it sure did seem like it), had passed quickly, as tornadoes generally do, and I crawled into my tent feeling as relieved as I ever had. There was still some subdued rain and distant thunder, but nothing like the intensity of when the storm had hit the shore with all its fury. So I curled up in my tent, which had truly proven itself a tent of tents, a champion that I gained a new admiration for in terms of its design and stability (it'd been manufactured to withstand alpine storms)—and fell into a deep sleep.

✳

THE MORNING DAWNED calm and misty. I was soon on the water paddling downriver through the mist, surveying the damage from the storm. Many big trees had been felled, though mostly from what I saw they were silver maples and cottonwoods, and not the sturdy oaks. A park along the river was flooded, its benches partly underwater, which must have been from the storm surge. I could hear the loud hum of generators at houses, which told me the power was still out. Many people in their backyards saw me pass in my canoe and gave friendly waves.

It turned out that the storm was one of the most powerful on record in Canada. Known as a derecho, it had spawned multiple tornadoes and torn a path of destruction almost a thousand kilometres long, with winds of up to a hundred and ninety kilometres an hour. Eleven people were killed, mostly by falling trees, although one victim was on a boat that sank on the Ottawa River. The extensive damage made it rank as the sixth costliest natural disaster in Canadian history.

Downstream I passed under a very high suspension bridge. The current was swift and the river busy with passing freighters that generated considerable wake. On my left was the historic city of Trois-Rivières. I'd always assumed that its name, "Three Rivers," refers to the three rivers that meet near the town: the St. Lawrence, Saint-Maurice, and Bécancour Rivers. But locals say this isn't the case and that the name actually reflects the illusion of seeing three rivers at the mouth of the Saint-Maurice, which are actually just separate channels formed by islands. Whatever the truth may be, it's a place that breathes history. Founded in 1634, it's Quebec's third-oldest town and was a flashpoint in many early battles in Canada's history. Throughout the 1600s the town faced fierce attacks by warriors of the mighty Iroquois Confederacy, which on one occasion killed more than half the town's male population. In 1652, the governor of Trois-Rivières was himself killed in one of these attacks. A hundred-odd years later, American invaders marched on the town during their first attempt to conquer Canada in the Revolutionary War. After a battle in the surrounding swamps, they were defeated.

I'd hoped that after Montreal's busy port, I wouldn't have to worry again about any shipping traffic. But this proved a vain hope: it turned out Trois-Rivières has a large industrial port that stretches more than a kilometre and a half. There were at least three freighters moored alongside it as I approached. Unlike at Montreal, here I'd have to canoe right below these steel giants. This was because the river was now too wide to make crossing to the far side feasible. And in any case, to do that would necessitate crossing the shipping lanes in the centre of the river twice—once there and again on the way back. So in practical terms there was no choice but to muster up my nerve and paddle as fast as I could right below the giant freighters.

Their bridges towered as high as a ten-storey building, making my canoe feel like some kind of pool toy beside such monstrous transports. I paddled hard and kept several hundred metres out from the port, in the hopes that this might buy me some time if one suddenly started to depart. Coast guard ships were anchored alongside the port as well, but I saw no signs of life from them. The engines on one of the freighters were loudly humming, which made me nervously redouble my efforts to escape from the port as quickly as possible. But even paddling at top speed, the fastest I could cover a kilometre and a half was about ten minutes—which felt agonizingly slow.

At last I reached the end of the port. After that I crossed the wide mouth of the Saint-Maurice River with its islands in the centre, one of which has a pulp and paper mill on it—logging has been a mainstay of the local economy for the past four centuries. From the water, the view of Trois-Rivières is dominated by the huge stone edifice of the Notre-Dame-du-Cap Basilica. The swift current propelled me past its lofty spire, while along the wooded riverbanks below it quite a few anglers were out casting. The forests around Trois-Rivières were still very swampy, but rich with wildlife. I photographed a bald eagle perched in a cottonwood growing out of the water. It was in one of these swamps that the explorer Pierre-Esprit Radisson while duck-hunting had been ambushed by warriors of the Iroquois Confederacy. He was taken back to their village and tortured, but showed courage so his life was spared, living happily ever after.

By mid-afternoon the skies were again looking threatening, with thunder rumbling faintly in the distance and a light rain falling. I landed on a small beach below the historic village of Batiscan, where an impressive stone church overlooks the river. I stretched my legs, ate my last apple, and examined the sky to judge whether it was safe to keep paddling. After the last storm, I was reluctant to push my luck, so I resolved to make camp at the first secluded place I could find.

Fortunately, just a few kilometres downriver was a forest at the mouth of the Batiscan River, which joins the St. Lawrence. The sandy soil and quiet woods here were so attractive that I felt almost blessed: it was one of the best campsites I'd ever come upon. A nice campsite is one of life's great pleasures, and having made camp early, I had plenty of time to make a cup of tea and enjoy it. I was heartened to see that the woods had many ash trees that were still healthy. The invasive beetles that have so devastated the ash forests elsewhere in recent years had not, as of yet, made it this far east. In the woods where I grew up had been many fine ash trees, and I'd mourned their loss to the beetles ever since. Seeing them again put me in a cheerful mood despite the impending storm—it was like meeting with old friends you haven't seen in years.

The threatening storm never materialized aside from some brief thunder and rain, but in the night the weather shifted and temperatures plunged. I woke up shivering in my sleeping bag and had to add extra layers. Since I'd cut yesterday short I rose extra early, at four-thirty a.m. to get underway. Downstream lay more beaches, but they weren't like any beaches I'd ever seen before: these ones, strangely, were in forests, with elms, ashes, and maples growing straight out of the sand. I found it such an intriguing landscape that I had to land just to explore the beachy woods a little. The extensive forests along the shore made for abundant birdlife. Plovers flying in formation passed low over the water, while grackles, robins, ducks, eagles, terns, and gulls were all to be seen. I also glimpsed some snow geese, which migrate to the arctic tundra and nest there in great numbers. But still no sign of any peregrine falcons, even though I was right on one of their main flyways north to the Arctic.

Downriver the unusual landscapes continued, where many slender, low-lying rocky peninsulas reached far into the water like the fingers of some giant skeletal hand. These peninsulas forced me to paddle far offshore to avoid them. At some of them the swift current rushed over sunken rocks, creating small rapids. After getting around these obstacles, the shoreline grew less wild and riverfront houses again appeared. Among them I saw an unmistakably ancient-looking windmill, which curiosity compelled me to land at. It turned out it was the Moulin à vent de Grondines: built in 1674, it's the oldest windmill still standing in all of Canada. The three-storey structure is made of whitewashed stone with a cone-shaped, wood-shingle roof. Flour was milled at it for over two centuries, and then when the mill was no longer needed, it was converted to a makeshift lighthouse to guide passing ships.

Beyond the windmill, as I kept paddling, I came across more vestiges of New France—old narrow seigneurial farms running down to the river and stone churches with twin steeples rising above small villages. The French had called their colony on either bank of the St. Lawrence "Canada," and the settlers here, cut off and isolated from their original homes across the ocean, rapidly developed their own separate identity. Within a generation or two they called themselves "Canadiens," the first people ever to do so.

At Portneuf the river turns abruptly east, and a very long quay runs out into the water. The gusting wind made detouring around it an exhausting task. Tied up at the quay was another coast guard ship as well as various fishing boats. The thought of fish made me hungry: I'd noticed that my food rations were rapidly dwindling. Luckily, I was almost at my next resupply. Before leaving home, I'd examined satellite images to find a post office nearest the water for a resupply. The one at the little village of Cap-Santé was right by the riverbank, so I'd asked Alexandria to mail a prepacked box of provisions to it for pickup. Its location a mere stone's throw from the river was perfect as it meant I wouldn't have to worry about leaving my canoe unattended for long. Cap-Santé was just downstream, so I looked about for a place to camp.

But it turned out that I'd made a mistake in my calculations—what I hadn't realized from the satellite image was that separating the post office from the water were *hundred-foot cliffs*. The topography of the St. Lawrence had changed dramatically from the swampy lowlands that I'd been passing through. Now the river was tucked below high cliffs on either side. There weren't any camping places anywhere within miles of where I needed to land—rocky boulders ran right down to the water.

Above the boulders were railroad tracks running parallel to the river, and immediately behind the tracks stood vertical cliffs.

Finally, just when I thought I was out of options, I found a little rocky beach where I could spend the night. The gravelly rocks weren't the softest, but this didn't bother me, since it seemed I was almost directly below the post office. I'd have to figure out some way to scale the cliffs to reach it, but that was a problem for the morning.

✳

AROUND THREE A.M. I turned over in my sleeping bag and drowsily blinked—the sound of lapping water seemed strangely close. It was a clear night without any rain and I'd pitched my tent about forty feet from the river. Puzzled, I unzipped my sleeping bag, letting the precious warmth escape, to open the tent door. I shone my flashlight out—and was astonished to see the waterline only a few feet away!

How could this be? I'd read that the St. Lawrence didn't become tidal until Quebec City, which was still another fifty kilometres downriver. But clearly that information was incorrect: the effect of the tides reached here. I did some mental calculations: tides change every six hours, and I'd landed late in the evening. Assuming that had been close to low tide, it must be past high tide now, meaning the water surely couldn't rise any further. Reassured, I lay back down in my sleeping bag. But the lapping didn't diminish—in fact, it seemed to come closer. I shone the light out a second time and was alarmed to see the water still inching closer to my tent. Leaving the warmth again I stepped outside. I found a distinctive white rock that stood out in the dark and put it on the waterline as a marker to tell whether the tide was still rising, or if it was just my imagination.

In another fifteen minutes I could no longer doubt it—*it was still rising.* My back was to the cliffs, and there wasn't anywhere to go. Unpegging the tent, I tried pulling it as close to the boulders as I could, but this bought me only a few inches. My canoe, too, I hauled up onto the boulders away from the rising water. I kept expecting to see the water recede, but to my astonishment it didn't. My rough calculations on the timing of the tides must have been off. I packed up my loose items, including my dry clothes that I used as a pillow and my sleeping bag, and loaded everything, except for the tent, into the canoe. That way I could still lie down in the tent, but be ready to leave at a moment's notice if the water kept rising. My hopes, however, were dashed: the tide seemed relentless, and when freighters passed in the dark, the wake they generated caused waves to reach even higher. I had no choice but to dismantle the tent and add it to the canoe. Finally, with all my stuff packed safely in the canoe, I climbed up onto the boulders, wrapped myself up in my warm jacket, and fell asleep on the rocks.

When dawn broke the tide had at last receded a half-dozen feet or so. I picked myself up from the rocks and looked about. It seemed obvious now, in the dawn light, that it was tidal here, but I hadn't noticed the night before when all my attention had been absorbed by the problem of the sheer cliffs. For breakfast I had my last granola bar, a few almonds, and a refreshing cup of green tea, then changed into my hiking boots and steeled myself for the climb.

I began by cautiously picking my way over the boulders to the train tracks above. It seemed the tracks weren't in use much, as no train had passed since I'd been here. Looking east down the tracks, I could see that the cliffs were sheer, with no prospect of climbing them. Things didn't look any better in the other direction. It seemed the best place to begin the ascent was right in front of me. Here the cliffs receded a little, with some thick bushes and tree cover that would give me handholds to pull myself up. It was exhausting, and I could appreciate why General Montcalm in the Seven Years' War had ordered a fort built at Cap-Santé. Its high cliffs constitute a formidable natural barrier, and with a fort on top, any attacking force from the river would be hard pressed.

As I neared the top of the steep slope there was a great deal of broken glass, old bottles, and rusty cans, forcing me to be careful where I grabbed. Garbage collection is very much a modern innovation; for generations, people simply tossed their refuse over local cliffs or into the woods. At last, huffing and puffing, I pulled myself over the top. I emerged right in front of a charming old house, in what seemed like a quiet neighbourhood. I'd come out just west of the post office.

I dusted myself off and walked down the quiet road toward it. This was the historic Chemin du Roy, the "King's Road." In the 1730s the French authorities had resolved to construct a road through the wilderness in order to link their little settlements along the river's north shore. At a time when travel by ship or canoe was the norm, it became the longest road in existence in North America north of Mexico. I saw several of the hydro poles along the road had been snapped like matchsticks from the recent storm, and there were quite a number of downed trees as well. The post office I found in darkness, the power still hadn't been restored from the extensive destruction wrought by the storm. Luckily, it was open.

I retrieved my precious box from inside. The clerk, a young woman, didn't speak any English (or in any case that's what she said), and I put my French to use. She didn't seem at all curious why a scruffy-looking stranger had come in to claim a mysterious box, which was just as well, as I lacked the vocabulary to explain things. With the box under my arm I disappeared back down the road.

It'd been hard enough scaling the cliffs with both hands free, but with a heavy box the odds of scaling back down without breaking my neck seemed doubtful. I contemplated throwing the box off the cliff, then climbing down and recovering it at the bottom. But this didn't seem like the best idea, as the box might smash open or get lodged in a tree branch. The dilemma resolved itself when I noticed on my return a narrow laneway leading down the cliffside. Whenever possible I try to avoid blatantly trespassing, but in this case it seemed called for. If I met with anyone, I'd just have to beg forgiveness.

The laneway led me down the steep cliff to a house perched in the woods at the bottom. No one seemed to be around. I cut through the forest and over the train tracks, then back down the rocks to my canoe. The tide had gone out in my absence; I'd have to portage everything about a hundred metres to reach the water. But first I emptied the resupply box into my canoe—it consisted mostly of granola bars, almonds, cashews, a bit of dried fruit, some green tea, toothpaste, a fresh pair of wool socks, some freeze-dried meals, and maps of my route ahead. Then I shoved the canoe in the water and was off again, heading for historic Quebec City.

15

TIDEWATER

THE TIDES MADE paddling much more complicated; I soon found that at low tide I had to go far offshore just to be able to paddle at all. Otherwise the water was too shallow and my canoe kept hitting bottom. At this point the river was roughly four kilometres wide, with a deep channel for the freighters out in the middle. Just past Cap-Santé a furious rapid-filled stream known as the Jacques Cartier River roars into the main river. Near its mouth the French army had built a fort in 1760 to try to stave off the British conquest of Canada. But by that point British armies were advancing from both directions up the St. Lawrence. The badly outnumbered French and Canadien forces held out valiantly, but in the end they were overwhelmed and by 1763 the British ruled all of "Old Canada" aside from a couple islands, Saint-Pierre and Miquelon, off the coast of Newfoundland, which to this day remain part of France.

As I continued downriver the landscape grew more dramatic: a lone blue mountain appeared on the horizon, while the riverbanks became more rugged and wooded. I landed briefly to explore a considerable nature reserve on the north shore, and was impressed by how luxuriant the forest seemed. There were old elms, birch, sugar maples, and ash. For the most part they were still the same woods I knew back in Norfolk County. But looking closer, I saw hints of more northern tidings and that the ecosystems were transforming: gone were the tulip trees, sassafras, and shagbark hickories, while pines, maples, and birches were becoming dominant.

By evening I could see the outskirts of Quebec City, and bobbing in my canoe on the swift outgoing tide and current, stared in wonder at a high train bridge running along the north shore. This was the Cap-Rouge trestle, which spans the Rivière du Cap Rouge valley. Built in 1908 as part of the transcontinental railway, it's still in use today.

Ahead the river narrowed and was spanned by two high bridges running parallel to each other, the Pierre Laporte Bridge and the Pont de Québec. The combination of outgoing tide and strong current made for turbulence under these bridges, which was considerably rougher than anything I'd encountered at the Jacques Cartier Bridge in Montreal. I paddled underneath, avoiding some rocks along the shore and the bridge pillars, then found myself canoeing along an artificial shoreline of high stone walls.

By now the sun was sinking below the horizon, bathing Quebec City in amber hues. From the waterline in a canoe, I could appreciate the dramatic setting of this storied city, and how it so impressed early travellers. No city in Canada, perhaps even in North America, has been more heavily fought over in its long history than Quebec, which owed its importance to its geographic position. It's a natural fortress, situated on high rocky cliffs where the St. Lawrence abruptly narrows, which made the site of great strategic value, since whoever controlled it could control the main water route into the continent. Cannons positioned on the high cliffs could sink any ships that might try to navigate the river.

Today the greater Quebec City area sprawls over some twenty kilometres of shore, and exhausted as I was and nearly nodding off in my canoe, with the sun setting I searched in vain for a spot to camp. With darkness coming on, there was no chance I could escape from the built-up city before nightfall, and as with Montreal, the commercial ship traffic at Quebec's port ruled out paddling in the dark. Beyond the bridges stood vertical walls that eliminated any camping prospects. A little farther downstream were some construction sites, and just as I contemplated the dismal prospect of sleeping at one of these gravel pits, I spotted the lights of a marina up ahead. With my last remaining energy I raced toward it.

The marina was in a small cove protected by breakwalls. Through the darkness I could make out that it was full of moored sailboats and yachts. I paddled silently alongside them, looking to see if there was anywhere I might camp. This marina happens to be in the exact spot where, in 1759, General James Wolfe landed his advance forces for his assault on Quebec. The cove is known as L'Anse-au-Foulon, but for centuries it was also called "Wolf's Cove" in reference to the fateful events that transpired here.

I beached my canoe at a very muddy boat launch. No one was around, but I climbed the launch to see if I could find someone.

A short distance away a light shone in front of what looked like a clubhouse, where two older men sat in chairs drinking. I felt slightly awkward strolling up to these perfect strangers and asking them in my broken French for permission to set up a tent on the grounds of a private club. It seemed only reasonable for them to tell me to scram as a scruffy trespasser and to find an actual campground. But their response couldn't have been warmer. They were not only quick to grant me permission, but they also showed me a tap alongside one of the buildings where I could replenish my water supply. I again felt blessed by the kindness of strangers, and went to sleep with the conviction that the world is filled with decent people.

✳

WHEN I WOKE at four a.m. the stars were still up in the purplish sky and I could see my breath inside my tent. There'd be quite a chill coming off the salty St. Lawrence, so I wanted to be as well prepared as I could. I pulled on the warmer of the two jackets I'd packed, with a fleece sweater and my merino wool base layer underneath. Then I packed everything up and carried it down to the muddy water's edge. The tide had come in considerably since I'd landed, which meant less distance for me to carry everything.

I set off paddling downriver with the outgoing tide. A few kilometres ahead were the Plains of Abraham, where the fate of empires hung in the balance one September morning more than a quarter of a millennium ago. The Plains sit atop the rocky promontory that Wolfe's troops had to scale, just outside the

Camping in a swampy section of the St. Lawrence River near Lac Saint-Pierre. The rich forests and marshes in this area form crucial migratory bird habitat.

Storm clouds gathering above the St. Lawrence River on May 21. This storm spawned tornadoes and caused considerable damage, but my canoe and tent survived.

One of my campsites along the St. Lawrence River in Quebec.

"I wanted one last look at the historic city, and turned around in my canoe just to gaze at the gleaming gothic turrets of the Château Frontenac, the castle-style hotel that sits atop the cliffs and dominates Quebec's cityscape. As I was looking back . . . I was startled to see the freighter I'd just passed abruptly pull out from port with remarkable swiftness and without any assistance from tugboats."

Hiking in the mountains along the St. Lawrence estuary in Quebec's Charlevoix region. "I kept going . . . reaching several rock outcrops with breathtaking views of the misty mountains around me and the foggy sea far below."

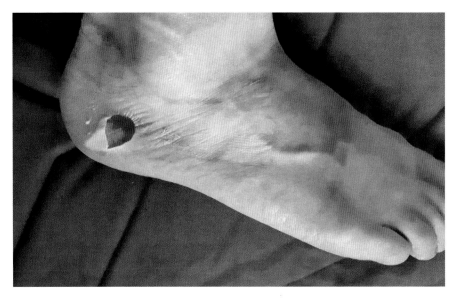

One of many blisters from long hours of hiking in wet conditions.

A porcupine near one of my campsites while hiking along Quebec's north shore.

June 1, Day 39: Making camp near a beautiful lake while hiking through the Laurentian Mountains.

Hiking the 389, the lonely road that runs north to Labrador.

Wading around the Marshall Rapids. "I inched forward cautiously, the dark, swirling waters rising almost to my chest. Ahead was the thundering roar of the rapids. With one hand I grasped the willow bushes along the shore and with the other the canoe . . ."

Paddling in the rain on the Menihek Lakes, with water accumulating under my seat. "Almost immediately upon entering the lake a heavy rainstorm soaked me and began filling up the canoe. I kept paddling regardless, pausing only to bail water over the sides as necessary."

A caribou swimming across a lake in Labrador. "Caribou are excellent swimmers, and this one didn't seem at all fazed by the thought of a long water crossing."

Hauling my canoe up a beaver creek as part of a series of portages to get over the watershed divide separating the Atlantic and Arctic drainage basins. "I found a second creek, this one choked with beaver dams and willows, that I had to paddle, pole, wade, and haul my canoe up while being attacked by blackflies."

"On a swampy island, I came upon a moose munching on some willows. After so much solitude, to have any company felt nice." On the hill behind the moose, tundra can be seen on the higher slopes, with subarctic forest lower down.

Portaging through an alder thicket. "The alder thickets virtually swallowed me up. They were taller than me, and inside them it was impossible to see which way to head— they were so thick that I couldn't see more than a foot in any direction."

July 11, Day 79: Slowing down to scout a rapid ahead on the Rivière De Pas.

city walls. After the British conquest, Quebec remained the capital of Canada, with the governor general (back when the position wasn't just symbolic) based there along with the majority of Canada's military and civilian administration. This state of affairs lasted until 1840, meaning that Quebec actually functioned as Canada's capital far longer than Ottawa has. (Quebec held the position from Champlain's founding in 1608 through to 1840, and again on a rotational basis in the 1850s and 60s, for a total of roughly 240 years.) At the far end of the Plains of Abraham, I could make out the star-shaped citadel that guards the western approach to the city and gives Quebec something of its medieval character. The fortress connects to the high stone walls that completely encircle Old Quebec—making Quebec North America's only walled city north of Mexico.

But I couldn't afford to get too absent-minded pondering these historic landmarks, as Quebec's port was as busy as any I'd seen. There were passenger ferries, tugboats, coast guard ships, and freighters all plying the waters. Unlike at Montreal, switching sides here was out of the question given how busy the narrow shipping lanes were—instead I'd have to paddle as fast as I could right by the port. I counted two giant freighters moored alongside it, which didn't seem too daunting. So long as one didn't suddenly depart, it should be safe to paddle below them. But as I swung a bit farther offshore a third freighter materialized a little farther down the port—then a fourth, then a fifth, and finally a sixth. I exhaled deeply; this was going to be daunting after all.

I mustered up all the courage I could, and started paddling steadily forward. A large passenger ferry sped across the river, taking commuters from Old Quebec to Lévis on the opposite bank. I drifted long enough for it to safely pass, then raced ahead. Immediately to my left was the historic Lower Town, with its narrow cobblestone streets and eighteenth-century architecture. It was here that Jacques Cartier spent his disastrous winter of 1536—when nearly a quarter of his band perished from starvation and disease—and where Champlain in 1608 stood down a mutiny among his crew by executing the ringleader and exhibiting his severed head on a pike outside the settlement's walls. Nowadays one hardly ever sees that kind of inspirational leadership in Canada.

A passing freighter snapped me out of these daydreams and forced me to be on guard. I let up paddling, tensely watching the giant ship to see if it intended to dock. A coast guard vessel sped by, generating more wake than just about any other boat that had passed me. That the coast guard paid me not the slightest attention I took as encouraging. Two other coast guard ships were alongside the dock: the *Pierre Radisson* and *Des Groseilliers*, named for the two colourful rogues and adventurers who'd founded the Hudson Bay Company in the 1600s. A third ship anchored at the dock bore the name of another 1600s-era Canadian explorer—the *Louis Jolliet*. Jolliet was born at Quebec in 1645, and had made a legendary journey of exploration by canoe to the Mississippi River. In Quebec, just about every ship, bridge, road, park, and building seems to be named after some historical figure.

Meanwhile another freighter appeared to be slowly working its way upstream, with two tugboats alongside it. It was moving at a snail's pace, and I raced by it in my canoe, desperate to finally get beyond the last of the busy port. I was almost at the mouth of the St. Charles River, which flows through Quebec City and joins the St. Lawrence, but there was one final steel giant moored alongside the dock. I'd have to canoe around it, and hesitated for a second to size it up: its engines weren't making any noise, and no tugboats were around it, so it seemed it wasn't going to depart anytime soon and there was nothing to fear. Feeling relieved, I paddled along its massive bulk, then skipped across the mouth of the St. Charles River toward an industrial area. I'd almost escaped the port.

But I wanted one last look at the historic city, and turned around in my canoe just to gaze at the gleaming gothic turrets of the Château Frontenac, the castle-style hotel that sits atop the cliffs and dominates Quebec's cityscape. The famous old hotel is named for the swashbuckling Count Frontenac, who in 1690 defeated an English attempt to capture Quebec. As I was looking back, and chiding myself that perhaps in retrospect there wasn't anything to fear from giant freighters, I was startled to see the freighter I'd just passed abruptly pull out from port with remarkable swiftness and without any assistance from tugboats. If I'd been only a little slower, I'd have been right smack in its path. I breathed a sign of relief and quickly paddled off.

Downstream the view was breathtaking: the river widened out dramatically, with the undulating peaks of the Laurentian Mountains running along the horizon and the pastoral landscape of historic Île d'Orléans midstream in the river. The wind was gusting, kindling whitecaps on the wide-open salty river, while a sailboat disappeared to the east beyond the island. I canoed by a beach, then aimed for the suspension bridge that links Orléans to the mainland. The island is something of a rural time capsule, with over six hundred heritage buildings and narrow seigneurial-style farms that date back to the 1600s. Its rural charms have long made it a popular destination.

I paddled under the suspension bridge, the gusts helping drive me along. The tidal effects were becoming ever stronger, with large mudflats appearing along the shore as the ebbing tide ran out. This complicated paddling, as low tide would prevent any easy access to shore given the quicksand-like mud.

Just beyond the bridge I had an excellent view of the roaring Montmorency Falls, which tower nearly a hundred feet higher than Niagara Falls. It was near this spectacular cataract that Frontenac's Canadian militia easily repulsed the landings of a New England invasion force. The New Englanders had appeared in the river with some thirty-four ships and several thousand troops, but their plan to capture Quebec and conquer Canada ended only in bloody disaster on these muddy shores.

The English made another attempt to conquer Canada in 1711, with a vast fleet of seventy-one ships and over thirteen thousand troops setting sail. But this mighty fleet never reached Quebec—it was defeated by the treacherous navigational hazards of the St. Lawrence estuary in one of the worst maritime disasters in British naval history. Stormy winds and thick fogs near Sept-Îles caused the fleet to wreck off the rugged shore. Almost a thousand soldiers and sailors drowned. This catastrophe ended the invasion. Not until the Seven Years' War would another major attempt be made to take Quebec. By that time the kingdoms of England and Scotland had united to form the United Kingdom, and with their combined might resolved to conquer New France, especially the largest colony, Canada. After first laying siege to France's Acadian settlements, in 1759 a powerful fleet of almost two hundred ships sailed up the St. Lawrence under General Wolfe.

The British first landed right beside the shore where I was now paddling at Beauport, but were fiercely repulsed by Canadien militia and French soldiers, who inflicted heavy casualties on the attackers. Wolfe, however, didn't yield. Instead, he spent the next six weeks marauding the countryside—destroying many Canadian villages and putting farmhouses to the torch—before launching his surprise night assault below the cliffs in September, which led to victory outside the city's walls and the capture of Quebec. In the battle, both Wolfe and the French commander, Montcalm, were killed.

Although the British now controlled Quebec, Canada's fate wasn't settled. In the spring, another French army travelled downriver from Montreal and attacked the British at Quebec. The resulting battle at Sainte-Foy was even bloodier than the Plains of Abraham. But in the end, the British prevailed and the conquest of Canada was complete. Battle-scarred Quebec City, however, hadn't seen the last of its wars. The Americans launched their own campaign to seize the city and conquer Canada in 1775. But in a blinding snowstorm their army was cut to pieces outside the city's walls.

The fierce gusts were driving me rapidly down the channel separating Île d'Orléans from the mainland. I landed twice to investigate the shoreline, but both times found it to be a quagmire of impassable mudflats that I sank into knee-deep. At high tide, landing wasn't an issue, as I could come right into the solid shoreline, but at anything less than high tide it was a serious struggle to reach some semblance of dry land.

The shoreline had gradually grown wilder, and now it was made up of forested marshes that looked like excellent water-fowl and other bird habitat. Duck hunting was plainly a pop-ular pastime judging by how many half-concealed duck blinds I spied in the marshes. The St. Lawrence estuary is a major stopover site for thousands of snow geese and ducks on their arctic migrations. It also happens to be the world's largest estu-ary, defined as a tidal mouth of brackish water where a river meets the sea. The rich waters of the estuary attract not only vast numbers of birds, but also many whales, Greenland sharks, fish, and other marine species. There were once vast popula-tions of walrus on the estuary, too—but their great bulk and slowness sadly made them easy targets for ravenous sailors and hunters, and by end of the 1700s they'd been extirpated. In the shifting sands along the tidal beaches it's still possible to find old walrus tusks.

The gusts were so strong now that, even though they were tailwinds, it was making paddling tricky. The extensive mud-flats running more than a kilometre offshore at low tide forced me to canoe far from land, which wasn't very comfortable given the whitecaps. But ahead of me was one of the most breath-taking vistas I'd ever seen: a dome-shaped, forest-clad mountain loomed up on the distant shore with a little village nestled at its foot, dominated by the steeple of some historic stone church. The distance I was at in my canoe concealed any signs of mod-ernity such as hydro poles or passing vehicles, so that the entire scene looked like some eighteenth-century painting come to life.

The St. Lawrence had now broadened to more than fifteen kilometres wide, feeling more like the sea than a river. It was clear that I wouldn't be able to continue much longer by canoe. The large waves, lack of freshwater, tides, and extensive mudflats along the shore all meant that canoeing was increasingly impractical. I'd need a ship to make decent progress on the estuary, and I had none. In any case, on the northern rivers flowing into the St. Lawrence are massive hydro installations that render canoeing impossible. The only choice would be to travel on foot: hiking through the mountains along the coast, then north until I'd bypassed the hydro dams, when I could resume paddling.

The falcons, too, leave the estuary at this point and make a sharp turn north over the mountains toward Labrador—and I wanted to follow them. So the time had come to bid farewell to my canoe and begin the really gruelling part of my journey.

I landed in the evening on the muddy tidal flats on the mainland just beyond the far tip of Île d'Orléans. It was an exhausting struggle to drag the heavily loaded canoe half a kilometre to a marshy shoreline while sinking into the mud. I made camp in an overgrown field on the edge of some woods, just outside the little village of Saint-Joachim. A hot cup of tea helped warm my chilled frame.

It was my thirty-second straight night in a tent since setting off from Long Point, and in total I'd paddled roughly twelve hundred kilometres. The Arctic was still more than two thousand kilometres away. Tomorrow morning I'd have to make what preparations I could to begin hiking into the mountains.

16

INTO THE MOUNTAINS

W HEN I WOKE in the morning, I paddled up a tiny creek snaking inland. It took me to an astonishing stone manor more than three centuries old. All around were fields and forests, though the manor itself appeared deserted. I knocked on the oak door, but no one answered. I wanted to find somewhere to store my canoe, paddles, and other gear I no longer needed so that I could lighten my load for hiking over the mountains. Stashing them in the woods didn't seem wise, given that I expected to be gone for at least two months. Once I'd bypassed the hydro installations and reached Labrador, I'd have to round up a second canoe to paddle the remainder of the way to the Arctic. I didn't exactly know how I'd find another canoe there, but I figured it couldn't be that hard—it's Canada, after all.

In a neighbouring field I came upon an old farmer on a tractor. He didn't speak English, but was as nice a fellow as any, and with my limited French, I managed to make plain what

I was after. He told me to follow him and pointed to a farm-house across the road. He rapped on the farmhouse door, and out came a man who introduced himself as Camille. He spoke excellent English, and showed the same kindness and generosity to a traveller as anyone I'd met. Not only did he kindly agree to store my canoe in his horse barn; he also refused any payment for doing so. Camille even offered me breakfast, which was very considerate—but I had a lot of ground to cover and had already eaten some almonds, so I had to be on my way. I promised I'd be back in a few months to reclaim the canoe, then bid farewell. It was a comfort knowing that I'd left it in good hands.

I set off hiking down the quiet country road. In the dis-tance loomed the green peaks of the Laurentian Mountains. I'd compressed everything I needed into my backpack, includ-ing my tent, an extra set of clothing, my sleeping bag, a first-aid kit, a fishing rod and a couple of lures, a pot to boil water, duct tape, paracord, a pocket flashlight, a few other survival items, and as much food as I could cram in. All told, it weighed about fifty pounds.

Along the road were signs indicating that the adjacent woods and fields were part of a protected National Wildlife Area, established in 1978 to preserve the marsh habitats here for migratory birds, including such arctic species as snow geese and peregrine falcons. A light rain began to fall and the weather was unseasonably chilly. I stopped to rest at a little bird observatory hut overlooking some marshy ponds. Some snow geese were at the ponds, and as I watched them, a fox dashed across an over-grown meadow, stalking the unsuspecting geese. I'd been inside for only a few minutes when an older man arrived on a bike.

"Bonjour," I said.

"Bonjour," the man replied.

"I speak only a little French," I explained.

"Oh no problem," he said. "Are you hiking?"

"Yes, into the mountains."

"Oh! Where did you start from?"

I explained briefly. The stranger introduced himself as Pierre and said he regularly biked here.

"The forests up the mountains are different; they're not like the forests down here," Pierre said. "They're very old."

"Old-growth forest?" I asked, excited.

"Yes." Pierre nodded. "Because the mountains are so steep, they were never logged. But aren't you worried about bears? There's lots of bears up there."

"Oh, I'm pretty used to bears," I said. Just last fall I'd had a grizzly charge me.

Pierre wished me well and warned me to be careful on the steep mountain trails in the rain. I thanked him and we parted ways, he riding back in the direction of Saint-Joachim and I heading for the mountains.

The quiet road led me to Cap Tourmente National Wildlife Area. It seemed I was the only visitor. I paid my six-dollar admission and then followed a laneway through rich marshes toward the start of the mountains. A high waterfall tumbled over distant cliffs while misty clouds draped the summits. Spring had arrived with fresh greenery everywhere and a variety of birds flapping across the marshlands. The misty day and vividness of the forests made everything seem uncommonly lush. I had the sense that I was passing through somewhere special. The Cap is indeed one of the most important birding sites in North America, and as such was the first place on this continent protected under the Convention of the Conservation of Wetlands of International Importance, also known as the Ramsar Convention, an international treaty signed in 1971. The combination of the salty St. Lawrence, sheer mountain cliffs, and marshy lowlands makes the area incredibly rich with birdlife. I was excited to see it while the spring migration was still in full swing. My sense of wonder only increased when I came upon a cottonwood of enormous proportions, with giant fungi growing out of it like shelves. This astonishing tree was the largest I'd ever seen in eastern Canada, looking like something out of a fairy tale. I set my backpack beside it for a sense of scale to photograph it.

This wasn't the only fascination at hand. Nearby stood a weathered stone farmhouse with a steep roof and gabled windows. A plaque explained that it was the site of Champlain's farm, which, with his keen eye, he'd established to capitalize on the rich soils here in 1626 to supply his fledgling settlement at Quebec with badly needed food. Though only a few years later Scottish privateers, the notorious Kirke brothers, attacked the farmsteads and put them to the torch. The Scots then captured Quebec itself (the first of the many attempts to take the strategic stronghold) and held it for three years before a treaty forced them to give it back. In those days, anywhere ships could reach was never entirely safe—coastal Canada was for centuries plagued by violent raids and plundering.

The trail led me into the woods to a smaller path. This second path led over the mountains, which run in a dark chain along the St. Lawrence. Given the rain and cold, the trail appeared

deserted. My legs burned with the weight of my pack as I began
to gain elevation. As Pierre had said, the steepness of the mountain terrain had saved these woods from the logger's axe, leaving them beautiful old-growth. There were scaly sugar maples,
tough ironwood, giant ash, and yellow birch. Fresh greens were
also coming up, which would provide a much-needed addition
to my diet. I found some bluebead lilies, the berries of which are
poisonous, but the leaves taste a bit like cucumber. They're good
raw and taste best when they first emerge in spring. Farther up
the mountain I came upon some high-bush cranberries; they're
pretty bitter, but these ones were from last season and had overwintered, which makes them more palatable.

The trail was very steep, and accustomed as I was to paddling, I had to unstrap my heavy pack and rest frequently. It'd
take a week or so to break my body in to the rigours of hiking
ten hours a day with a heavy load. The trail I was following connects with a section of the Trans Canada Trail, the network of
trails that stretches across the country. This was perfect for me,
as it meant that I could follow it for a long way through the
mountains. Eventually it would come to an end and I'd have to
find other ways to make progress—a combination of local trails,
back roads, cutting across fields and forests, railroad tracks, or
anything else. But there was no need to worry about that now.

As I ascended higher the forest changed from broad-leaved
deciduous trees to hemlocks and pines, then finally spruce thickets. The rain turned heavy; even with the shelter of the spruces,
I was soon drenched. I kept going, though, reaching several
rock outcrops with breathtaking views of the misty mountains
around me and the foggy sea far below. I could see freighters

passing along the stormy estuary, which in this area is notoriously treacherous.

Along the mountain ridges the trail became more challenging, with some very narrow sections and boulders that I had to scramble over. At several steep sections, ropes had been fastened to make ascents and descents a bit easier, though I was a little unsure of trusting my safety to them. The first one I came to was hanging over a precipitous drop; it looked very old and timeworn, and in any case seemed too short. Instead, I used some spruce roots growing out of the cliffside to carefully lower myself down. The rain had made everything extra slick. Only when I reached the bottom did I realize why the rope had seemed short: it had snapped in two, and the other half was lying on the rocks. I continued deeper into the mountains.

These rugged peaks are part of the Charlevoix region, which has some of eastern Canada's highest summits. Near their centre lies a massive asteroid crater, which flattened a huge area when it struck three hundred and fifty million years ago. These mountains also happen to be one of Canada's most earthquake-prone regions, with the Charlevoix Seismic Zone running right through them. Earthquakes occur every year, including on occasion highly destructive ones. A huge magnitude 7.9 quake struck the area in 1663, triggering numerous landslides and levelling entire mountains, as well as damaging buildings as far away as New England.

That evening, with the rain still coming down steadily, I made camp in the shelter of some thick spruces. Despite the heavy rain I was able to keep everything dry inside my tent, and once I'd changed into my extra set of clothes, I was soon warm again. There's something about cold, rainy nights that just make a tent seem all the cozier.

It was good that I had my fill of wonder early in the mountains, as the following days were as miserable as any I'd ever faced. I'd fallen asleep with the hope that the morning would dawn warm and sunny, so that I could dry out my tent and clothing. But when I woke the rain was still coming down and the temperature was only three degrees above freezing. I had to steel myself to pull on my drenched clothes from the day before, since it was critical that I keep my tent clothes dry for sleeping in. I motivated myself with the thought that—unpleasant as it was to don wet clothes in three-degree temperatures—the sun might come out later. Alas nothing of the sort happened—to my surprise, the heavy rain lasted all day and into the night. This unseasonably cold weather and rain continued the following day, too. It rained more than I could have thought possible. The unusual conditions prompted Environment Canada to issue heavy rainfall warnings for the area. The alerts noted that the ground was already saturated from prolonged rains, and without the capacity to absorb more rainfall, flooding was likely.

When I hiked down the mountain valleys into the sodden gullies, it was impossible to keep my feet dry—puddles and pools were everywhere. The moss-and-lichen-carpeted ground felt like one giant sponge oozing water. Every step on the saturated ground soaked my boots. The rain made my backpack waterlogged and therefore heavier, forcing me to rest frequently. But whenever I did I had to rub my arms to stay warm, as the cold temperatures left me shivering. At the higher elevations or in the deeper woods there was still thick snow, so I avoided these areas as much as I could. On the bright side I had no trouble finding drinking water—at night I just filled my pot from the rain puddles and boiled it up for tea. As an added bonus, here in the mountain forests I had my choice of any wild tea I liked. My favourite is yellow birch; the fresh leaves and twigs make a sweat, pleasant brew.

The woods had transformed once I'd come over the first mountain and left the sheltered St. Lawrence Lowlands—gone were the familiar broadleaf trees like beech and cottonwoods that I'd seen since setting off on Lake Erie. Now the area had a distinctly more northern character: I'd reached the boreal forest, the world's largest forest. It's dominated by conifers, especially spruce and balsam fir. The wildlife was different here, too—I saw the skeleton of a moose in the woods, killed, it seemed, by a hunter. There were porcupines in the trees, and wolves and black bears stalking silently through the shadowy thickets. Spruce grouse flocked from branch to branch while red squirrels chattered noisily as they scurried up and down the trees around me.

On the third rain-filled day I came out of the mountains at the little town of Baie-Saint-Paul, which sits nestled in a mountain valley where the rapid-filled Gouffre River flows into the St. Lawrence estuary. In French, "gouffre" means abyss or chasm. The river was named in 1608 by Samuel de Champlain, who in his journal described seeing it from the deck of his ship: "There is a small river which enters far enough inland, & we have named it the river of the abyss, especially since across it the tide runs marvellously, & although it faces calm, it is still very excited, having great depth there." At certain times the tide causes a whirlpool near the river's mouth, which was reputedly the terror of local sailors, who had to time their navigation just right to avoid it. The bay's many shipwrecks testify that not all were successful.

I passed through town quickly—stopping only at a gas station to buy some delicacies, mainly chocolate bars—then cut cross-country. The terrain was very rugged here, with high rolling hills and an ever-increasing amount of dark spruce forests that I passed through. The long hours hiking combined with the incessant wetness left my feet looking terrible. Blisters formed around my heels, a result of the foot rubbing against the boot all day long. No matter how broken in boots might be, blisters are hard to avoid if it's raining constantly. The wetness also caused an ugly-looking rash all over my feet, which after several days had a stench of decay about them. If there was any upside to my hideous-looking feet, it was that the sight of them quite put me off my appetite.

The rain let up that afternoon after three days of constant wetness. When the sun finally crept out, it felt wonderful. I made camp in a clearing in the woods that had been recently logged. A tumbling little stream provided drinking water, while songbirds fluttered among the trees. It seemed as if the area had been clear-cut in preparation for someone building a cabin on the spot; at least, that was my guess. In any case, I spread my tent out to dry and put my wet clothes on saplings to catch the sun's rays. My aching feet I washed in the cool waters of the stream, then cleaned the sores with alcohol wipes and applied an antifungal cream from my first-aid kit to treat the rash.

The warm sunshine had a rejuvenating effect on me, and I was half in a daydream when I chanced to look up and see the silhouette of a long-winged, sleek-looking bird flapping across the sky. I jumped up, grabbed the camera from my backpack, and snapped at the passing bird before it vanished into the clouds. I thought I'd spotted a peregrine falcon. But when I zoomed in on the blurry image on the camera's digital screen, I realized my excitement had gotten the better of me. It had only been a hawk. Still, I felt I was getting closer to the elusive falcons.

17

CÔTE-NORD

T HE WEATHER IMPROVED markedly over the following days, with only sporadic rather than continuous
rain. The scenery was charming, with forested mountains and
some wonderfully shaped peaks, including twin peaks like a
saddle near the small village of Les Éboulements. In French,
"les éboulements" means "the landslides," a reference to the
1663 earthquake that levelled the area. Luckily for me there
was no trouble finding trails to follow—the Trans Canada Trail
had come to an end, but there were ATV trails I could take
through the woods or fields, and when these weren't around
it was easy to locate back roads or hydro cuts running parallel
to the main roads that kept me headed in the right direction.
I passed through several small villages, some with New France–
style houses and historic churches, which gave a general sense
of timelessness to these quiet places. Farms were scattered along
the lower slopes, with dandelions coming up in the meadow
mountains. There were wheat fields, sheep farms, and a few cow

pastures as well. The rugged hills made hiking with my heavy pack rather exhausting. But on the bright side, there's nothing quite like punishing physical exertion to help one sleep soundly.

Finding campsites was never difficult. There were always forests at hand whenever I halted for the night. I'd often hear the eerie calls of owls echoing out of these woods, giving me a thrill before turning in for the evening. Whenever I camped near marshes or streams, the forest seemed almost alive with the *peep, peep, peep* of spring peepers, a type of chirping frog. These little frogs are remarkably hardy, and live farther north than most frogs can tolerate. In the bitter cold of winter their bodies produce a natural "antifreeze" that allows them to survive frigid temperatures without organ damage. With the spring thaw they come back to life as if by magic, filling the forest with their nightly calls. A third call that frequently echoed from the darkness around my camps was a strange low drumming that sounded like a small engine starting up. These calls are made by male ruffed grouses rapidly beating their wings, which they normally do just before sunrise and sunset. They're striking birds that are generally found only in large, undisturbed forests. Unhappily for the grouses, many of these same forests that I camped in were in the process of being logged.

Seven days after setting off from Saint-Joachim I reached a beautiful little lake in the mountains. I camped beside it, and felt I'd made quite a discovery when at the base of an oak tree I stumbled upon a glossy green plant—it was prince's pine, also known as pipsissewa. This little plant was once a popular tea. I excitedly plucked a few leaves and brewed them up in my pot while sitting beside the lake.

My feet, meanwhile, were very blistered, raw, and pain-ful. By the end of ten hours' hiking each day I'd be limping. Normally in these circumstances you'd want to take a few days off to let your blisters heal, but to make good time I was deter-mined to keep hiking regardless, since I missed my family. To do so, I'd pop the blisters, drain them, and cover them with foam bandages to protect the raw skin underneath. Then, to prevent any further blisters from forming, I'd duct tape over the back of my feet. The duct tape prevents blisters by providing a protective layer that stops any friction from the boot against bare skin (crazy as it may sound). This method worked toler-ably well, and while I was still sometimes in discomfort, I was able to average anywhere from nineteen to thirty kilometres a day depending on the terrain. Luckily, the relatively drier spell allowed my hiking boots to dry out, and with the antifungal cream, my rash subsided.

The next day I reached Baie-Sainte-Catherine, a small town nestled at the foot of the mountains on the St. Lawrence coast. It's named after a shipwreck, the tragic *La Catherine*, which ran aground here during a fierce storm in 1686. I followed a rugged trail over the mountain to the ferry terminal at the Saguenay River, which flows through a fjord into the St. Lawrence. A short ferry ride took me across the narrow fjord to the historic village of Tadoussac. Founded in 1600 as a fur-trading post, it's one of the oldest French settlements in Canada. The early days of the settlement were none too cheerful: only five of the orig-inal sixteen colonists survived the first winter, and then Basque whalers attacked the French ships there. The Basque were attracted to the area for the same reasons tourists are today:

whales (though the Basque harpooned them instead of photo-graphing them.)

Daydreams of food were never far from my mind. When canoeing, I'd been under tight enough restrictions on how much food I could reasonably pack. But hiking is even more restrictive; not only does it burn enormous amounts of calories, there just isn't space enough to carry as much food as ideal. I was eating just one meal a day plus snacks, which left me ravenous. Even supplementing my meagre rations as much as possible with wild edibles (bead lilies, a few types of berries, some roots), fish from the rivers, and anything I could get from whatever gas stations or stores I chanced to pass, I was constantly hungry.

But on occasion I received unexpected assistance. The trail I was following linked up several times with the main road that winds along the St. Lawrence, and at one of these points I followed it to a rundown store that was boarded up. I was resting here out of the rain, my pack beside me and my back to the derelict building, when a trucker happened to pull in. He asked me in French what I was doing, and after I'd explained as well as I was able, he seemed surprised and curious. When he pulled his vehicle around to leave, through his open window he called out to me, and then tossed down a yogurt. It was a windfall that made my day.

That night I camped at the base of a mountain in a thick stand of aspens. It was bitterly cold and I woke up several times shivering. Cold nights like this only made me hungrier, since the body is forced to burn more calories to stay warm.

Even though I wasn't in a canoe, it turned out wind could still be a factor, and stiff headwinds slowed my progress the next morning. Worn out by the bitter gusts, when I needed to rest I'd find a spot in the forest, toss my backpack aside, and collapse on the moss. The soft sphagnum moss, which grows in dense carpets across the boreal forest, at least made my rests comfortable. I'd usually lie with my head against my backpack, but sometimes I'd reverse and put my head in the moss and my feet on the pack instead, as elevating the feet helps reduce throbbing and swelling caused by long hours of hiking.

At certain high points I had sweeping views of the St. Lawrence estuary, and could just dimly make out hazy mountains on the far shore, now nearly fifty kilometres away. The weather remained cool, around ten degrees, and rainy. I passed through the little village of Les Escoumins, where a small pharmacy allowed me to replenish my supply of blister bandages. The constant hiking wasn't giving much time for my blisters to heal, and the return of wet weather didn't help.

Beyond the village was a rough trail running parallel to the estuary, with numerous little creeks draining across it that I had to jump over. It seemed I wasn't the only one on this trail—a large bull moose had followed it, leaving rain-filled tracks. Some bushwhacking up and over a steep hill took me down to the shoreline, where I camped on the outskirts of the little village of Saint-Paul-du-Nord. I thought the saltwater might do my feet some good, so I soaked them in the chilly water for as long as felt tolerable. The wild shore, encircling hills, and quiet, deserted cove all reminded me of the kind of place where pirates might have once come ashore to hide treasure. The St. Lawrence estuary was for centuries the great highway into the heart of Canada. Ships rich in cargoes of furs, fish, and timber plied these waters in the days of the French Empire. But such merchant vessels in turn attracted pirates, with the St. Lawrence at one time swarming with them. Whether any pirates ever actually anchored in this remote spot I had no idea, but the mere thought they might have lent a certain charm to things as I pitched my tent.

It rained heavily overnight, drenching everything. The morning dawned on another cold, wet day, which my rain pants and jacket proved unable to withstand. Although these modern synthetics are great for light or sporadic rain, they inevitably wet through if exposed to a continuous heavy downpour. Only traditional rubber rain jackets seem able to cope with that much water, but they have their own downsides of being heavy and not great for physical exertion. So like most things, there are trade-offs either way. I had to bushwhack once more, this time through the sodden forest to link up with another trail that would continue leading me northeast, further soaking my boots and pants.

My spirits were cheered when I came to a bird sanctuary situated on the edge of an extensive tidal marsh—but the overcast skies and drizzling rain made it difficult to spot any birds. Side trails running parallel to the main road made hiking relatively flat and easy, as the mountains had receded from the coast and the ground had become marshier. Farms had disappeared and there were more and more signs of logging. The forest still had a few lingering hints of southern woods; I passed wild cherry trees, dogwood, and jack and white pines, as well as plentiful bead lilies to snack on.

In the evening, red squirrels kept me company, chattering up a storm around my tent, as did songbirds singing among the trees. Whenever possible I tried to halt for the night beside a stream, so that I could fetch water for boiling a freeze-dried meal and tea. On occasion, though, I had to settle for murky swamps.

The next morning, June 6, I passed through the little town of Forestville, picking up a much-needed resupply of granola bars and dried fruit from its grocery store. But towns were becoming fewer and farther between, which often weren't really towns at all now, but just labels on the map that didn't seem to correspond to much of anything. The population along Quebec's remote north shore has declined substantially over the last three decades, leaving some hamlets to almost disappear.

Having hiked another twenty-four kilometres, I made camp in some deep fir and spruce woods, the air filled with their sweet fragrance. After munching on some bead lilies and sarsaparilla roots, which taste a bit like parsnips, I fell fast asleep. But less than an hour later, a loud crash outside my tent startled me. I clenched my knife and rose to my knees in a defensive posture, half expecting a bear to come plowing in. Normally whenever I found bears creeping around my tent in the dark, it was only the slightest hint of movement—leaves rustling, a branch snapping—that alerted me to their presence. So on second thought, the sudden crashing I'd heard might be something else. There were plainly a lot of moose in the area, judging by how frequently I'd seen their tracks. And while moose are also almost uncanny in their ability to move quietly through forests, when they're startled, they create a tremendous racket. So it was probably only a bull moose, which something had frightened. This reassured me, and when no further noise followed, I lay back down and fell asleep.

＊

I WOKE IN the morning to unfriendly skies—more rain it seemed. This motivated me to pack up quickly before my tent got waterlogged again. I stored my tent in a waterproof bag that I attached to the outside of my pack. At night, the bag doubled as food storage, since I figured it would at least partly dim the scent of food to animals. Luckily, I was able to get everything stowed away before the downpour began. It soaked me, but at least my tent was dry.

A cold wind was blowing off the sea, and the temperature never climbed much above freezing, so not only was I soaked but chilled, too. Some rugged trails and back roads led me toward the outskirts of Papinachois. But the rain was so heavy that it created puddles and pools nearly everywhere, which became impossible to avoid. My boots soaked right through, and I was as wet as a lobster. The miserable weather caused me to halt earlier than I normally would, this time making camp in the shelter of some thick spruces. The inner branches of spruces will often stay dry even in downpours, so fortunately it wasn't difficult to make a comforting fire. I warmed myself with a cup of tea and cooked my last remaining freeze-dried meal: a delightful vegetable lasagna.

The rain still continued the next day as I trudged wearily along toward the outskirts of Chute-aux-Outardes, a small village near the mouth of the Outardes River. This river, like most others along Quebec's north shore, has been dammed for hydroelectric development. As far back as 1544 French explorers had noted the Outardes River on their maps, but the present name doesn't seem to have taken root until the early 1700s. "Outardes" is a common slang term in French for Canada geese. I spotted several of them flying overhead as I made another rainy camp in the woods near the reservoir created by the dam. A chorus of spring peepers called in the forest, while moose tracks were more plentiful than ever.

I hoped the morning would bring better weather so that I could dry out, but it proved only colder and wetter. Hiking through so much rain was exhausting, especially on a cold day, and with my feet already blistered and sore, I figured some rest might now do me good. The rain remained steady all day, but I snoozed in my sleeping bag and enjoyed some spruce tea boiled up on my tiny camp stove, which was small enough to set up within arm's reach of my tent's door. This felt wonderfully luxurious, but I was nearly out of food, with just a few nuts left. I was about twelve kilometres from the outskirts of Baie-Comeau, the largest town on Quebec's north shore (population about nine thousand). I intended to bypass it by turning north along some back roads to link up with the 389, the lonely road that runs north to Labrador. But before I could do so, I'd need a proper resupply of Clif bars, nuts, and freeze-dried meals. Alexandria had mailed in advance a box of these precious provisions to the post office on Baie-Comeau's outskirts for me. After that, it would be six hundred kilometres before I'd hit another town.

The next day, June 11, at last dawned sunny, and so I hiked into the outskirts of Baie-Comeau in good order, chatting with several friendly locals along the way who—seeing my scruffy appearance and outsized backpack—inquired curiously where

I'd come from. They seemed surprised by my answer. One old woman standing on her driveway, who saw me passing by, seemed to want to ask me every question conceivable, of which I understood less than half. But my lack of comprehension didn't sccm to dampen her enthusiasm at all, and she talked up a storm for a good fifteen minutes, before I could politely continue.

At the post office I was relieved to find my package was safe and sound, and I quickly emptied the precious contents into my depleted pack. Afterwards, knowing I'd soon experience hunger like never before, I treated myself to a grand feast in the form of a Tim Hortons brunch.

Then, the sun shining on a fine morning, I picked my way along a trail leading north of town to a rough road under construction. There'd be no cell service where I was headed, and my route was bound to become much lonelier and wilder. But I took heart that I was on the path of the falcons, and that there'd hopefully be better weather ahead.

18

NORTHBOUND

T HE NEXT COMMUNITY, Labrador City, a small mining
town, was exactly 588 kilometres away. The most I could
reasonably cram into my backpack was food for two weeks—
and that was if I limited myself to a single meal and eight
granola bars per day. That'd be enough, but just barely, to keep
me going. However, I wasn't sure I could actually cover that
much distance in just fourteen days. To do so, I'd have to average a good forty-two kilometres a day, with no rest days.

So far, I'd only managed to hike an average of twenty-five
kilometres a day. That slower pace was partly the result of rough
trails and sometimes none at all, so with a road to follow I could
be assured of improving my pace. But I'd still need to increase
my daily distances pretty substantially, or else risk running out
of food. Of course, I could try to supplement my rations as
much as possible by foraging for wild plants—but there aren't
many calories to be gained in bead lilies, sarsaparilla roots, and
cattail tubers. In any case, these would peter out as I went north,

since they don't grow at more northern latitudes. I had my fishing rod, but fish don't provide all that much in calories either, and fishing takes time, which would detract from hiking. More promising were a couple of gas stations and truck stops scattered over the six hundred kilometres separating me from the next town. I could count on finding at least a meal or snack at these places, which would help stretch my supplies a bit further. But on the whole the hike was bound to be difficult: I told myself to look upon it as a simple matter of putting one foot in front of the other, and I'd get there eventually.

I took a shortcut out of Baie-Comeau to a rough road that was not yet open and still under construction. Dynamite was being used to blast a path through the solid rock to build the road. Luckily for me, it was a weekend, so the construction was halted and everything was deserted. It looked a bit like some post-apocalyptic landscape, given that the heavy machinery, haul-trucks, and backhoes were just left there unattended. A two-and-a-half-kilometre hike over this unfinished road would allow me to link up with the 389.

Once I'd reached it, I no longer had any cell reception. I followed the narrow road's gravel shoulder, passing thick spruce forests on either side dotted with moose tracks. The weather was warmer than it'd been lately, and clouds of blackflies soon materialized. These pesky bloodsucking insects normally emerge in mid-June, and now they were out in droves. In a canoe I could partly escape them by paddling offshore, but here I was at their mercy. Even putting on my mesh bug net did little to stop them from crawling underneath or biting through it. I was soon covered in their itchy bites.

After eight hours of hiking I reached a bridge over the Manicouagan River immediately below a huge hydro dam, the Jean-Lesage generating station, or Manic-2. It's one of five mega dams spanning the river. Nearby was a campground and small diner. I'd hoped to get an extra meal here, but I was out of luck: a sign on the door stated it was closed. So I made do with my granola bars and kept going.

That evening I made camp in the woods beside a little alder-lined lake. A small campfire allowed me to boil water and cook one of my freeze-dried meals while driving off some of the bugs. I'd made it only thirty-two kilometres. But I took encouragement in the knowledge that my heavy pack would get lighter each day as I ate up my rations, and that as it did, I'd be able to travel faster.

When I woke in the morning it was to the steady drone of millions of mosquitoes. I lingered in my tent for a few minutes, just to breathe freely. It soon turned into a hot day, which, combined with the incessant swarms of not only mosquitoes but blackflies, drained my energy. There were some consolations, though. The wind occasionally provided relief from the bugs, and birds sang from the branches overhead: I saw gray jays, robins, song sparrows, and even some goldfinches. Meanwhile goldeneye ducks swam in the beautiful lakes that I passed.

Twice I stopped at lakes or creeks to pump water through my hand-held carbon-filter purifier. It's not an easy operation— you have to push hard, and it can take twenty minutes of strenuous effort just to fill up one bottle, all while being attacked by blackflies. So when I halted for the third time at another lake, exhausted and dehydrated as I was, I decided to risk things and drink straight from it. This saved me a lot of effort, and I trusted I'd likely be fine, as I'd never had trouble in the past drinking untreated water in Canada's wilderness.

That night a smoky fire helped drive off some of the black-fly clouds, and just to be safe, I purified two pots of water by boiling it. This was much faster and easier than the hand-held pump. The ground in the woods was uneven, with a steep slope, but at least it was soft. I'd managed to hike thirty-eight kilometres; better, but still not quite good enough.

A light rain fell overnight, making my bag heavier in the morning. The bugs were again relentless in their assault on my neck, face, ears, hands, legs, and anywhere else they could get at. Mentally I just told myself to block them out, think of something else, and keep trudging on. If the bugs had any upside, it was that they motivated me to keep moving. I passed over numerous swift-flowing creeks, which explained the intensity of the blackflies, as they only lay their eggs in running water (unlike mosquitoes, which breed in stagnant water). I noticed as well a number of bear and wolf tracks along the gravel shoulder of the road. It was nice to know I wasn't alone.

In the afternoon I came to a compound on the side of the road that had a fuel depot along with parked trailers, mobile homes, and trucks. As far as I could tell it functions as a base of operations for some of the hydro personnel and other workers. In any case, thankfully I was able to purchase some chocolate bars, nuts, and water here, which would help stretch out my rations.

But it was increasingly clear that if I continued to get swarmed by bugs all day, I'd have a hard time reaching Labrador. I had a neck bandana—the tube kind you pull over your head—and I decided to turn it into a mask to help protect me from the blackflies. I cut eye holes and a mouth hole, then pulled it over my face. Over top I wore my mesh bug net and my hat. This was a vast improvement, reducing the bites on my face, ears, and throat. The only downside was it restricted my vision, and it was hot and uncomfortable. But this seemed a small price pay to gain some relief.

That night, for the first time on my journey I had trouble sleeping. My throbbing ears were so swollen from blackfly bites that it was painful to lie on either side. I tossed and turned for hours until I finally drifted off.

Fortunately, the next morning dawned cooler and windier, which brought relief from the bugs. My improvised mask also helped a great deal, making my hike an altogether more pleasant experience. As I continued north the terrain became increasingly mountainous, with more bear and moose tracks as well as ravens atop the spruces. It seemed somewhat ominous how the ravens eyed me from their perches, squawking as I passed below. Ravens are carrion birds, living off the carcasses of dead animals. I imagined they were saying to themselves, "This one can't last much longer. We'll soon eat well."

After covering another thirty-eight kilometres, I made camp in a mossy forest near a little spring-fed stream. Dehydrated as I was, I once again drank straight from it. If it had been a slow-flowing creek or some stagnant beaver pond I would have been more hesitant. After refreshing myself from the stream, I was surprised to find that there were still some wild cherry trees this far north. Their pink blossoms added a dash of colour to the otherwise grey woods. They reminded me of the woods back in

Norfolk County, where wild cherries are common. I gathered some cherry wood to burn in my fire, which filled the air with a sweet fragrance. To sit on mossy ground by a cherry fire further reminded me of how comfortable camping could be. There were even some bluebead lilies nearby to munch on.

I had a restful night's sleep on the soft moss, which was a good thing, as the return of warm weather the next day brought back the blackflies. My mask protected my face somewhat, but the flies seemed to compensate by shifting their focus to crawling under my clothing and biting my legs and arms. With the mask on I was sweating twice as much, and the only water sources were sometimes miles apart.

I'd been staggering on for several hours, my water bottle empty, sweat dripping down my face, my body itching from the bites, when I heard a vehicle approaching. In these vast solitudes, surrounded by millions of acres of forest, any approaching vehicle could be heard from miles away. I paid it no attention, and just kept hiking.

An SUV materialized; it passed right by me, kicking up a cloud of dust, then thirty feet ahead it stopped and abruptly reversed. When the driver had backed up to where I was standing, the window went down and I looked up to see a young man behind the wheel. He seemed surprised to see someone beside the road.

"Bonjour. What are you doing?" he asked me in French.

"Hiking."

"Is everything okay?"

"Yes."

"Where are you heading?"

"Labrador."

He stared at me. "Labrador! That's hundreds of kilometres from here."

"462 kilometres," I replied. (I'd been counting down the exact number since Baie-Comeau, which was easy to do since every two kilometres there'd been a roadside marker.)

"Do you need anything? Can I help in any way?"

"If you have any water you can spare, I'd definitely appreciate it."

He quickly fetched a bottle of water from the trunk and handed it to me; I was so parched I drank the entire thing in one go. Then he generously handed me a second one, which I poured into my empty bottle. After that he gave me an apple, which I devoured on the spot—it tasted like the best apple I'd ever had. Finally, he pulled out some bug spray and gave that to me as well. It felt like Christmas. I was almost at a loss for words.

"What's your name?" I asked, after expressing my hearty thanks.

"Steve," he replied.

"Do you work for hydro?"

"No, I work monitoring forest fires."

"Oh. Are you anticipating fires here?" (I figured it would be good to know if I'd have to run from a fire.)

"No, we're expecting lots more heavy rain."

This was a relief. Well, sort of. Better than a forest fire in any case.

He then asked my name and I told him.

"Adam?" he said, looking puzzled.

"Yes."

"That's strange. My wife and I are expecting our first child, and Adam is the name we chose," Steve explained. He remarked it seemed an odd coincidence that in such a remote place as this, he should happen to meet someone of the same name. I agreed it was probably unlikely. Steve then wished me well, and drove off while I resumed hiking.

A while later I came upon a stream flowing beside the road, which I could see plainly, was full of trout. It seemed this was my lucky day: the fish would make a nice meal. But just as I was preparing to bludgeon one with a heavy stick (the shallowness of the pool suggested this method), I heard the rumble of another vehicle.

A few minutes later I was surprised to see it was Steve again. I wondered what could have brought him back. Once again he stopped next to me and put down the window.

"This may sound strange," he began, "but as I was driving I just kept thinking how odd it was to meet you here. And I was wondering if you'd mind if we took a photo together? I'd like to tell this story to my wife."

After such gifts as water, an apple, and bug spray, it was impossible to refuse. In truth, of all the kind people who'd crossed my path, Steve's assistance, coming as it did in such a lonely and remote place when I was at my lowest ebb—exhausted, bug-bitten, and hungry—made me feel I'd be forever in his debt.

Steve took a quick selfie with me on the side of the road and asked if he could do anything else to assist me. Since leaving Baie-Comeau five days earlier I hadn't been able to contact Alexandria. Steve explained that where he was headed—a fire-monitoring base—it was possible to send messages. So I gave him Alexandria's number and asked if he could send her a text. Steve said he'd send her the photo he'd taken to prove I wasn't dead yet. Such consideration was touching. Then he climbed back into his vehicle, wished me good luck, and drove off down the dusty road.

I was on my own again, but didn't feel alone in spirit— such kindness had given me a renewed energy. I trudged on for another ten kilometres before halting for the night in the woods beside a little stream.

19

BOREAL

T HIRTY MORE KILOMETRES of rough hiking up and
down steep hills left me sweaty, parched, and with blisters
forming at the ends of my toes. A gnawing hunger was my constant companion, and even with my allotted eight granola bars
and one freeze-dried meal a day, I felt ravenous. On the bright
side, the duct tape had succeeded in preventing any new blisters
forming around my heels. In the afternoon a heavy downpour
drenched me (as Steve had foretold), forcing me to make camp
early. The extra rest was welcome, though, as it allowed me to
collect water, make tea, and recuperate for the many miles that
still lay ahead.

The rains lasted most of the night and into the next morning, with at times a torrential downpour that reduced visibility
to near zero. Given the circumstances, it seemed prudent to wait
for the storm to pass before setting off again. It wasn't until mid-
morning that I was finally able to shoulder my pack and resume

hiking in what had become a mere drizzle. I didn't mind this, as it helped keep me cool and diminished the blackflies.

A sign indicated that a few kilometres ahead was another hydro dam, the massive Manic-5. This spurred me on, as near it was a truck stop, where I hoped to find something to eat. When I reached it, it didn't disappoint. The small store had as fine a selection of granola bars as any connoisseur could wish; I bought a dozen. There was even a cafeteria-style restaurant, where I was able to obtain such rare delicacies as a burger and fries. I left feeling full for the first time in a week, hiking off toward the giant hydro dam.

A bridge led me across the turbulent river immediately below the dam, which holds back millions of gallons of water. It's the largest dam in the world of its kind, stretching the length of a dozen football fields and towering as high as a sky-scraper. It took more than a decade to build, opening in 1970. The grey skies and drizzling rain made the huge structure seem slightly menacing, especially in contrast to the encircling for-ests. With the hum of machinery and the sound of the turbu-lent river below, I felt vaguely nervous trudging beneath it. I kept picturing the dam suddenly bursting, unleashing a tsunami right at me. I tried to laugh at the absurdity of my own fears, but when I noticed red signs indicating evacuation spots above the high-water mark in the event of an emergency, I didn't feel entirely reassured.

The road wound up a steep hill on the opposite side of the bridge. When I finally reached the top, sweating despite the cool weather, I saw that beyond this point the road was unpaved. It was merely a rough gravel lane disappearing into the distance over what seemed like an endless sea of forested hills and misty mountains. I hiked late into the evening, with the rain continuing off and on, until I finally stopped for the night in a soggy forest beside a swirling stream. I was too exhausted to cook anything, and in any case the lunch had filled me up. So I skipped dinner and instead just boiled up black spruce tea, which is rich in vitamin C, and this felt as satisfying as anything. In any case, I'd been failing to hit the forty-two-kilometre mark every day, meaning I had no choice but to cut back on rations.

Temperatures plunged again overnight, with cold air coming down from the north and more rain. When I woke, shivering in the grey dawn, I told myself not to worry; hiking would keep me warm. But it turned out that in these wild, windy mountains it was too cold even for that. Temperatures were hovering just a few degrees above freezing, with a wet snow that utterly chilled me.

Alone all day with my thoughts, my mind would often roam over the mysteries of this ancient land: to my left, screened by dark forests, was the so-called "Eye of Quebec," a massive asteroid crater that from space looks like a giant eye. The construction of the Manic-5 dam had flooded the crater, drowning thousands of acres of forest. Wandering in such a place makes you feel very small.

On the high slopes the road was windswept and exposed, and the drizzling snow and chilling winds forced me to seek shelter in the woods during my rests. I'd rub my arms and sit under a spruce just to warm up a little and get out of the wetness before resuming my trek. To my surprise I noted a few more stunted black cherries this far north, though they were becoming much rarer. There was also mountain ash (the orange berries of which are edible but not particularly tasty), and the odd jack pine and white birch. Along the streams and creeks were often alder thickets, and sometimes trembling aspens. But in these austere north woods it was mostly balsam fir and black spruce, which is fantastic if you enjoy conifer tea.

The road was increasingly rough, with many loose rocks, some of them fist-sized, scattered all over it that left my ankles quite sore. It wasn't very comfortable to hike on, especially ten hours a day, ascending and descending steep terrain. When I took rests, to ease the throbbing in my feet I'd elevate them on my pack. On the other hand, as the road became rougher, the scenery became more spectacular, with glistening snow-clad mountains and island-studded blue lakes stretching endlessly toward the horizon. Wolf and bear tracks were also becoming more common, and for nearly an hour I followed the tracks of some enormous wolf that had sauntered right along the road.

Despite my sore feet and the road's unevenness, my pace was improving. I was roughly at the halfway point when I came upon a little roadside establishment, the last one for several hundred kilometres. It seemed about the loneliest place imaginable: just a gas station and a little house that doubled as a tiny store. Luckily, I reached it just before it closed for the day and procured a bounty: a sandwich, a muffin, several chocolate bars, an orange, and an apple, which would stretch my dwindling rations a bit further. But after this last outpost, things were bound to get tougher. Not only were there no further waypoints where I could supplement my rations, but the terrain was becoming ever more mountainous.

A cool, windy day spent passing beneath these mountains at least brought me relief from the blackflies. I managed to cover another forty-two kilometres, halting for the night in a wooded valley by a stream.

Oddly enough, at intervals through the day, I'd heard a strange snapping noise coming from somewhere in the woods. When I first heard it, I didn't pay it any attention and just kept plodding along. But when I heard it again, I paused and cast a glance into the dark forest flanking the road, eyeing the spruces and tamaracks suspiciously. The snapping, occurring at occasional intervals, was too loud to be an insect, and I knew of no animal that made any sound like it. I never did figure out what made it, accepting it as one of life's mysteries.

The weather in these windy mountains was even colder, and alongside the road were often thickets and steep slopes that forced me to bushwhack or climb inland to find suitable spots for pitching my tent. At night the damp ground sapped heat from my body. To stay warm I had to bundle up in three layers and spread out my reflective emergency blanket to help insulate myself from the ground.

It took another forty kilometres of weary hiking to bring me out of the last of the high mountains into some flatter, swampier forest. Near here the winding road led to the former site of Gagnon, a ghost town. Founded in 1957 to mine iron ore, in its heyday Gagnon had everything from a hockey arena to schools, churches, an airport, and four thousand residents. But when the mine closed in 1985, the entire town was dismantled and abandoned. Almost no trace remains—the quiet forest has reclaimed the townsite. Not a house or a building still stands, only some overgrown sidewalks endure. It was with something of an eerie feeling that I walked these cracked paths along a lonely stretch of spruce woods.

With the towns of southern Canada now far behind me, sometimes an entire day or more would pass without me uttering a word, especially since I didn't even have a canoe to talk with. But the landscape itself held such a deep fascination that my mind was always active, brooding over the things I saw: the shrieking ospreys overhead, the industrious beavers in the weedy ponds I passed, the spiders in the thickets, the various species of trees, the animal tracks I'd cross. People are naturally keen observers, but living indoors dulls our perceptions. Spend enough time outside, though, and it's like a whetstone on an old knife, sharpening our perceptions up again. It's remarkable living outdoors how quickly you become attuned to things around you: from the subtle shifts in the wind to the smells of certain trees in the breeze to the different varieties of rocks.

When I'd put the ghost town behind me, I heard a vehicle approaching from a long way off, the sound echoing eerily across the vastness. When it came into view I was surprised to see a car with Alberta licence plates. It passed me, then a hundred metres farther along it stopped, did a U-turn, and drove back. Inside were a young couple. It perhaps would've been reasonable for them to suppose they'd encountered a crazy drifter on the outskirts of a ghost town in the middle of nowhere, but instead they pulled over and asked if I needed anything. Their names were Vincent and Tinesha. It had been a while since I'd passed any creeks, so I asked if they had any water. Vincent stepped out and fetched some from a cooler in the back. After downing a few sips, I asked what they were doing so far from Alberta. Driving to Labrador to visit family, they told me. After I'd finished the water, they kindly wished me well and drove off.

Such generosity on the part of travellers and locals alike continued over the remaining distance of my solitary hike. The following day, June 22, was another cold and rainy one, but with my increasingly light pack I had no trouble covering ground. I kept track by the two-kilometre roadside markers, stopping for the night at the first creek I'd come to after passing the forty-two mark. The forest was subtly changing again; the trees were growing smaller and more thinly spread, a result of the harsher conditions and shorter growing seasons. The wildlife were changing too: for the first time I saw a caribou run out of the woods, pause and stare curiously at me, then vanish into the spruces. There were also more lakes, with beavers paddling along their surface and eagles gliding overhead.

By this point I was nearing the vast mining complex around Fire Lake and Mont Wright, some of Canada's largest iron mines. The mines are elaborate outposts, with facilities for rotating workers to live in. Some fly in or come on trains that haul the iron ore down to the St. Lawrence coast, while others commute to Fermont, a small mining town on the Labrador border.

A cold rain was coming down steadily when I saw a dump truck approaching from the direction I was heading. These dump trucks, as far as I could make out, haul gravel and sand to the mines or places along the road where it's needed.

When the truck reached me its driver stopped, leaned over from the driver's side to the passenger window, and said with a kind look, "Let me help you a little." He tossed down a brown lunch bag. I opened it and beheld its riches: a sandwich, two cookies, and an apple.

"Thank you!" I exclaimed.

The driver merely waved and drove off. I was so ravenous that I devoured it all right on the spot, feeling extraordinarily grateful for the kind-hearted driver. Nor was this all—later in the day, a second dump truck came along. Without asking any questions, the driver simply tossed from the window a second lunch bag to me. In French he wished me good luck, then he waved and was off. Inside the bag was another sandwich. Two meals in one day felt like an unheard-of extravagance, and I could barely fathom such a windfall.

That evening the weather improved, but with it came storms of blackflies and mosquitoes. Given that I'd already eaten twice that day, I decided to skip cooking a freeze-dried meal and instead dive straight into my tent to escape the bugs. The freeze-dried meal I could save for another day, which seemed prudent. Plainly it would take me longer than the two weeks I'd hoped to reach Labrador City. Although I'd been averaging forty-two kilometres a day since the halfway point, my slower progress at the start had set me back.

The morning dawned overcast, with another heavy rain setting in just as I got my tent down. The rain lasted all day, chilling and drenching me. I seldom stopped to rest, forcing myself to keep hiking to stay warm. I passed through desolate areas that had been burned out by forest fires, charred dead trees still standing as far as the eye could see. Seeing such vast swaths destroyed by fire had the upside of making me grateful for the rain. In dry weather, forest fires travel remarkably fast, and on foot, there'd be little I could do to escape one.

Around mid-morning I was climbing a long hill, my backpack drenched and heavy, when the chest strap suddenly snapped off. This vital strap helps keep the pack tight to a hiker's body, reducing back strain. Once they snap off, it's hard to improvise any decent replacement, as the way the buckle connects to the shoulder strap doesn't really permit for tying it. I fixed it up as best as I could, but it wasn't as tight as before. As a result, I had to use my hands to pull on the shoulder straps.

By the afternoon I'd reached signs for the Fire Lake mine. I could hear heavy machinery in the distance, and train tracks now crossed the road at several points. These trains are for the mines; I saw one of them, it was a long series of open cars loaded with iron ore. The ore is mined in the mountains, then transported to blast furnaces to make steel. This created a dilemma for me in terms of finding drinking water, as creeks adjacent to the road are contaminated by the mining operations. In sharp contrast to the clear streams I'd been drinking from, the ones I saw now were either a reddish colour or muddy from runoff. I hadn't used my water purifier for days, since it was so cumbersome, and had just been drinking straight from the creeks. I thought about trying it now, but its effectiveness at eliminating mining toxins was highly questionable.

Since drinking from the contaminated streams didn't seem advisable, I became parched and light-headed as I trudged wearily along the increasingly rough, pothole-filled road. But luck, it seemed, was on my side: a car appeared, stopped, and when the window came down, a young woman behind the wheel spoke to me in French. She was in the process of driving from Baie-Comeau to Fermont, the mining town. She generously offered me two bottles of water, which I used to fill up my empty one. When I thanked her, she said it was nothing and wished me well. This kindness from a total stranger did more than stave off dehydration—the positive feeling it gave me made it easier to ignore the blisters on my feet and keep going.

The rain let up in the evening, and I made camp in a sparse forest covered in lichens and mosses. Despite the wetness, dry branches underneath the spruces let me kindle a warming blaze. Parched as I was, the water I'd been given by the sympathetic driver hadn't lasted long. Now I searched in all directions for more, yet the streams were still filled with runoff from the mines. I tried shaking the spruce boughs to collect the raindrops in my cooking pot. This method was slow and yielded only a few sips, and was less appealing when spiders kept falling in. My hunger had made me desperate for one of my last remaining freeze-dried meals, but to cook it I needed a least a few litres of water. A long detour into the sodden forest finally led me to a bog that didn't seem connected to any polluted stream. On the other hand, it was stagnant and foul-smelling. I debated the prospect of using it to cook with, but at last my hunger overcame my objections. I scooped up the dark, muddy water, trekked back to where I'd set up my tent, and boiled it. It may have been my famished state, but the freeze-dried rice and vegetables tasted as delicious as any meal I could recall.

In the morning I had to put my damp clothes back on, since the rain had again soaked through my rain gear, and I didn't dare wear dry clothes hiking. These precious luxuries I sealed up in a vinyl waterproof bag so that I'd have something dry to wear at the end of the day. A few hours of hiking brought me within sight of a large grey mountain. I'd reached the outskirts of the Mont Wright mine, one of Canada's largest open pit mines. Like the one at Fire Lake, it mines iron ore. Perhaps it was just dehydration, but the grey skies and dark mountain looming on the horizon, with its slopes stripped of trees, conjured in my mind strange visions of dwarves toiling under it.

Around mid-morning a dump truck heading to the mine passed me. The friendly driver pulled over to ask in French if I needed anything. I made a gesture for water. He didn't speak English, but he held up a Coke can. I appreciated this, but declined, since I didn't want to dump Coke into my water bottle, which I couldn't clean anytime soon. The driver had nothing else, and drove off. A few hours later, I was surprised to see the same driver coming back down the road. He pulled his truck to the side, and motioned me to come over. Then he tossed down three water bottles! I was ecstatic at such kindness; he must have returned to their base of operations and rounded them up for me. The driver seemed the silent type, but his kindly look said it all.

A short time after this, two white pickup trucks came by. On the truck doors in French were the words "Innu Nation, Rights and Territories," with the logo of the local Innu band council. The Innu, also known as the Montagnais and Naskapi, historically ranged across northern Quebec and southern Labrador. The two trucks parked on the shoulder and their drivers got out, one who looked perhaps in his sixties, the other around thirty. They asked me in French if I was the hiker who'd come all the way from the south. I nodded. Now they waved excitedly to the vehicles, and out came two women, one with a baby in her arms and the other holding a large plastic bag.

They gave me the bag, and I was stunned to see it was loaded with sandwiches, cookies, cakes, oranges, apples, and juice boxes. It turned out that apparently rumours of some strange character slowly trekking north had been circulating for weeks, with sporadic reports of sightings. In an isolated place like this, news travels quickly, and the various passersby who'd stopped had relayed things. Apparently to hike the road was unheard of, especially at the height of blackfly season, and had made me something of a local curiosity. They asked what could have motivated me to undertake such an ordeal, but my limited French made explaining difficult. I said something about following falcons, which seemed to make them think I was maybe not entirely right in the head, but in a harmless sort of way.

They wanted photos with me, and I was a little surprised when they asked if I'd hold the baby for one. I obliged, though it stirred pangs of heartache for my own little one back home. On the bright side, it motivated me to get moving again, as I wanted to get home sooner to him.

A few hours later, as I was still hiking along the road, I looked up at the sound of another approaching vehicle: it was the two trucks from the Innu nation again. The same two men got out as before. It turned out that they were father and son. The elder of the two explained in French that if I wanted a break they would give me a ride to the nearby mine, where they could provide me with a room, a hot shower, food, and a place for the night. Such hospitality was heartwarming, but I shook my head. Thinking that perhaps I was concerned about interrupting my hike, the younger of the two grabbed a flag from the back of the truck and indicated that we could stick this in the shoulder of the road to mark the exact spot. They explained that, if I so wished, they could drop me off right here again, so that I could resume my hike. I thanked them, but still declined, trying to explain as well as I could that I was perfectly happy. They relented, wished me well, and said they'd check up on me again the next day to see if I needed anything.

Several more truckers encountered me, stopping their big rigs to speak with me. After so much solitude, it felt a little awkward to be the subject of such attention. But I tried my best to be sociable and explain succinctly in my limited French what I was doing. They were all very considerate, and I found their well-wishes and enthusiasm heartening. Other trucks passed with their drivers slowing down and giving me thumbs-up gestures; it seemed they must have heard about me from their colleagues. To be cheered on felt nice, and I made camp feeling the warmth of this reception alone in the forest.

But that night I ran into some trouble pitching my tent. The tent has only a single interconnected pole, with an elastic cord running through it and small metal rings that snap it altogether. This makes it fast to set up and take down. But probably from repeated use in cold weather and strong winds, one of the connecting ends came off inside the tube, making it impossible to set up properly. I tried various tools on my Swiss Army knife to retrieve the end part from the tube, but none were slender enough to fit in. When this failed, I experimented with sticks, but these proved too bendy and weak to force the broken part out. What I needed was a steel awl, but I didn't have one. I made the best of things by jerry-rigging the tent as well as I could. It was rather misshapen now, and not as roomy on the inside. If the wind rose, my confidence wasn't high that it would stay up. But it seemed well enough for one night.

In the morning, when I looked into my food bag, I found that even with the unexpected help I'd received, my rations were nearly gone: I was down to just two granola bars. It'd been a very cold night, which left me craving more food.

I ate one of the bars, then staggered on for more than forty kilometres again, feeling as thin as a rail. The cold day at least took care of the bugs, though it made me hungrier than ever. I was thirsty too: my concerns about drinking the water near the mines had apparently proven well-founded, as there were now big red signs warning not to drink from the lakes. Luckily, that afternoon a trucker rumbled down the rough road, pulled over, and handed me a large bottle of water and a bag of oatmeal cookies. Like the other truckers, he was a man of few words, but the silent nod he gave said it all. Truckers, spending a lot of time alone on the road, perhaps can relate to a solitary wanderer and maybe for that reason seemed inclined to help me.

The oatmeal cookies made for an excellent dinner in the forest, and when I brewed up some spruce tea for vitamin C, I felt quite satisfied. The next morning, June 27, with my backpack emptied of all provisions, I hiked the last thirty kilometres out of Quebec and into Labrador. It had taken me sixteen days instead of the fourteen I'd hoped for, and sixty-five days since I set off from Long Point.

A sign along the road noted the invisible boundary with a nod to Labrador's nickname: "Welcome to the Big Land." Light rain greeted me as I crossed it, but this didn't bother me; having bypassed all the hydro installations, I was excited to end this long portage, find a canoe, and paddle to the Arctic.

20

THE BIG LAND

FOUNDED IN 1960 by a mining company as a temporary encampment in the wilderness, Labrador City grew into a permanent settlement with a population today of roughly seven thousand people. Mining for iron ore remains the basis of its economy. The town sits on Little Wabush Lake, which was perfect for my purposes, as I could launch a canoe from it and paddle the remaining twelve hundred kilometres north to the Arctic—well, in theory anyway.

I followed the main road into town. My first order of business was to visit the post office, where I'd asked Alexandria beforehand to mail some paddling supplies and food rations. After that, it seemed important to find an actual canoe.

But before I could attend to these things, my ravenous appetite demanded attention. Right on the main drag was a Pizza Delight, and while normally I'd avoid these kinds of fancier places, my hunger led me into it. I ordered and devoured a whole pizza, feeling wonderfully restored afterward.

Then I headed to the post office to retrieve my things.

"Oh, you're *Adam*?" said a young employee, when I came in to claim my supplies.

"Yes," I nodded.

"We wondered who'd claim these things," she said, pointing to a pair of paddles taped together and a plastic barrel with a harness around it. The barrel was crammed with granola bars, nuts, freeze-dried meals, a life jacket, rope, duct tape, and a few other essentials.

"I'm afraid I can't lift it onto the counter. You'll have to come behind and get it."

"Sure," I said.

"What's in it, anyway?" she asked.

"Oh, mostly food and camping supplies."

"Didn't guess that."

"What did you think?"

"Rocks. We thought you might be a geologist."

"No." I shook my head.

"You're camping somewhere around here?"

"For a little bit," I said vaguely.

She looked at me as if she expected a further explanation.

"I'm canoeing to the Arctic," I added.

"You're flying to the Arctic and then canoeing there?"

"No, I'm canoeing to the Arctic from here."

She stared at me blankly for a second. "That's possible?"

"Well, there's enough lakes and creeks that if you keep going north you'll get there eventually," I said. "By the way, you wouldn't happen to know anywhere I could find a canoe, would you?"

"A canoe?"

"Yeah, I don't actually have one."

"Sorry." She shook her head. "No."

I asked if it'd be all right if I left the barrel until I could round up the things I needed, principally a canoe. The friendly clerk said that this was no problem. After thanking her, I headed off.

Outside the post office, I considered my options. Only one store in town sold canoes, the Canadian Tire. But their canoes are far too heavy and slow for expeditions, with cupholders and backrests and a design that makes them impractical for anything other than a leisurely afternoon. Absent-mindedly I cut across the parking lot, wondering where I might be able to find one. It seemed it might prove harder than I'd thought. Then I chanced to look up and saw, lying overturned in the grass beside a building, *two red canoes*. At first I thought I might be hallucinating, but when I walked up and kicked them, they felt real. To stumble upon two canoes a stone's throw from the post office seemed unfathomable, and though I'm not overly sentimental, I almost had to look skyward and wonder if someone was looking out for me.

But I was getting ahead of myself. It was one thing to find a canoe, another to acquire it. The two canoes were similar in length, around fifteen feet, the same as my own. One was fibreglass, which is fine for casual paddling, but wouldn't last long on northern rivers laced with rocks and rapids. It'd be punctured and destroyed. The other one was considerably more promising: it was an Old Town, manufactured of tough Royalex, very similar to my own canoe. It was exactly what I wanted—even the right colour. I walked farther along the building and saw that it was a Leon's furniture store. Inside I asked if anyone knew about the canoes and if they might be for sale. An employee told me they belonged to the store's owner, though he wasn't sure whether he'd be willing to sell them. I was told that if I came back later he'd be in and I could ask myself.

With time on my hands, I went to explore the nearby lakeshore to find where I could launch a canoe, once I managed to get one. It was only a five minute walk to the lake, which was thickly wooded with alders and spruces. I followed a faint trail through a thicket, then along the water to a spot that looked suitable. As I stood gazing out at the lake, a black and white bird swooped down and landed in the shallows with a raspy call. It was an arctic tern: they migrate to the Arctic in June, make their nests, then fly south in the fall. Seeing it now made the Arctic feel, for the first time, not so impossibly far—if I could just get a canoe. The area seemed deserted, so I made myself comfortable in a little nook under a big spruce tree. Later two anglers came along and started casting from shore. They saw me, and perhaps owing to my wild and unkempt appearance, seemed to think I was a hobo. Glancing at my watch, I figured I'd better get back to the Leon's before it closed.

When I returned to the store, another employee informed me I could find the owner at the back. He looked busy and perhaps not in the best mood. In response to my inquiry about the canoes, he said curtly that they weren't for sale. I said I'd pay a fair price, but he told me it made no difference. Canoes, he said, were hard to come by here, and he wasn't going to make a trip to Baie-Comeau anytime soon to get another one, which he'd have to do if he sold one of his. My heart sank; it seemed my luck had at last run out.

But I explained that I'd come a long way, and that I was determined to keep going all the way to the distant Arctic. This seemed to spark his interest. He asked to see my route on a map.

"All right," he said after he'd scrutinized the map I'd brought up on my phone. "I'll sell you the canoe."

"Thank you, thank you!"

It turned out that I'd stumbled upon another generous individual. His name was Ken, and luckily for me, once we started talking, I realized that I'd met a kindred spirit, one who enjoyed adventures as much as I did and was going to help me after all.

"Here," he said now, motioning me to follow him into a back office. "I've got some leftover energy bars and things. Take these."

"Are you sure you don't need them?"

"Not as much as you will," Ken said. "What else do you need?"

"I have to hike over to Canadian Tire and buy a belt," I explained. I'd lost so much weight on my trek north that the piece of paracord that usually kept up my khaki pants was no longer cutting it.

"I've got one you can have. Try this on." Ken tossed me a brown sport belt.

"Gee, thanks," I said, threading it through my pants. It fit perfectly.

"What else?" Now he was sorting through some desk drawers. "Bear spray? Bear bangers? Matches? Batteries? Take what you need."

"Well, one thing I could use are blister bandages," I said.

Ken had some of these and handed them over. As he was helping me with these things, he offered to deliver the canoe to the lakeshore for me, and even said he could install some foam kneepads below the seat if I wanted them—most long-distance paddlers use them, and I had them in my own canoe. But I felt like I'd already asked for too much, and said this last wasn't necessary. After all, it was only twelve hundred more kilometres to the Arctic, so what was the worst that could happen to my knees?

"What else?"

"Well, I have to find a steel awl to fix my tent."

"Oh, I might have one." Ken rifled through some drawers, but no luck.

"That's all right. I'll walk over to the store to see if I can find one."

"When do you intend to set off?"

Ideally, I wanted to leave immediately, but by the time I had everything rounded up it would be too dark. "First thing tomorrow," I said.

"In that case, come here and we'll give you breakfast first. Then we'll drop the canoe off at the lake for you."

"Thanks!" I said, feeling hugely fortunate to have not only found a canoe, but to have found someone so willing to help me.

✳

THE MORNING DAWNED with overcast skies threatening rain, but the clouds couldn't dampen my excitement. I met Ken at the store at seven; he let me in and sat me down in the back where there was a kitchen. Joining us were Ken's partner, Cindy, her father Steve, and Ken's border collie, Bella. Over bacon, eggs, and toast we discussed bears and canoe tripping.

With the warmth of their reception and their excellent breakfast filling me up, I felt prepared for anything. We loaded Ken's canoe into the store's delivery van, and he drove it the short distance down to Little Wabush Lake. Then I hauled it through the marshy reeds to the water's edge and loaded everything in while Bella, the border collie, sniffed around inspecting things. They seemed to meet with her approval.

A short distance away a float plane bobbed on the water, moored to a dock. There aren't many roads in Labrador, and most of the territory's immense 294,000 square kilometres are accessible only by air, including the entirety of its northern part, which has no roads at all. Ken and Steve told me that just a few years earlier a float plane had crashed in a remote lake. There were no survivors, and despite an extensive search, the plane's wreckage had never been found. It was a stark reminder of the vastness of the land that I was planning to cross alone.

Once I had the canoe loaded up, Steve took a photo of Ken, Bella, and me. The kindness and help I'd received from them, as well as everyone else so far on my journey, resonated a little more just now, knowing that in the lonely wilderness that lay ahead of me, assistance from others would likely be a thing of the past, and that Ken and Steve were probably the last people I'd see for a while. They wished me well.

With that, I waved farewell, stepped into the canoe, and pushed off from shore.

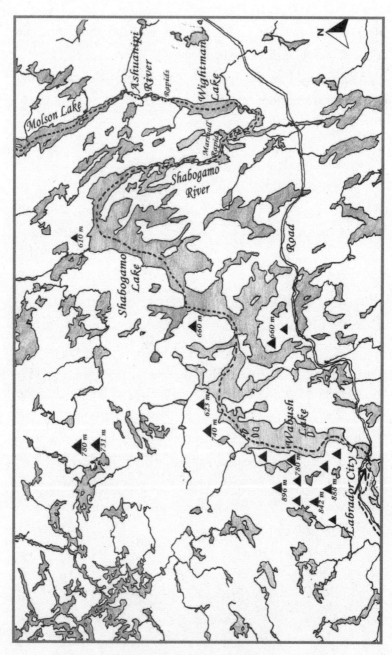

**ADAM'S ROUTE FROM LABRADOR CITY
TO MOLSON LAKE.**

21

LAKES AND RIVERS

A DRIZZLING RAIN fell as I paddled away. At the "Narrows," just on the outskirts of town, I passed under a road bridge and then a train bridge, which took me into a wilderness lake surrounded by spruce-clad hills. It was remarkably quiet, with no other boats in sight. To be back in a canoe felt glorious; certainly, my sore legs and feet appreciated the change.

As I drew strokes I got to know my new canoe: it was similar to the one I normally paddled with a few notable differences. It was half a foot longer and quite a bit heavier, weighing around ninety pounds. But by far the most important difference was its depth. This canoe had a much sleeker, shallower design than my usual one, which made it faster. I noticed almost at once how much more swiftly it moved through the water. This extra speed would be an asset, but it came with a significant trade-off: the lower sides made the canoe more vulnerable to waves. I'd have to be mindful of that when crossing the large windswept lakes that lay ahead.

But for the moment at least, there was little to fear. The winds were relatively light, without any whitecaps. The lake's zigzagging course meant my direction of travel alternated frequently, so that at times I'd be slowed down by headwinds while at other times I could enjoy the wind at my back. Once I'd put some distance between myself and the town, I was surprised to see how mountainous the terrain was, even more so than I'd realized hiking. The perspective granted from the water, far out on a lake, really allows for an appreciation of the surrounding topography.

Iron hills and dark cliffs rose precipitously above the green forests: it's this geology that's responsible for the town's existence. Beneath the hills lie some of the world's richest iron deposits. Looking back at the distant western shore, I could see signs of that mining activity. The mines on the outskirts of town cause considerable runoff into the lake, including a vast area of shore that's been transformed into a morass of mud. When I passed it I found the water to be a murky reddish colour, and I had to canoe to the lake's centre to get away from it.

By evening I'd paddled about thirty kilometres. Normally, I'd want to paddle more than that, but I'd had a bit of a late start, and more importantly I'd happened to come upon what looked like a gorgeous camping place. It was a little beach in a quiet cove with big boulders arranged almost as if by a landscape artist along the sand. The small beach backed onto a rich, verdant-looking forest of spruce and fir. In picturing Canada's wilderness, beaches probably aren't the first thing that come to mind. But over countless centuries, the powerful winds that generate whitecaps on big northern lakes have also moulded numerous alluring sandy shores, ones that can seem almost tropical (if not for the clouds of blackflies and freezing temperatures).

Although beaches are ideal for launching canoes, sand tends to get into every little crevice, making everything heavier, and at night, the sand loses heat quickly. So, I pitched my tent in the forest just above the beach. I'd found a perfect patch of level ground in the woods: a real luxury on an expedition. Most nights I had to make do with sleeping on lumpy ground or slopes. (The tent's pole I'd repaired practically as good as new using an awl I purchased in town, keeping it with me should I need it again.)

Since I'd had breakfast, I didn't bother with dinner. There was no longer any prospect of further resupplies, so the food I had in my barrel had to last however long it might take me to reach the Arctic. Much would depend on the wind. Fortunately, the last couple months seemed to have accustomed my body to living off less food.

In the morning, I continued paddling northeast through Shabogamo Lake. The scenery looked like something out of a dream: the sky was filled with puffy grey clouds interspersed with patches of sun that illuminated tabletop mountains and rugged hills. Wooded islands lay scattered through the lake, and ancient forest crowded close to the water's edge.

The lake's snaking course meant I was at turns battling stiff headwinds, and then racing with tailwinds as I'd round points and bays. Throughout the morning the wind increased steadily and the skies grew darker, with sporadic rain. The gusts were reaching fifty kilometres an hour, which is normally far too strong for a little canoe to handle. But luckily for me I'd reached a point where the lake runs almost straight north, so that the gusting wind was now in my favour.

Still, wind in my favour or not, I was slightly apprehensive about canoeing in such conditions. If a wave caught me the wrong way, I'd be swamped. But the gusts came only at intervals, and during the lulls in between I dismissed my own concerns as too cautious. It would be a shame, I told myself, to huddle on shore rather than continue on my way.

Things went smoothly until I reached a large bay. The main body of the lake curved to the east, so I'd have to cut across the bay to reach the shore I needed to follow. This meant an open-water crossing of about a kilometre—no big deal in calm conditions, but a little trickier in roaring winds. To make the crossing, I'd have to turn into the wind, letting it hit me broadside. If I didn't turn, the wind would drive me far into the bay, trapping me at its end until it slackened enough to paddle back out.

A lull made conditions seem not as bad, so with a confident stroke of my paddle I set off on the crossing. But within a short distance the wind picked up. It may have been that on account of closely hugging the shore until now, I'd underestimated how fierce the wind was far from land. The canoe rolled up and down on the incoming waves, which were hitting my starboard side. A roaring gust nearly knocked off my hat; I tossed it into the canoe to keep the wind from claiming it. The waves were pushing my canoe into the big bay, and I had to exert all my strength just to stay on course for the far shore.

I thought the howling gusts couldn't get any stronger, but around the halfway point across, the intensity suddenly ratcheted up another notch, kindling whitecaps. Huge surging waves slammed into the canoe, spilling over the side. In an instant, the situation went from challenging to terrifying. With a shudder I realized just how big the difference was between my sturdy, deep-sided canoe and this much shallower one. Abandoning any thought of making the far shore, I swung my paddle to turn the canoe toward the bay's end; this way I could at least go with the wind rather than into it sideways. As I pivoted, the canoe surged forward, the bow getting air as it crested the waves.

My whole body was buzzing with a tingling sensation. With everything I had I was navigating as best as I could to keep the canoe from swamping. Then another, still stronger gust roared, and mentally I accepted that I was going into the frigid water. There was no avoiding it now, so it was best to prepare myself for it. In a flash I visualized what it would entail and what I'd have to do to survive. Inside the canoe was my backpack and the watertight barrel. I'd have to sacrifice the backpack and let the waves claim it—but once the canoe filled and turned over, I could grab it with one hand and the floating barrel with the other. Then, kicking frantically with my feet, I'd swim for dear life toward the shore—half a kilometre away.

Odd as it may sound, once I'd accepted this was to happen, I was able to battle the monstrous waves with greater calm. I didn't allow myself to think I'd keep the canoe from swamping, but I did tell myself, "a little farther, and the swim won't be as bad." The gusts I estimated had to be fifty, perhaps sixty, kilometres an hour. I inched closer to the rocky shore, but landing would be difficult. Jagged rocks loomed out of the turbulent water, breakers smashing into them. I took a deep breath, scouted a passage, then went for it. I squeezed between the surf-pounded rocks, then landed.

After hauling the canoe up, I turned and looked back with a shudder at the wild, storm-tossed water I'd crossed. The howling winds were bringing more rain clouds in my direction and for the time being I was trapped. I raced to find somewhere to set up my tent. The shore was a scattered mess of rocks, and when I pushed into the woods, the ground rose abruptly, with nowhere to set up a tent. Camping on the exposed shore was the only option.

The tent would fly off like a kite if I wasn't careful, so I pinned it to the ground with my knees as I spread it out. It would never stay up without stakes, but the ground was too rocky to drive them into it. Instead, I lashed the tent to my overturned canoe on one side and the heavy barrel on the other. A third guy line reached a spruce sapling on the forest edge. Then, as the rain intensified, I crawled in as fast as I could.

A few pools formed around the tent's edges, but I was able to stay dry by spreading out my emergency blanket. Since I'd skipped dinner the night before, I snacked on some pumpkin seeds, almonds, and cashews, feeling a bit like a squirrel holed up in a tree. I figured I'd be stuck here until at least morning, but to my surprise the winds slackened by evening and the rain stopped. Tempting as it was to stay warm inside the tent, I forced myself to break camp and set off. The dangerous waves I'd faced had convinced me that I couldn't afford to squander any calm conditions on Labrador's notoriously windy lakes, if I wanted to reach the Arctic before winter.

I paddled for another three hours, with the wind later dying entirely. This brought out vast mosquito clouds, but on the bright side I spotted an eagle and a loon hailed me with wild laughter. For miles the lakeshore was nothing but steep banks with dense thickets of spruces and firs, or else swampy marshes offering nowhere to camp. I ended up having to pitch my tent on a steep, overgrown slope. This didn't make for a very comfortable sleep, as in my sleeping bag I kept sliding down the tent to the bottom.

When I woke in the morning, rather sore and stiff, I found myself huddled against the tent wall, having rolled back down the slope again in the night. One bad night's sleep on a gruelling journey isn't too troublesome, but back-to-back nights start to become problematic. When in the morning I crawled out of the tent into a mosquito cloud, it was with the conviction that I'd have to find a better spot for the next night.

Twenty kilometres of paddling in a cold wind brought me to Shabogamo Lake's end. It drains into a river of the same name, which I headed down. Dark spruce forests enclosed its course. An abundance of rocks in its shallow waters made navigation challenging; in a few sections I had to get out and splash ahead, pulling the canoe with a rope behind me. Other rapids I canoed through, until the river emptied into a small lake.

So far, there hadn't been anything too dangerous, but at the end of this lake lay a stretch of whitewater labelled on the map as "Marshall Rapids." Generally, if rapids are important enough to be labelled with a name, it's a good indication that they're dangerous. I unfolded my topographic map in the canoe and examined it: the contour lines indicated a ten-metre drop in elevation over a few hundred metres of river, suggestive of some serious rapids indeed. Before leaving home I'd printed satellite

images of the most important sections of the route I intended
to take. These, along with the maps, had been in the barrel
Alexandria mailed. Looking now at the satellite image, I could
see the squiggly black line of the river suddenly transform into
a white blur.

I proceeded downriver cautiously, sticking to the left bank
so that I'd have an escape route. Soon I could hear an ominous
roar; then, just a little farther, the river's dark waters appeared
to vanish over a precipitous drop, water and spray shooting up
into the air above it. I'd seen enough rapids to know that this
was probably something very hazardous, but one can never quite
tell with rapids until you get right up alongside them. So with
infinite caution I canoed along the bank until I reached a small
cove immediately above the roaring water. Here I landed, pulling
the canoe onto some rocks, then tying it to a willow. If I didn't
tie it up and the current knocked it loose, I'd be stranded.

With the canoe secure I bushwhacked ahead. The forest
was an almost impenetrable thicket, with sharp, poke-your-
eye-out branches everywhere, jagged rocks and boulders scattered about, and no trail or path of any kind. With considerable
effort I worked my way to a spot with a view of the rapids. One
look at them and I knew there'd be no chance of paddling:
it was one of the wildest, most terrifying stretches of violent
water I'd ever seen. Huge standing waves, swirling cauldrons of
eddies, and fallen logs swaying over the vortex all combined to
make it a perfect storm. The seething river squeezed narrowly
between the shore and a spruce-covered island lying midstream.
"Marshall Rapids" seemed a very unfitting name. I wasn't sure
how they acquired that label; perhaps it was the name of some

early surveyor. Personally, I would have gone with something more descriptive like "Death Rapids" or "Deadman's Rapids" or "No Hope of Surviving Rapids."

Since paddling was out of question, I'd have to go around. But carrying the ninety-pound canoe, backpack, and barrel through the impenetrable thickets—all while being eaten alive by bugs—was a daunting proposition. At least three separate trips, plus two more backtracking, would be required. It'd take at least the rest of the day to do. If only there was another way: I paused and stared at the roaring vortex carefully. Perhaps it might be possible to float the canoe down the side, controlling it with a rope while I hopped along the boulders. I'd used this method on some of my past expeditions, but it's fraught with hazards—if the canoe catches a rock or a wave, it'll tip. I stared at the swirling currents, realizing reluctantly that there were just too many waves, fallen logs, and dangerous ledges along the shore for it to work.

But I wasn't prepared to give up just yet. If I could paddle to the small island in the river's centre, I might be able to cut across it. I contemplated this for a few minutes, only to concede that this wouldn't work either. The odds were I'd be caught in the powerful current and sucked into the deathtrap downstream. This left me with only one other option to avoid a pathless, bug-infested portage—try taking the unknown channel on the far side of the island. If I paddled back upstream a safe distance, I could cut across to the opposite bank. This would let me reach the island's far shore, and there was a chance the current might not be as bad there. From where I was standing, the island's trees screened that other channel, but it seemed the majority of the river's surging water was being diverted into the near channel I was standing beside, leaving less to crash over the far one. Attempting the far channel seemed my best choice, so I climbed back through the woods to my canoe and untied it.

The swift current forced me to paddle upriver before I could cross. When I reached a point where the current seemed manageable, I struck out from shore, angling my canoe slightly upstream to compensate for the current (what canoeists call "ferrying"). When I neared the far shore, I jumped out onto the rocks. The banks unfortunately were too steep and cluttered with deadfall and willows for me to hike and guide the canoe in the water with rope (what canoeists call "lining"). Instead, my only choice was to cautiously wade in the water, edging along the shoreline, while grasping the canoe for balance (what canoeists call "insanely stupid").

I stepped out into the frigid water, shuddering with the shock of the cold. A few steps and it was up to my waist. The river bottom was a nightmare of jagged crevices, which it was easy to get my foot wedged in. I inched forward cautiously, the dark, swirling waters rising almost to my chest. Ahead was the thundering roar of the rapids. With one hand I grasped the willow bushes along the shore and with the other the canoe, holding onto it for dear life. Then I edged toward the roaring water. With any luck I might be able to squeeze through; without luck, and I might find myself trapped in some deadly current.

22

ASHUANIPI RIVER

I HAD TO edge my way forward at a snail's pace through the rushing water, trying not to slip, or bang my shins on rocks. All the while, I kept my eyes sharply focused on the river ahead, trying to read the current and see whether it was shallow enough for me to keep wading down the side. The fearsome roar of the main channel, where the water surged high and fierce, lay directly across from me. I could barely stand to look at it, knowing as I did how deadly it was. Luckily, as I'd guessed from the satellite image, most of the water was thundering down that main channel on the far side of the island, so the side I was edging along wasn't nearly as deep or dangerous. If I could just manage to get all the way down it, it'd save me a long and difficult portage.

But another step took me into a pool that proved deeper than I'd guessed, forcing me back. The shore was a barrier of deadfall and willows; my only choice was counter-intuitive: edge farther out into the stream, where I could see rocks beneath the surface, which I'd be able to stand on. I did so as carefully as I could, shuffling forward, using the canoe to steady myself. The wet rocks made it easy to slip and smash my head off a boulder, which I thought it wise to avoid. The canoe repeatedly snagged on rocks, forcing me to heave and pull to get it loose. After a lot of readjusting, hauling, and pushing, I floated my canoe through shallow rapids to a rock ledge that created a small waterfall. I hopped up to the edge of it, then tried to push the canoe down it. It scraped ominously over the jagged rocks, but I couldn't get it over the ledge.

I'd have to go ahead and heave the canoe from the front. But beneath the ledge the river was too deep for me to stand in. With my best acrobatic performance, I had to jump from the ledge onto another boulder below. From there, I was able to pull the canoe forward, trying not to tip it in the process. A few more manoeuvres and I reached the end of the channel's rapids. It had been a hard struggle, and a little stressful at times when I thought I might slip on the rocks, but I felt hugely relieved to have made it through the Marshall Rapids without a portage.

Beyond the rapids the river widened into a tranquil section dominated by a steep, dome-shaped mountain. I canoed through the shadows cast by this lofty peak toward an outlet filled with forested islands. According to the map, the Shabogamo River at this juncture joins the larger Ashuanipi River. The Ashuanipi then flows almost due north through a chain of long lakes, alternating with rapid-filled sections connecting them. My plan was to follow it. From my canoe, though, it was hard to tell where the one river ended and the other began: a maze of small islands made it all seem like one. In any case I paddled on, weaving between islands and canoeing through minor rapids. Mergansers and loons drifted among the islands, while robins and sparrows flitted among the spruces.

After a big bend, the Ashuanipi River flows into a long lake, marked on the map as Wightman Lake. I reached it by evening, and was pleased to find beautiful sandy beaches along its quiet shores. I made camp on one for the night, kindling a smoky fire to drive off the clouds of bugs that materialized soon after I landed. After my last night on the steep bank, I was looking forward to a comfortable sleep on more or less level ground. This time I set my tent right on the beach, since the woods were too thick. A little sand getting into things didn't seem a bad price for a restful night.

Sometime after I'd fallen asleep a noise outside woke me: something was creeping in the dark through the thick bushes behind my tent. I fumbled for my pocket flashlight and the reassurance of my knife, then unzipped the tent door. I shone the light at the bushes, spooking a big black bear that ran off as soon as I did. The fact it ran off easily was encouraging: that generally means it's a timid bear not looking for any trouble. I rolled over and went back to sleep.

✳

IN MY POCKET journal I noted the date: July 1. That morning back in April when I'd wheeled the canoe down the road at Long Point felt impossibly far away now, and here in this far-flung, isolated, and solitary northern forest, it seemed almost surreal to think back to the times when I'd paddled through densely populated cities.

I canoed north through Wightman Lake, admiring the forested hills and mountains surrounding it. The lake empties into a narrow channel, which is considered part of the Ashuanipi River. Whatever one considers it, I knew it had potentially dangerous rapids on it. I could see hints of them on the satellite image I'd printed: little white blurs scattered over a twisting two-kilometre section like booby traps on an obstacle course. When travelling alone in a place where there are no park rangers, no roads, no trails, no help at all—the margin for error is very small. Northern rivers like this one, with its frigid, hypothermia-inducing water temperatures, powerful currents, and legions of jagged rocks, are unforgiving.

It was with some trepidation, then, that I headed down the narrow, snaking river, keeping close to the right bank in case I should have to land quickly. The river curved ahead, making it impossible to see what lay around the bend. I could hear rapids, though, and the current was already swift. So I steered my canoe into some shallow rocks, leapt out, and hauled it up safely. There was no choice but to go ahead on foot to scout things out. Some bushwhacking led me up a moss-covered hill, then along the river, which was now partly screened by willow bushes. I had to cut back down the hill and push through the willows to get a proper view of the current. Sure enough, I could see some dangerous rapids that looked too risky to run alone with a shallow, heavily loaded canoe. But I could also see parts that didn't look as threatening, and these, I felt, I could safely handle.

A hybrid approach seemed warranted: I'd paddle cautiously down the right side, hugging the shore, and when I couldn't paddle I'd wade with the canoe along the edge. This would, hopefully, spare me a long portage through the pathless forest, which I was keen to avoid now that I no longer had a cart and instead had to carry everything individually (the cart I'd left behind with Camille back in Saint Joachim, as it'd be of no use in a trackless forest).

When it came to wading, on my past expeditions, I'd experimented with just about every type of system to stay dry and stave off hypothermia. Sometimes I'd use traditional hip waders, on other occasions I'd gone with more expensive neoprene suits with detachable water boots. Each had their pros and cons, but no matter what I went with, it seemed over the course of a very long journey they'd always get torn and punctured. So for this journey, knowing the importance of travelling light, I'd broken with my normal custom and not packed waterproof waders of any kind. Instead, I'd just found a pair of cheap water shoes of the sort people wear at the beach. The shoes had been in the barrel Alexandria mailed to Labrador City. My theory was that since any waders inevitably punctured sooner or later, I was actually no better off than if I'd merely had water shoes. I'd also figured that although the waters in the far north would be frigid, as long as I moved fast to stay warm, hypothermia wouldn't be a concern.

Well, as it happened, temperatures turned out to be consistently ten degrees below seasonal norms—making things much chillier than I'd anticipated. But sometimes you just have to make the best of things. The shoes were light, easy to slip on and off, and let me move over the rocks with greater agility than I could in heavy waders.

I canoed along the riverbank, edging slowly down as the roar of foaming waves appeared mid-stream. When it was no longer safe to paddle, I steered the canoe into some rocks and leapt onto them. Then with one hand grasping the canoe's bow, I inched out into the cold, swirling water. As far as possible I tried to walk along the rocks to spare myself the cold. But despite my best efforts I frequently had no choice but to get wet.

When I'd made it to about the halfway point, the river curved sharply again, concealing what lay beyond. I'd have to land and scout ahead again. With luck I might be able to paddle the remainder of the rapids, or failing that, at least continue wading. As I was scampering up the mossy bank into the thicket, I startled an animal. It spooked me when it uttered an odd shriek, then jumped through the trees like a giant squirrel, before vanishing. It took a second before I realized what I'd seen—a pine marten. They resemble a weasel and are about the size of a cat, living in trees and preying on squirrels. Their speediness and tree-dwelling habits mean that they're not often spotted.

When the marten had gone, I jogged ahead to see if it was safe to continue downriver. But my scouting was cut short when I came to a roaring creek rushing through a small gully. I had to find a spot where I could jump across. I found a better vantage point, and assessed the rest of the rapids in the main river. It'd be a bit dicey, but it looked like I could make it through with the same combination of cautious paddling and wading.

It proved hard work getting through the remainder of the rapids—my shins, legs, and feet took a beating among the underwater rocks. It was difficult to avoid slipping in the roaring current; by the time I reached the end I'd acquired scrapes and bruises to go with my earlier blisters. But it was a toll I was happy to pay if it spared me a whole day of portaging.

The river emptied into a small almond-shaped lake, before continuing through an outlet on its far shore. I paddled down the outlet cautiously, not knowing whether more rapids were in store. There weren't any marked on the topographic map, but these maps are often inaccurate or incomplete. A few eddies and swifts appeared where the water rushed over exposed rocks, but I snaked around these without trouble. The current was swift and I flew along in the canoe, soaking in the dramatic, ancient landscape all around me—the rugged, rocky hills old beyond memory, and the silent forest with its shadow-filled thickets.

The sky had grown dark and the winds were picking up. Here on the narrow river I wasn't as vulnerable to the wind, but ahead were long, stormy lakes I'd have to navigate. As I neared the start of these lakes the river began to gradually widen. On the eastern shore a smaller river roared in with whitecaps, and looking incongruous in a wilderness of trees and rocks, I saw that a train bridge spanned it. These tracks run hundreds of kilometres north through the wilderness to an ultra-isolated mining community, one that has no road access at all, Schefferville. It's the most isolated rail line in North America, possibly the world. The trains transport iron ore blasted at the remote mines, and the tracks lead right down to the Gulf of St. Lawrence, where the ore can be loaded onto huge freighter ships. If you look at a map of this rail line through Labrador's wilderness, you'll sometimes see towns labelled on the map that don't actually exist. Places like "Livingstone" and "Ross Bay Junction," mere phantom towns that may once have been some isolated camp or a collection of cabins, but that's it.

On the forested shore below the roaring stream stood a rotting dock jutting into the water with a small, half-sunken boat tied up to it. Intrigued, I paddled over to investigate. Through the spruces I could see a ramshackle cabin; perhaps it was the home of a hermit in need of someone to share lunch with. But when I climbed ashore, it seemed no one had been here in years. The dilapidated cabin's roof had collapsed, with rusted tools, mouldering clothes, and other debris scattered about. It looked as if bears had torn the place apart. Bears are remarkably good at sniffing out any food stored in backwoods cabins—sometimes tearing the door off to get at it. Whatever food might once have been here had long since been devoured.

Returning to the canoe, I set off in heavy rain toward Molson Lake, the first of the long lakes through which the Ashuanipi River flows. The wind was gusting so ferociously as I entered its wide expanse that it made for horizontal rain. Luckily, they were tailwinds; otherwise I'd never have been able to paddle such a big lake in gusts this powerful. As it was, the roaring wind was still something of a challenge. But I paddled hard and bailed as much water as I could. With the shallower canoe, I had to bail more often since it filled up quicker. The wild weather continued all day as I battled my way down Molson Lake's thirty-kilometre expanse. Toward its north end is a veritable labyrinth of dozens of islands, which makes it easy to get lost. Hidden somewhere in them the Ashuanipi River flows out again, and finding its outlet was my goal.

I kept to the northeast, until the roar of rapids told me I'd found the right course. The lake had narrowed back into a river, with some dangerous rapids hidden among the islands. There was one short but deadly-looking rapid with an abrupt ledge where the swirling current plunged into an eddy. I couldn't paddle through it and nor could I wade around it; I had no choice but to portage through the woods. Fortunately, it proved to be a short portage, which I managed quickly.

The wind died in the evening, giving the mosquitoes a chance to come out in droves, though the rain continued as I found myself in the midst of another island maze. Most of these islands were full of little mossy hummocks, with dismal camping prospects. I finally settled upon one with a small hill in its centre. It took a bit of effort to make a fire and boil water given the sodden forest and heavy rains, but my appetite drove me on. On the upside, the island was full of fragrant Labrador tea shrubs, so with their glossy leaves I brewed up a pot of tea.

On a long journey, I was likely to call home for the night many beautiful spots that I'd be only too happy to linger at, but by equal measure there were bound to be uncomfortable, boggy, mosquito-filled ones too, and this place was one of the latter. It may have been the dreary weather, or the clouds of mosquitoes, but the atmosphere of the island I found disagreeable. The thickets and mossy hummocks made it hard to move around, and in spite of myself, I kept having to glance over my shoulders at the bushes to make sure I was really alone. Accustomed though I was to solitude, the claustrophobic island gave me an uneasy feeling.

To put my mind at ease, I tried talking to my tent and canoe while I broke some spruce branches for the sputtering fire. But they had little to say, and the sound of my own voice in this silent wilderness seemed only to reinforce the isolation of the place. At last I gave up trying to make the wet, uneven forest feel homelike, and instead drank my tea inside the tent. A good night's rest, I told myself, would make me feel better come morning.

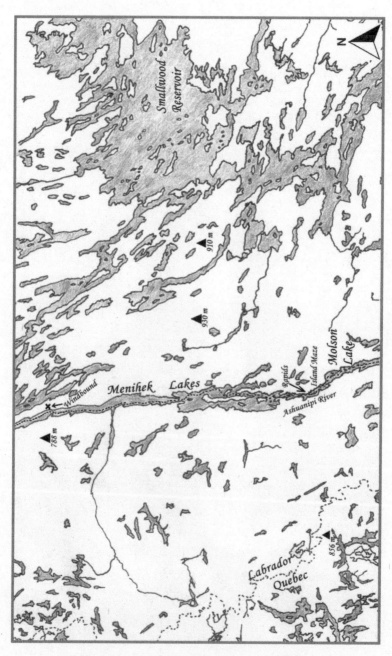

ADAM'S ROUTE FROM MOLSON LAKE
TO THE MENIHEK LAKES.

23

ISLAND MAZE

IN ALL THE thousands of miles of exploring I'd done I
couldn't recall ever encountering such a bewildering maze
of islands. What made things particularly confusing was not
only the swampy, monotonous character of the countless
islands, but the numerous dead-end bays and the lack of perceptible current to indicate the correct way to head. I weaved
between the islands, navigating the best I could, having to
frequently consult my map to make sense of things. It was
another overcast, rainy day, such that I began to think no other
weather was possible.

Hidden in the labyrinth of islands I was surprised by the
sight of something jarringly out of place: a small collection of
cabins. It looked like a fishing outfitter's camp. Remote camps
like these can be found at various backcountry lakes or rivers,
and are generally accessible only by float planes. They cater to
anglers looking for trophy fish. The camp appeared deserted,
but I landed to investigate anyway.

I soon saw that unlike at the decrepit cabin I'd come across earlier, this place had taken precautions against bears: wooden boards with numerous rows of jutting nails lay on the ground in front of all the doors and windows, making it impossible for a bear to approach without stepping on them. There was no sign of anyone having been at the camp for some time. I cautiously stepped over the booby-trapped boards to open a cabin door and let myself in. On a table were some expired painkillers and peanuts. There were magazines too, and the dates on these were likewise from several years earlier. My guess was that no one had come here since before Covid, as travel restrictions had hobbled outfitters. After eating a jar of expired nuts, I left, remembering just at the last second about the nails. In the nick of time I sidestepped to avoid them, then returned to my canoe.

Downstream the maze continued, the current alternating from barely perceptible to roaring rapids. I ran one set of rapids sandwiched between islands, zigzagging as well as I could to avoid smashing into rocks. But a second, larger set was too risky to paddle. Luckily, I was able to line and wade my canoe down the side, thereby avoiding an arduous portage. Among the forested isles bald eagles hunted for fish, while flocks of mergansers and goldeneye ducks drifted among the weedy passageways.

By midday I'd at last found my way out of the labyrinth and into a chain of vast lakes: the Menihek Lakes. Despite the plural name, it's actually one very long lake, measuring over a hundred and ten kilometres long, and averaging two to three kilometres wide. From space, it looks like a giant slash mark across Labrador's wilderness, as if someone had swung a sword at the forest. Something like this did happen, in a sense, only it wasn't a sword but rather a giant glacier that sliced out this lake ten thousand years ago. I was a little apprehensive about paddling through such a long lake, as its peculiar shape could potentially make it a nightmare if the winds went against me. If the prevailing winds should come out of the north, they'd be able to sweep down almost the whole length of the lake, blowing with great force and generating impossible headwinds. But I'd carefully studied the maps and satellite imagery before leaving home, and any other route I could devise would be similarly fraught with challenges. This one happened to be the most direct route north, and for that reason I resolved to take it. On the bright side, at least there weren't any freighters to run me over.

Almost immediately upon entering the lake a heavy rainstorm soaked me and began filling up the canoe. I kept paddling regardless, pausing only to bail water over the sides as necessary. Fortunately, the rain didn't last long, and when it passed I was astonished to see what to me had become the rarest of sights—the sun. I made the most of it by spreading my wet clothes out in the canoe, including my soaked gloves and socks, and let them dry as I kept paddling.

Along the shore were ocean-like beaches, with huge amounts of driftwood heaped up from the powerful winds. Shrieking arctic terns along these sandy shores further made me think of the seacoast. Meanwhile, beyond the western shore rose majestic mountains, ominous-looking storm clouds gathering about their grey summits. I'd decided to follow the eastern shore, though it was a gamble, as if the wind came from the west it could pin me down. If it came from the east, I'd be relatively sheltered. If the winds came from the north, which was likely, I'd be in bad shape regardless of what side I was on.

It was clear the sunshine wouldn't last: those distant storm clouds swirling above the mountains were heading in my direction. I paddled as hard as I could to cover as much distance as possible before they came any nearer. By mid-afternoon thunder was rumbling; I landed to wait for it to pass. As I hauled my canoe up the rocks and looked about, I noticed huge chunks of iron scattered along the lakeshore, ranging from fist-sized to enormous boulders four or five feet wide and almost as tall as me. They testified to the area's rich, naturally occurring iron deposits. But they made me somewhat apprehensive about the gathering storm. Sitting on an iron boulder in lightning seemed one of those things in life that is best avoided. So as the storm arrived I headed into the forest, away from the exposed rocks. Of course, sheltering under trees in a lightning storm isn't usually considered the best thing to do either. I settled for lying under a balsam fir bush, which was low to the ground but quite effective at screening me from the rain.

A half hour later the storm passed and I returned to the canoe. The skies were still clouded over and more storm clouds were already on the horizon. But the camping prospects in this iron-filled place weren't great, and I was eager to cover at least a few more miles before another storm struck. With this thought I raced on as quickly as I could, paddling northward until coming to a small bay with a pebble beach. I landed on shore just as the first bursts of thunder echoed over the lonely land. Then a lighting bolt struck the forest uncomfortably close. This storm was much nearer than the first one. I grabbed my backpack and barrel from the canoe, tossing them under a bush. My tent I didn't feel safe setting up with its metal pole at the height of a lightning storm.

Instead, I sat on the mossy ground under a low spruce to screen me from the lashing rain. There's something peculiarly forlorn, I thought to myself, about huddling in a storm in a sodden forest alone in the wilderness. But as soon as the storm passed, and I had a roaring fire to warm myself, a pot of spruce tea boiling, and my snug little tent up, I felt much better and enjoyed the majestic feel of the wild landscape.

It proved a very cold night. I had to sleep in my wool toque with my sweater's fleece hood up, and with my jacket on too, to achieve some semblance of warmth. The temperature was down to zero degrees, but the damp, mossy ground felt even colder. My hunger contributed as well—the one meal and eight granola bars, plus a few miscellaneous nuts, were barely cutting it. But for the moment, I worried less about food than the wind.

I was up before five the next morning, July 3, which at these northern latitudes was no problem as the sky lightened early. The morning was wet and windy. I shivered as I took down my wet tent and packed it up. A granola bar for breakfast and some lukewarm tea in my thermos, which I'd brewed the night before, didn't warm me up much. It was a gusty morning, with the wind coming from the west. Ahead of me was a large bay. If I kept tracing the shoreline like I'd been, I'd exhaust myself paddling all the way around it. But to cut across its mouth was distinctly risky—it was more than two and a half kilometres wide. With my previous brush with danger crossing the smaller bay earlier, I didn't like the prospect of attempting this one.

264 | **WHERE THE FALCON FLIES**

The map indicated a large island lying in the middle of the lake: I could use it as a safety net, canoeing out to it first and then zigzagging from it to the lake's far shore, bypassing the giant bay. Island-hopping like this would replace the two-and-a-half-kilometre open-water crossing with a couple of one-kilometre crossings instead (first from the shore I was on to the island, then from it to the opposite shore). I also wanted to abandon the lake's eastern shore that I'd been following up until now, and get to the western shore. The reason was the wind direction—it was now coming hard from the west. This meant whitecaps hitting the eastern shore, but at least some protection from them if I could get across to the far side. Anyway, that was the plan I worked out over breakfast. And before I could get cold feet about it, I zipped up my life jacket, stashed my thermos in my backpack, loaded everything into the canoe, then grabbed my paddle and shoved off.

The harsh wind bit into my face, but I pulled up my hood to protect myself. It was an exhausting struggle to paddle forward, with waves constantly threatening to drive me into the rocks. An hour of difficult paddling brought me to the point where I judged it best to attempt the crossing to the island. I took a deep breath, then with all my strength spun the canoe directly into the waves and began paddling as hard as possible into them. When the gusts came, progress was impossible; my furious strokes did nothing other than hold me at a standstill. But when there were lulls, I'd inch forward, panting heavily, paddling furiously. It was nerve-racking when I reached the middle, but I tried to keep my eye fixed on the distant island.

I finally reached it, exhausted from the struggle, yet I couldn't rest. The second and more dangerous crossing was still ahead of me. I didn't dare land on the island because I knew time wasn't on my side: as the morning warmed up, the waves would only grow bigger. If I stopped, the wind might trap me. So I paddled along the island's shore until I reached its tip. It was time to cross the open water again, this time for the far shore. The shape of the lake made this crossing much rougher, as the wind had a larger section of water to gather force over. The gusts were so strong that I couldn't paddle directly over the shortest course, but instead had to turn into the wind slightly and take a more roundabout crossing to manage the waves. With aching muscles, at last I made it to the opposite shore safely.

This western shore protected me from the waves, but not from the wind, which remained bitter and fierce all day. It wasn't possible to drift at all; if I did the gusts would threaten to blow me far out into the lake. I had to exert half my strokes just to counteract the effect of the gusts, the other half to inch the canoe forward. The heavily indented nature of the shoreline—it was riddled with peninsulas, islands, and rocky shoals—greatly complicated my paddling efforts. Every time I came to one of these points or obstructions, I'd have to detour around it, first turning with the wind, then engaging in an all-out, exhausting paddle against it to finish the turn around the projecting point. At least the unusually cold weather and blustery conditions meant there were no bugs.

The western shore had a rather bleak aspect; parts had been burnt over by past forest fires, while elsewhere the harsh conditions had left even non-burnt areas with not much more than thinly scattered, stunted little spruce and tamaracks. Eventually I came to another large bay, and had to cut across it to continue north. Storms clouds were now filling up the western sky, with the wind bringing them straight for my path. But I calculated that it'd be safe to cross the bay before the storm could arrive. In any case, I had to cross, since there was nowhere to stop on the marshy shore.

I was making my way across this windy water, feeling quite serene despite the wet conditions, when nearly four fifths of the way along, I chanced to casually glance over my shoulder and shuddered in horror at what I saw—*the storm clouds had rapidly gained on me, and were much closer.* Above me, ahead of me, and to either side were just the same dismal rain clouds to which I'd become so accustomed, but the ones immediately behind were menacing, dark, and stormy. If they caught me while I was still on the water, I'd be in serious trouble.

I paddled frantically on my knee with every ounce of energy I could muster, stroke after stroke, without letting up, racing for dear life to reach land before lightning struck me. I had two paddles with me, both mailed by Alexandria to Labrador. A light, racing one made of carbon fibre, and a traditional one made of wood. It was the racing one made of carbon fibre that I was using now, which let me paddle faster. But I was painfully conscious of the fact that carbon fibre is an excellent conductor of electricity, and that every time I rotated paddle sides I was literally holding a lightning rod above my head in the middle of the lake with a lightning storm bearing down on me. After debating for a moment, I tossed the paddle down and grabbed the wooden one. It was slower, and wood (especially when wet) still conducts electricity well, but it made me feel a little better. I kept paddling frantically, with the wind all of a sudden increasing dramatically, knocking my hat forward. The chin strap was luckily around my neck. I was right on the storm's edge. I wouldn't make the mainland before it caught me, but a tiny island lay ahead, so I aimed for it. With the storm so close, I didn't dare raise the paddle above my head. Instead, using J-strokes I moved the paddle forward and back without drawing it out of the water. The storm was nearly atop me, the island just a little farther . . .

24

WINDBOUND

I LANDED ON the island's beachy shore just as the storm
struck. It was terrifying: thunder boomed and the trees
swayed violently. I hauled the canoe up to the edge of a steep
cliff, then huddled beside it. I clenched the canoe tightly, fearful
that it would blow away and leave me stranded here. The heavy
rain and blowing sand made it difficult to see, but I kept my
head down and my hood up to try to protect my eyes.

The storm fortunately blew past quickly; I could see the
outline of its dark clouds in the otherwise grey sky clearly as
it moved northeast across the landscape. When it'd passed,
only a light, drizzling rain remained. Comforting as it may
have been to stay put, I immediately relaunched the canoe and
kept paddling. Everything I'd seen so far had convinced me
that the Labrador plateau was as stormy a place as any, and that
this was no time to linger, especially with my limited food
rations. I needed to press on as fast as I could, lest even worse
weather arrive.

I canoed as long as I could bear it in the cold, wet conditions, paddling for thirteen hours. But the harsh wind made my progress slow, and I only managed to cover forty-five kilometres. A drawback of this canoe, I'd noticed, was that it accumulated water faster than my other one. This was not only due to its shallower design, but the position of the seat. Inevitably, some slight amount of drippage from paddle strokes falls into any canoe. With my regular canoe, I'd switch paddle sides in one smooth motion over my head, which would generally prevent most of the drippage falling into it. But this canoe's seat was situated farther up, so that no matter what I tried more drippage would land in it. Combined with the incessant rain and waves, the result was a pool of water that would always settle right at my feet. Fortunately, I'd packed a pair of knee-high, waterproof socks. They were pretty good, except that long hours kneeling in the puddle invariably caused them to soak through, leaving my feet numb. What I needed was a sponge or towel to absorb the water beneath my seat, but I had none. Bailing the water, which I did regularly, kept it from getting too deep, but even with bailing there'd always be a small amount that was too shallow to scoop out.

I made camp late in the evening on a little patch of sand beneath some tangled forest. Luckily, there was plenty of driftwood washed up, so making a nice warming fire didn't take long. I built mine beside a boulder, to heat the rock up and reflect it back at me. My "waterproof" socks I turned inside out and stuck on willow branches, steaming them over the fire to dry them. When I was warmed up sufficiently, and had eaten my allotted freeze-dried meal (a lovely lasagna), I crawled into my tent. It was another cold night, and I had to sleep in three layers to stay warm.

✳

A FROST FORMED on the tent overnight. There was no morning sun to thaw things out, and the unfriendly skies suggested I could soon expect more rain. I had to stamp my feet to warm myself up as I took down my frost-covered tent at five a.m.

Given the chilly conditions and imminent rain, I knew I had to do something to deal with the problem of water accumulating under my canoe seat. In such cold weather I couldn't afford to let my socks soak through again. From the forest I gathered some sphagnum moss to lay down under my canoe seat. It's incredibly absorbent, and would act as a sponge. Then for a little extra protection I cut some green willow shoots and broke them in half. These I'd lay down atop the sphagnum moss. That way, when I knelt in the canoe, I'd be elevated on the willows above any remaining water.

The ferocious winds made paddling difficult, with gusts over fifty kilometres an hour. There was little to be done against such gusts, and I barely seemed to inch forward despite my rapid, frantic strokes. An island chain in the lake's centre at least enabled me to cross safely to its eastern shore, which was the side I needed to be on to reach its still-distant end. By late morning, though, the wind was so strong that paddling became impossible: I was windbound. I made the most of the break by brewing Labrador tea over a fire and cooking a freeze-dried meal of mac and cheese. I justified eating my allotted meal now since I was ravenously hungry, plus if the wind died in the evening, I'd be able to take full advantage of it since I wouldn't need to set any time aside for dinner.

Yet the wind showed little sign of slackening. After an hour on shore, feeling rather angsty to be trapped on land, I convinced myself that I'd detected a slight moderation in the gusts, and on that basis relaunched the canoe. But the relentless gusts and whitecaps made paddling almost impossible. My strokes barely drove the canoe forward, and panting with exhaustion, within an hour of setting off again, the howling wind completely defeated my best efforts. I had to concede I was expending calories I could ill-afford on an exhausting struggle with precious little to show for it. Since setting off that morning I'd made it only thirteen kilometres.

If I was to be windbound, I'd hoped to find a nice place, but the roaring gusts pinned me on an inhospitable, rock-bound coast. To make camp I had to portage my gear up a steep embankment into thick, sodden woods. Just as I was hauling the canoe up the bank, I heard a crack: the canoe's wooden yoke had broken loose. The yoke helps give the canoe stability, but more importantly makes it possible to balance it overhead when portaging. On the other hand, with no trails to speak of and dense thickets nearly everywhere, most of the time carrying the canoe overhead wasn't an option anyway. I'd just have to drag it from now on.

When I pushed into the woods, I saw there was no level ground, and the firs and spruces were huddled so close together that I could barely erect my tent. But once I crawled inside and arranged my emergency blanket, rolled up my extra clothing for a pillow, and spread out my sleeping bag, it felt as comfortable as anything. I spent the rest of the day napping and taking notes in my journal, since the wind gusts never relented. In the evening, they were still no better, and waves continued to pound the shore.

All through the night, in fact, every time I chanced to roll over on a tree root and wake up, it was to the sound of the wind roaring. I put my hopes on a morning calm, but none came. If anything, the ceaseless roaring only grew louder and fiercer. I was trapped: windbound for a second day. Since I couldn't go anywhere, I slept in, stirring myself at noon to leave the shelter of the tent and make a fire. I purified several pots of water and tried to dry some of my wet clothes, despite the rain.

With the wind as bad as it was, it would likely take longer than I'd anticipated to reach the Arctic. So I figured that for now I'd forgo cooking any of my meals, and just rely on my snack food. But when I unscrewed the barrel lid to examine things, I was alarmed by how empty it looked. I dumped everything out to take a tally. It was as I'd feared: my rations were less than what they should have been. There was barely enough for seven granola bars a day, a few Ziploc bags of nuts and seeds, one bag of jerky and dried fruit, and just fifteen freeze-dried meals. I must have somehow miscounted these back in April when I'd sealed them away to be shipped out. All told, it seemed certain that I'd run out of food before my journey was over. This meant I had no choice but to cut back on my already meagre rations. If I could have, I would have fished, but it was too windy even for that.

To my astonishment the wind was still gusting on my second night at the spot. I fell asleep with the same hope as before:

that the dawn would bring calm conditions. Around three a.m., things suddenly became quiet, and I knew the wind had slackened. Not wanting to be stuck here for a third day, I raced to take down my tent and portage everything back to the water's edge. Although it wasn't dead calm the winds were lighter than they'd been for days, and I was determined to make the most of it.

I launched the canoe and began paddling. There were still headwinds, but they weren't enough to stop me. It turned into another grey day, cold and overcast, with fantastically shaped clouds above and snow-capped mountains looming along the opposite shore. Thoughts of food constantly drifted across my mind, as I had to limit even my granola bars despite craving more to eat.

Three hours of hard paddling brought me to the tip of a long peninsula, which I rounded into a big bay. I'd nearly finished my journey up the lake. Somewhere on its far shore, hidden from view by islands, lay a small hydro dam, at least small relative to the gigantic ones I'd passed earlier. This ultra-isolated dam isn't connected to the main North American electricity grid; rather, it was built in the 1950s by the Iron Ore Company of Canada to provide power for their mine and the company town they'd created, Schefferville. The fly-in community of Schefferville wasn't on my route, as it's another forty kilometres north of the dam. Whether I'd encounter anyone at the dam or not I wasn't sure; I didn't know if it was staffed by workers or merely automated.

I'd have to portage around the dam. But fortunately, the distance was short, and I suspected, in this highly remote place, there wouldn't be any pesky fencing or other safety features to interfere with my portaging plans. Still, as a rule it's prudent not to just blindly canoe straight up to a hydroelectric dam in the middle of nowhere. So I approached in a roundabout way. If there was a strong current above it, I figured I could back out before it was too late.

To reach the dam, I first had to round a swampy island. As I was doing so, a caribou emerged from the woods and began swimming across the lake. Caribou are excellent swimmers, and this one didn't seem at all fazed by the thought of a long water crossing. Its path intersected mine, and as we passed each other I wished it good morning, and it grunted something in reply. It seemed curious but wary, and veered away as I paddled by.

When I'd finished my transect of the bay, in the distance I could make out the hydro dam. It looked jarringly out of place, like something in a science fiction movie. Amid a thin line of spruces sat a low grey structure with radio antennas, towers, and supporting structures around it. I slowed and approached cautiously along the shore, the drone of falling water and machinery becoming audible as I neared.

Not knowing how dangerous the current was from the hydro intake, as I came abreast of the dam, I swung away from it, paddling farther out. Even keeping my distance, it was nerve-racking to paddle in front of it, since I had no way of knowing whether it might suddenly suck more water in or otherwise do something unexpected. On its far side there seemed to be a floodgate where water was siphoning off. An earth dike had been built up along the lake's swampy eastern shore, and this difference in elevation meant the water thundered out down below.

Beside the dam I saw a small boat launch and landed at it. It seemed no one was around. Standing up after having been cramped in the canoe for the past six hours, my feet were numb from wetness and my legs felt wobbly. I hadn't realized how cold it was until now. The sphagnum moss and willow branches had worked tolerably well at first in keeping my feet out of water, but over such a long stretch my waterproof socks had soaked through once again.

I hiked up the dike to get a lay of the land. Train tracks ran right over the dam; they were the same ones I'd seen earlier, the ones that run all the way to the mines at Schefferville. There were some buildings a few hundred metres away, and a gravel clearing below in the forest. On the lower side of the dam were furious whitewater rapids, but luckily it didn't look as though I'd have to portage very far to be on my way again.

Just as I began doing so, a white truck rumbled up a gravel laneway toward me. The driver put down the window; inside were four workers in hardhats and orange vests. They were the first people I'd seen since leaving Labrador City.

"Hello," they said.

"Hello," I said casually, as if this was a totally ordinary occurrence.

"What are you doing out here?" asked the driver.

"Paddling to the George River," I said.

"That's a long way from here."

"Not as long as where I've come from."

"Where did you come from?"

"Lake Erie."

"What?"

"I've been travelling for two and a half months. I left Lake Erie in April, and I've paddled and hiked 2,400 kilometres to get here."

"My god. Do you need anything?"

"I'm pretty well equipped," I said, but as I did so I thought of my numb, wet feet, and how the weather had been much colder than anticipated. If it was still this cold when I reached the Arctic, my toes would probably fall off.

"Well, actually, if you happen to have any rubber boots you don't need, I could use them."

"What size?"

"Eleven or twelve would do."

I'd left my insulated paddling boots back at Camille's farm, and since then I'd had only my hiking boots, as well as the wading shoes mailed to Labrador. But neither of these were keeping my feet warm.

"I'll see what we can find," replied the driver. "We'll also help you get that canoe around the dam."

One of the workers got out of the truck; the rest drove off toward the buildings. The one who stayed behind was named Paul. He was from Newfoundland, he told me, as were most of the workers. Paul and I chatted while we waited for the others. He explained that the camp at the dam operated from May to November, but not in the depths of winter. The workers came in and out by helicopter, or sometimes by rail. He also mentioned that one of his ambitions was to hike across Newfoundland with his son; I readily agreed that this was an excellent idea.

When Paul saw that I was planning to haul my canoe across the gravel to the far side of the dam (which was the only option now that the yoke had broke), he told me to wait where I was and that he'd go fetch his truck to ferry it over for me. I said this wasn't necessary, but in his kindness, he insisted that it was no problem.

I stood waiting alone for some time by the dam, wondering what could be taking Paul so long. I started to think he'd forgotten about me. Just as I was beginning to haul the canoe down the gravel lane, Paul re-emerged in a pickup truck. He stepped out to give me a hand with the canoe, and held a large plastic bag out to me.

"What's that?" I asked, as he handed me the bag.

"Food," said Paul.

I looked in it and saw that it was loaded with sandwiches, cookies, crackers, chocolate, canned meat, and other delicacies! That's what had taken him so long: he'd gone back to their base and rounded up all this food. I was desperately hungry, but I didn't want to be a nuisance so I hadn't asked for any food, plus I thought I'd already asked for too much with the boots. But Paul had probably guessed by looking at me how hungry I was. I could have almost cried at the sight of food, but as it was, I merely laughed with joy.

"Thank you!" I said. "This means a lot."

"There's enough there to last several days, if you use it sparingly," Paul said kindly.

Then we lifted the canoe into the back of his truck. Since it was only a short distance we didn't bother strapping it down, and I just walked behind holding the end to make sure it didn't fall out as Paul drove at a walking pace. When we reached the clearing in the centre, the others came by, along with several more workers I hadn't met yet. One of them, a generous indi-vidual named Blair, was carrying a pair of rubber boots for me. They were brand new, and still had a price tag on.

"These were the best we could find," said Blair, handing the boots to me.

"Gee, thank you," I said.

"I hope size twelve is fine."

"No problem."

"They're steel-toed and steel-plated," added Blair.

This made them rather heavy, but on the bright side, nail bear traps outside cabins would no longer pose any danger. After I accepted this gift, the workers asked to pose for a photo with me. We took a group shot, and I thanked them all, but Blair and Paul especially, for their kind assistance. Truly, it felt like my birthday receiving such gifts as food and boots, and if I'd known I could expect such generosity, I would have made a point of visiting hydro dams sooner in my life.

Then Paul and I continued to where I could launch the canoe. While I was packing everything into it, he asked if there was anything else they could do for me. I said I could barely thank them enough for what they'd already done. I couldn't find the right words to convey just how much the food and boots meant to me—half-famished as I was, chilled and shivering from wetness and cold, they were gifts that only someone in a similar state could appreciate. I remarked to Paul how every-one I'd met on my journey so far, from the biggest cities to the smallest towns, from Lake Erie to the middle of nowhere, had shown me such utter kindness and eagerness to help.

"You know why that is?" asked Paul.

"No," I said. In truth I'd never really thought about it, other than to think people in general are naturally good, warm-hearted, caring sorts.

"It's because you're doing what we all dream of," he explained.

I'd never thought of it in that light. Whether this was actually the case or not, I didn't know. But regardless, I did know how grateful I was for the help I'd received. More than alleviating hunger or discomfort, the morale boost whenever someone did a kind thing or wished me well was worth more than anything.

Before pushing off from shore, I asked Paul if he knew the forecast. He told me more stormy weather was expected, and added, with a nod to the bag of food he'd given me, that there were many bears in the area.

"Thank you!" I said again.

Paul waved from shore. "Good luck!"

**ADAM'S ROUTE FROM THE MENIHEK LAKES
TO THE RIVIÈRE DE PAS.**

25

NORTH BY NORTHEAST

RAPIDS ROARED DOWNSTREAM of the dam. I hovered in my canoe just before the turbulence, taking a moment to scout out the route that looked best: left, then right, then right again, then straight through the middle.

My course set, I paddled into the waves, carefully weaving between the rocks. The channel was wide enough that I could zigzag between the boulders pretty easily; at the bottom the rapids spit me out into a wide pool. Ahead were forested islands and numerous bays, part of a long chain of vast, interconnected, oddly shaped lakes that together represented the most challenging navigational part of my entire route.

I had to find a way northeast to the Torngat Mountains, where the falcons nest. I'd tried to devise the shortest and most efficient route possible, which meant cutting diagonally across Labrador's interior through lakes and rivers until I could get over the watershed divide. But studying the maps, I'd always half dreaded reaching this point: even with a bird's eye view on a map, it was a confused mess of geography, a byzantine riddle of strangely-shaped lakes that together looked like a two-sided comb with long, finger-like bays. Or perhaps more like claw marks from a giant bear. If I were to get lost anywhere on my journey, it'd be in this immense puzzle. What made these lakes particularly problematic was the sheer length of their dead-end bays, some of which went on for more than thirty kilometres. If I failed to find the right outlet it could take days of back-tracking to correct the mistake.

Already I could see that I'd have my work cut out for me. Below the rapids lay the first of many lakes, called Marble Lake. My GPS showed an outlet toward the north end, but when I traced out the shore, no outlet was to be found. Bewildered, I did it a second time, which was exhausting, and yet still no outlet. Finally, checking my GPS, compass, and map, I came to an unsettling conclusion: *the maps and the GPS were wrong.* The GPS showed water where there was only solid land.

I'd seen this sort of thing before, though one could be forgiven for thinking that in the twenty-first century such cartographic blanks might be a thing of the past. They aren't. Sometimes when map errors occur it's a result of fluctuating water levels, but in this case the record-breaking rain had risen water levels to the highest they could be, so that couldn't explain it. Instead, it might well have been a matter of beavers gradually transforming the shape of the lake. Their engineering works can be quite extensive, and over the years enough mud, rocks, logs, and other debris can build up on their dams to the point where they become solid land, with trees taking root. That seemed to be what had happened here.

I portaged across a narrow bit of land not on the map, which took me to a small lake on the other side. From here, it took educated guesswork to figure out the route I should take, as the GPS was again of little help. It showed this lake as being connected to a larger one, which it wasn't. Instead, a second portage, hauling the canoe across a marsh, took me into another lake. From here a tiny, meandering creek, in places no more than a few feet wide and intersected by several beaver dams, flowed out. I squeezed my canoe through the creek until it led to what was labelled on the map as Astray Lake. It was a maze of islands and bays, surrounded by majestic green hills that made me think of the Scottish Highlands. This weirdly shaped lake eventually connected to another one, Dyke Lake, which I reached late in the evening. The shore was very swampy and thickly wooded, without a single place I could set up my tent. This forced me to paddle well after dusk, searching for anywhere to camp. Several times I landed on shore to investigate possible sites, without any luck.

At last, weary and exhausted, having paddled for fifteen hours, I settled for a giant slab of rock. There wasn't any dead wood at hand, and the mosquitoes and blackflies were as thick as storm clouds, but with the food Paul had given me I didn't need to cook anything. Instead, I ate the sandwiches, saving my freeze-dried meal for another day. Then I dove into my tent to escape the bugs.

※

JULY 7 WAS another frost-covered morning. Such cold weather was unusual for this time of year, even at these latitudes. I didn't mind the cold though, since it dispelled the bugs and let me breathe freely without swallowing mosquitoes. In the frosty morning I continued to navigate the large, island-studded lakes, cutting down on big open water-crossings by aiming for islands to break up the expanse.

When I reached a wide channel connecting some of the bays, to my surprise I discovered that the current was now flowing against me. This was bound to happen sooner or later, as all this water drains out to the Atlantic coast, but in these labyrinthine lakes it was hard to keep track of exactly what watershed I was in. I'd passed from Petitsikapau Lake into Freeman Lake, and now found myself confronted by shallow rapids that I had to pole my way up, standing upright in the canoe and jabbing off the river bottom with my wood paddle. A second set proved too strong for that method, and I could only get up them by wading along the edge. Not long after this roared a still more powerful section of whitewater connecting two lakes. There was no way to canoe or wade up it.

So I landed below the roaring water to begin what I suspected would be a gruelling portage. The weather had warmed enough to bring out blackflies and mosquitoes, which attacked me as soon as I landed. I strapped on my backpack and pulled the mesh bug net over my head, then set off into the shadowy forest. The uneven ground and thickets made hiking difficult; in places I had to crawl forward under fallen trees, and in other places, over them. This made for slow going, so after half a kilometre I set down my pack and examined the nearby river. It seemed I'd bypassed the worst of the rapids, and could, if I stripped down to my boxers, wade with the canoe the rest of the way. Even with the frigid water and the possibility of slipping and smashing my head off a boulder, this seemed more appealing than portaging.

I returned to fetch my next load, the plastic barrel, only to halt midway at the sight of something: *bear droppings*. They looked fresh. I poked at them with a stick: still gooey. I cast a suspicious glance at the bushes around me: a bear was somewhere nearby. It may have followed me on the first trip with the backpack, or it may have picked up the scent of my food, especially the sandwiches given to me by Paul, which I'd left back at the canoe. I was unarmed aside from my trusty pocket knife. Accustomed as I was to wandering alone in bear territory, I seldom gave bears a second thought. The bear spray was stored in a mesh pocket of my backpack at the far end of the portage.

I found myself a sturdy stick and rock, then, making some noise to hopefully frighten off any bear in the area, at a double pace I hurried back through the forest to where I'd left my canoe. Bears are remarkably smart and stealthy, and although my stick and rock made me feel better, probably the bear would try to take me from behind; springing out of a thicket at my back. My food rations I expected were already ripped to shreds.

But I found the canoe and food untouched. I cast more suspicious glances around: perhaps this bear didn't care for Cocoa Puffs, cookies, and sandwiches?

Shouldering the barrel, I set off again. The alder thickets along the river made me uncomfortable: it would be easy for something to lurk within them unseen; plus, the roar of the rapids would make it impossible to hear anything approach. I pushed on quickly until the sight of a track in the moss brought me to a stop: it was a bear track all right. Tracks don't imprint long in moss, so this was obviously fresh. I hurried ahead to the spruce thicket where I'd left my backpack. Reaching it, I set down the barrel and grabbed the bear spray. I clipped it to my belt. Reassured, I returned for my last load: the canoe.

Dragging the ninety-pound canoe through tightly packed rows of spruces, deadfall, and alders proved difficult. The canoe constantly got stuck between trees. Huffing and puffing, I'd have to climb over deadfall to get to its stern, then flip it on its side or otherwise readjust it, to try to jam it through. Pulling, pushing, and bending spruces out of the way, I struggled to make headway. And with my hands full with the canoe I couldn't swat away the blackflies, which swarmed around me. If a bear was watching, it'd be the perfect time to catch me off guard.

Finally, I managed to get the canoe over to where I'd left the other loads. The thickets crowding the banks made relaunching into the river challenging, and I had to batter a passage through to the water. The current was rip-roaring, but I tossed my pants into the canoe, switched into my wading shoes, and plunged in. A half kilometre of difficult wading in frigid, rushing waters brought me to the next lake.

Not until I was back in the canoe paddling far from land could I forget about the bear. I'd reached what's called the Iron Arm, a massive bay of the vast Attikamagen Lake. The Iron Arm is just one of its many large bays, in this case almost forty kilometres long. Dramatic mountains rose on either side of the long, narrow Arm, with dark forests below them. As I worked my way down its length, the calm conditions ended and a strong wind picked up. The icy wind slowed me down, while the skies clouded over ominously. I'd thought I might make it a whole day without rain, but this proved wishful thinking.

I camped in thick woods on shore. Before I could start a fire a downpour drenched everything. Cooking was out of question, so instead I just ate more of the food Paul had given me. But this created a dilemma about what to do with the wrappers and the rest of the food. Normally I'd burn the wrappers to destroy any scent, so no bear could smell them in the night. But the heavy rain ruled that out. The bag and everything in it that Paul had given me was soaked, and I was reluctant to put it inside my plastic barrel. The barrel partially dimmed the scent of food, but I also used it to store things that needed to stay dry like camera batteries, first-aid kit, and warm gloves. So I didn't want to get the barrel all wet. When I was hiking without a barrel, I'd just leave my food in a waterproof bag outside my tent at night. But given the fact that there were clearly many bears in the area, this wasn't an appealing option. None of the surrounding trees were suitable for tying the food off the ground—a bear would be able to climb and get it down easier than I could. I at last resolved the dilemma by deciding I could store the garbage and still-packaged food underwater for the night. This would elimi-nate any scent. I waded into the lake and then used some rocks to secure the bag on the bottom. When I was sure it couldn't float loose, I took cover in my tent.

*

IT WAS ANOTHER cold, rainy morning. At this point, I was at a loss to account for such record-breaking amounts of precipitation.

It had rained for weeks with scant interruption, and all spring and summer had been unusually wet. On the upside, I didn't have to worry about sunburn. I packed up my camp in the rain, trying my hardest to roll up the tent while somehow keeping the inside semi-dry. Then I flipped the canoe back over, pushed it to the water's edge, loaded everything into it, and waded out to recover my bag of food and garbage. The rocks had held it securely, and luckily, no bears had sniffed it out in the night.

Temperatures were again in the single digits, and I could see my breath as I paddled down the remainder of the Iron Arm. When I'd nearly reached the end of it, I saw a couple dozen small cabins on the opposite shore. From the distance I was at, they looked deserted, perhaps on account of the bad weather. Now I turned northwest, into the main body of Attikamagen Lake. Just as I entered its wide expanse the rain turned heavy and the wind picked up. I shivered in the cold and kept paddling. What made navigating these large lakes challenging was their huge bays, which on a map look like a giant paint splatter. If I played things safe and stuck close to shore (never a bad idea when travelling alone in the wilderness), the total distance I'd have to cover would increase severalfold. In contrast, if I rolled the dice and left the safety of the land, cutting straight across open water and avoiding the long bays entirely, it'd shave a huge distance off my total route.

I chose to roll the dice. The wet conditions, and vast distances still ahead of me, made this option too difficult to resist. Still, I tried to minimize the danger by angling my canoe toward islands, if there happened to be any, or by turning into the bays slightly with the wind, in case I should capsize. The first sizable crossing was almost two kilometres from point to point, which, in the driving rain and wind, was not a pleasant experience. I'd paddle as hard as I could to get through the open water quickly, then rest and catch my breath when I was closer to land. After a few minutes I'd have to summon up my courage and energy for another crossing, and repeat the process until I'd reached the end of Attikamagen Lake.

The heavy rain left me drenched. My system of sphagnum moss and willow shoots wasn't able to cope with so much rain. And even though I had rubber boots and waterproof socks, on the big open water crossings the runoff in the canoe would slosh down the boots as I knelt. I bailed water frequently, but it came down steadily all day. My feet were numb, and I had to stamp them in the canoe to try to get some feeling back.

Fortunately for my wet feet, by the afternoon I'd reached Attikamagen Lake's end and began the process of bushwhacking, portaging, and poling my canoe up creeks and through small lakes to get over the watershed divide. The first creek I came to was short, and I managed to pole up it with my wood paddle, using it to push off the shallow bottom while I stood up in the canoe. This brought me into a small lake, labelled as Mole Lake on the map, which was only a couple of kilometres wide. To get out of it, I found a second creek, this one choked with beaver dams and willows, that I had to paddle, pole, wade, and haul my canoe up while being attacked by blackflies. It brought me into a lake that didn't even have a name on the map. This nameless lake I paddled through too, finding another beaver creek at its tip. This one took still more effort to fight my way up, standing in the cold water and heaving my canoe up and over beaver dams, then squeezing through narrow, snaking passages. Eventually, the alders and willows smothered the creek entirely and I was left hauling the canoe over fallen logs and across mossy hummocks until I emerged into a more sizable lake. This one did have a name, Fox Lake; I paddled diagonally across it in the rain.

From here the next creek was totally impassable; there wasn't enough water to float a boat, and the alder thickets were too dense to squeeze through. Luckily, this didn't matter as the distance was short, and I could just as easily portage my three loads through the sparse forest to yet another lake. Outside the alder swamps the trees were thinly scattered, and the ground so utterly smothered in white caribou lichens that it looked like snow. These hardy lichens flourish across Canada's north, making up the primary diet of grazing caribou. I tried eating them too. They don't taste that great and have little nutritional value (to a human), but when you're hungry, they're more or less edible if you boil them.

The short portage brought me to another unnamed lake on the map. To have gotten this far was, literally, a watershed moment: once I portaged out of this lake, I'd no longer be in the Atlantic watershed. Beyond it, all the lakes, creeks, and rivers flow north into Ungava Bay and the Arctic Ocean. You wouldn't know it to look at it, though, as these inconspicuous little swampy lakes are all ringed by tamaracks and black spruce, and in these remote regions there are no signs to mark or announce anything. Personally, I prefer it that way.

To cross the divide would involve a half-kilometre portage, as usual in three trips, one for each load, plus two backtracking trips to get the next load—so five trips total. In other words, to advance half a kilometre on the map would require two and a half kilometres of portaging. I began with my easiest load, the backpack, setting off through the sodden spruces and over some rocky terrain. The rocks made twisting an ankle easy, so I had to pick my way carefully. The second load was the barrel, and then the last and hardest, the canoe. I dragged it behind me through the forest, up and over little hummocks, across marshy alder swamps, and over the rocks to complete the portage.

In the process, I'd crossed not just the watershed divide separating two vast drainage basins; I'd also left Labrador behind and passed over the invisible boundary back into the vastness of northern Quebec. The imaginary line separating the two provinces isn't marked, but it's based on the watershed divide. The Atlantic side is Labrador, the Arctic side Quebec.

Quebec's immense far north region, which I'd now reached, is known as Nunavik. The name means "great land" or "big land" in Inuktitut, the Inuit language, and it's an apt one. Nunavik covers almost half a million square kilometres, and it was this great land that now lay before me.

26

SUBARCTIC

THESE ISOLATED LAKES, seldom seen by humans, were
a bird paradise. Horned larks and pine grosbeaks sang in
the spruces; young eagles hunted fish; and loons, mergansers,
and goldeneyes drifted on the water. In the misty grey clouds
I spotted what at first glance looked like a soaring peregrine
falcon, but a second look convinced me it was a northern gos-
hawk. Goshawks are impressive hunters; they prey on other
birds, and have been known to attack humans who get too close.
Other wildlife were around too: beavers swam in the lakes, and
in the silent forests unseen were phantom-like lynx and wolves.
The wolves hunt caribou and moose, while the lynx prefer snowshoe hares. While portaging, I spotted a few of these hares. Their
coats are brown in summer to blend into the forest but turn
white come winter.

The first lake I reached across the watershed divide was
labelled on my map as Lac Snowshoe, and it quickly led me
into a second, interconnected lake. I paddled across it in the

rain before finding a small creek draining out of it. I headed down this creek without giving it much thought, like I had with the others. But the current was quite swift, and to my surprise, it soon increased even more, then large rapids roared ahead. Given the swampy conditions I wasn't expecting such a swift drop in elevation or such challenging rapids, but I was trapped in the current now and had no choice but to run them. Probably the heavy rain had transformed the creek by raising water levels.

I dropped to my knees, angling my paddle to slow the canoe's pace, and taking a second to read the jagged rocks that loomed ahead. There was one smack in the middle of the creek sticking up like an iceberg. Smashing into it would do considerable damage. One major concern when paddling rock-infested rapids is avoiding "pinning" a canoe. This happens when a canoe strikes a rock and the force of the current spins it sideways, causing it to tip, flood with water, and then "pin" against the protruding rock. The rushing water's force can be so strong as to fold the canoe in half (and crush a human body if it gets between the canoe and rock). Canoes can get bent around like horseshoes; some popular whitewater rivers have veritable graveyards of pinned canoes. With a group of people it's sometimes possible to dislodge or winch a pinned canoe free. Alone, I'd be in serious trouble if my canoe pinned on a rock.

With that in mind, I zoomed down through the rapids, feeling a bit like a ball in a pinball machine, snaking left then right, avoiding the obstacles. The speed of the current shot me through quickly; I had little time to react. My canoe came within inches of several sharp rocks, but in the nick of time I managed to avoid them. Then in a blur, the roaring current spat me into the next lake.

It was nearly dark, and a light rain was falling, so I made camp not far from the rapids. I found a perfect little spot with level ground to sleep on. The triumph of running the rapids, crossing the watershed divide, and best of all finding a flat spot to sleep on made me particularly cheerful. I celebrated with a cup of spruce tea, a freeze-dried meal, and a nice blazing fire before turning in for the night.

＊

OVER THE FOLLOWING two days I continued to work my way through a chain of lakes connected by a swift-flowing river known as the Rivière De Pas, which is full of dangerous rapids. I was now in the subarctic taiga, the spruce and tamarack forests that lie just south of the Arctic. The trees were generally smaller and more thinly spread, with the notable exception of bushy willows and alders, which in wet places form suffocating thickets. Pines, firs, and cedars had all disappeared entirely, as they can't survive in these harsher, more northern conditions.

The rain and misty skies made these lonely lakes feel particularly wild and forlorn. Small mountains loomed around them, their higher slopes almost barren, with just a few stunted spruces clinging to the rocks and occasional patches of snow. Below the mountains and along the lakeshores were extensive alder swamps. Passing through these vast solitudes made a strange contrast with the crowded cities near the start of my journey, and when I camped in quiet woods or along deserted lakeshores, I'd reflect on how different it felt from when I'd slept, say, under the Burlington Skyway. It seemed doubtful that anyone would bring me Tim Hortons now.

After a few days I didn't see much wildlife, which gave the area an even more deserted, lonely feel, accentuated by dismal grey skies and sporadic rain. On some of the larger lakes I had to once more battle fierce winds and large waves, to the point where I'd nearly give up and stop early for the day. What saved me from this was the twisting, meandering course of the lakes. The wind was coming out of the north, so sometimes, depending on a lake's shape, I'd get some relief if its shore turned in a different direction. More challenging were the narrow connecting channels between the lakes, which were increasingly laced with rapids. Some of these I paddled, trying my utmost not to swamp in waves or smash into rocks. Others were too risky to canoe, but in my boxers and wading shoes I managed to wade along their rocky shorelines. The frigid water chilled me though, and by the end of the day my feet and shins would be battered from repeatedly banging into underwater rocks.

A couple of rapids were too dangerous for this method, and I had no choice but to haul my three loads through swampy forests to bypass them. The first of these was easy enough, but the second was longer and more difficult. Blackflies and mosquitoes dined on me without mercy, and I tripped several times when hauling the canoe over fallen trees. On the bright side, once when I fell I landed right in a patch of lingonberries. They're one of my favourite berries, and although they don't ripen until August, the little burgundy-coloured berries often overwinter on the plants. This improves their cranberry taste, and I happily feasted on the ones I'd landed on.

Finding decent places to camp proved more of a challenge. The shore alternated from steep slopes to swampy marshes, and I generally had to settle for one or the other. At one little lake, after days of nothing but trees, mountains, and water, I was surprised to see some derelict cabins. It was an abandoned fish or hunt camp, which would have been accessible only by float plane. But it looked like it hadn't been used in decades. The cabins were decaying and falling apart, the encircling forest swallowing up the site.

The weather remained cold and very rainy, so that some days, with nothing but willow bushes on shore, I had to forgo the comfort of a fire. I'd eaten up the last of the food Paul had given me, and was down to just my dwindling rations. I was always hungry, even after devouring a full freeze-dried meal.

By July 10 I'd reached the last of the chain of lakes, after which the Rivière De Pas comes into its own, running wild in a snaking course northeast. Its narrow path is a mix of whitewater rapids and more tranquil stretches. In one of the latter, on a swampy island, I came upon a moose munching on some willows. After so much solitude, to have any company felt nice. But my attempts at conversation ended in failure, as the moose merely stared at me, then vanished into the woods.

The rapids, meanwhile, were getting more serious and more frequent. Some were so long that they stretched over two kilometres, which made properly scouting them out beforehand impracticable, particularly since the shores were often impassable boulder fields or impenetrable alder thickets. This forced me to err on the side of caution (well, relative caution) and forgo attempting to paddle many of them. From what I saw, they were far too dangerous to paddle anyway. Instead, I hopped along the rocks, guiding my canoe wherever possible with a rope in the water, but more often than not having to switch into my wading shoes and plunge into the cold water to haul it along.

In several rapids I encountered difficulties with this method. Huge boulders would sometimes loom out of the river near the shore, blocking my route, the water too deep or dangerous to wade around them. When this happened I'd have to perform a mini portage, unloading my canoe and carrying the loads a dozen metres ahead to a place where I could resume wading. My back became a bit sore from staying hunched over for hours, which I had to do in order to haul the canoe over rocks, or to control it in the currents. A few times, despite my best efforts, I'd lose my footing and slip under the water, gasping at the shock of the cold.

Each day the river seemed to get more challenging, with some rapids so large and fearsome that I had no choice but to make long, arduous portages inland to entirely bypass them. A few of these portages lasted over a kilometre or two in length, and I had to camp in the middle of one. On a positive note, when I did paddle, the river's current was so fast that I practically flew along. I managed to cover fifty-three kilometres on July 10. The next day was a little harder with more portages, but I still clocked forty-five kilometres.

But on July 12, I encountered such long, roaring, and dangerous rapids that I had to spend many hours on shore bushwhacking through bug-infested woods, hauling through alder swamps, and in some places climbing steep, rocky cliffs to get around them. It was certainly a contrast to when I'd portaged around Niagara Falls with my own police escort. The hardest part was right by the river, where the alder thickets virtually swallowed me up. They were taller than me, and inside them it was impossible to see which way to head—they were so thick that I couldn't see more than a foot in any direction. I needed a machete to get through, but I had none, so instead I used my canoe as a battering ram and hammered down the alders in front of me with it.

When I eventually emerged from the alders, I found myself confronted by a steep hill enclosing the river. Exhausted, I had to haul each of my three loads up it, and then into a forest littered with deadfall, sharp branches, swamp pools, and moss-covered boulders. The canoe would often snag on tree branches or wedge between spruces, forcing me to flip it on its side to squeeze through. It was a gruelling challenge to heave it and the other two loads over, but luckily in the forest I found more lingonberries to snack on and even a few red currants. I was further excited to spot a frog—a spring peeper—which astonished me as I hadn't seen any in weeks and didn't think they could survive this far north. On the other hand, the blackflies were draining my blood, and I felt practically woozy by the time I staggered down a steep, boulder-lined hill back to the river's edge. I still hadn't bypassed the last of the hazardous rapids, which roared away as far as the eye could see. But the sun was fast sinking below a mountain on the opposite bank, and I had no choice but to camp among the boulders for the night.

A fire helped warm my chilled frame, and rooting around in my barrel, I dug out a precious delicacy that I'd been saving for a particularly tough day: a pack of dried mangoes. They tasted like heaven, and immediately made me feel better. Some rain developed, driving me into the tent, where I finished the delicious mangoes. Possibly it was unwise to eat them in my tent, especially since the roar of the nearby river made it hard to hear any animal approach. But I was too tired to give it much thought, and fell into a deep sleep despite the hard ground.

After another day of navigating rapids and dealing with unseasonably cold weather and rain, I finally paddled down the last of the Rivière De Pas and came to a spot where it joined a larger waterway—the mighty George River. It was this historic river that I planned to follow north to the arctic coast.

27

NUNAVIK

WITH A LENGTH of nearly six hundred kilometres and a drainage basin of more than forty thousand square kilometres, the George is not a waterway to be taken lightly. It's wide and powerful, with hundreds of whitewater rapids and frigid waters that make hypothermia easy. Even in July, as I soon saw firsthand, long slabs of ice remain along the river's rock-strewn shores. At least thirteen paddlers have died attempting it, and it's not generally considered the wisest thing to do alone. Fierce north winds further complicate paddling, while the last part of the river has strong tidal effects from the ocean, not to mention the occasional polar bear.

Back in 1838 the Hudson's Bay Company established a fur-trading post on the George River's mouth near the arctic shores of Ungava Bay, just one of the hundreds of posts that the company operated across Canada's hinterland. However, the remoteness of the George River made it unprofitable, with few trappers ever showing up. Historically the Naskapi lived far to the south in the boreal forests, and with the wisdom that comes from living off the land, were reluctant to risk a journey to such an isolated post, especially since there were already much closer ones in central Labrador. The George River, too, with its countless bad rapids, wasn't very suitable for birchbark canoes, given that the nearest birch trees for repairs were located many hundreds of miles away. The Naskapi were also the hereditary enemies of the Inuit, and as their oral traditions testify, deadly raids were once common between them. This naturally only added to the Naskapi's reluctance to journey north. As for the Inuit, they too, already had more accessible and important trading posts located farther west. As a result, just four years after the George River post was established, it closed down. In the 1870s the Company experimented with reopening it, but it was just as remote and no more profitable, so it was soon abandoned again. It was later re-established a third time, though less as a trading post than a fishery station to capitalize on the richness of the offshore tidal waters.

One of the better-known stories connected with the river is that of the ill-fated Hubbard expedition, and the bitter rivalry it later provoked. In 1903 the American explorer Leonidas Hubbard, along with his friend Dillon Wallace and a Canadian guide, George Elson, sought to explore the George River. They took a steamer to central Labrador, then set off by canoe for the river. But they never made it: starvation caught up with them long before even reaching it. The caribou herds they were hoping to hunt failed to show up, and one by one, they steadily weakened. Hubbard starved to death, Wallace became too weak to walk, while Elson, famished but still staggering, eventually stumbled south to a post for help.

This tragic failure, however, wasn't the final act in their story. Hubbard's iron-willed widow, Mina, vowed to finish what her husband had started and explore the river he'd failed to reach. Meanwhile Hubbard's friend Wallace, who'd survived the first expedition, albeit barely, also resolved to finish the journey. But Mina didn't like Wallace, and indeed blamed him for tarnishing her dead husband's memory. The result was that they launched separate expeditions the same year to the George River. Elson, the Canadian guide who'd been the real hero of the first journey, agreed to lead Mina's party. With his abilities, they eventually succeeded in travelling down the river, though more than once rapids nearly killed them. Wallace, with a companion, managed to canoe the river too—but also nearly died when his canoe overturned in rapids. Their rival journeys would later inspire other expeditions to attempt the George River—not all of which were as lucky.

At the point where I reached the George it was more of a lake than a river, and wind, rather than current, was the main factor to deal with. On the map this wide, windy section is indeed labelled as a lake, almost sixty kilometres long and up to two and a half kilometres wide. This shape makes it susceptible to the prevailing north winds. Over centuries the roaring wind has weathered the shores here into fine sand, even piling up considerable dunes. It was an exhausting struggle trying to canoe up the lake into the howling gusts, which by midday had grown so ferocious that paddling was impossible. I experimented with sloshing ahead on foot, dragging the canoe behind me with a rope. This method worked remarkably well—for about thirty feet, at which point a wave splashed over the canoe and a second one came over my boots, soaking me.

After this it seemed best to wait until the wind slackened. I was windbound on a long, sandy beach hemmed in by willow and alder thickets. Rugged, ancient mountains encircled the lake, their lower slopes covered in spruce forests, while higher up were windswept tundra and scattered boulders. With the wind pinning me on shore, I decided to explore on foot some of these surroundings. I assured the canoe that I'd be back in a few hours.

It wasn't long before I came across some very large wolf tracks in the sand. The wolves of these northern regions are the largest in the world, growing to monstrous sizes by feeding on caribou and moose. Some of the largest on record have tipped the scales at 175 pounds, or roughly twice the size of an average German shepherd. I pulled the collar up on my jacket as the icy wind kicked up sand, obscuring the tracks.

Farther ahead were bear and caribou prints. Caribou, also known as reindeer, are often considered an iconic northern species, although they actually once ranged as far south as Ontario's Algonquin Park, Nova Scotia, and even Prince Edward Island. Of all the members of the deer family they're by far the most curious, which often leads them to walk right up to humans. This makes them easily hunted. For that reason they generally survive today only in remote, isolated places. The George River herd, which ranges across the lands I was now travelling through, was until recently the world's largest. But its numbers have dwindled from an estimated 800,000 in the 1990s to fewer than 10,000 today, a staggering decline fuelled by unregulated hunting with modern technology, notably snowmobiles, motorboats, and aircraft. The tracks I'd found were evidently some of the survivors.

Some predict that history will repeat itself and that the caribou in the north will suffer the same fate as they did in the south. However, examples have shown that caribou, if protected, have a remarkable tendency to bounce back.

Luckily, late in the afternoon the wind slackened enough for me to resume paddling. Given the wind direction and the shape of the lake, I resolved to cross to the western shore and follow it, as high hills along it would at least partially shelter me. Paddling along this shore in the rain I spotted a huge black bear. As soon as it saw me, it turned and vanished into the alders. The rain soaked me, but it passed later in the evening, and at the same time the wind died away, bringing out immense clouds of mosquitoes that made the sky hum with the sound of millions of beating wings.

I stopped for the night on a small beach surrounded by willow thickets that were so thick they could have hidden a hippopotamus. I didn't suspect any were around, but bears were a distinct possibility. My wet clothes I tossed onto a willow bush to dry in the smoke of my fire. The insect clouds drove me into my tent early, where I had to spend twenty minutes just squishing the bugs that had come in with me.

The next day was another rainy one, forcing me to bail water as I continued to battle the wind. The river still resembled more of a lake set amid ancient mountains than an actual river, although it had narrowed and now had a perceptible current. But so far I had yet to encounter any of its infamous rapids. Near its northwest corner I came upon a small cabin; the door and windows were entirely boarded up, doubtless to protect it from marauding bears. The George River is famed among anglers for its excellent trout fishing, and along the river's nearly six-hundred-kilometre course, usually where it flows through small lakes, are a few camps accessible by float plane. But these are generally in season only in August, when the blackflies and mosquitoes aren't as suffocating. The rest of the year they're boarded up like the one I saw, or else protected by ranks of nails.

Suitable campsites, I was finding, were in short supply, as much of the shoreline was smothered in willows and alders or else chaotic boulder fields. Not wanting to get caught in another storm, when I finally came upon a tiny patch free of willows, I made camp early. That night, temperatures dropped to freezing, and this far north where the trees and moss had thinned considerably, I found the ground even colder. I put on all the dry clothing I had to stay warm.

✳

AFTER THREE DAYS of canoeing the wide, windy expanse of the George River, on July 16 I reached a point where I could see ahead the glint of moving water, and knew I'd finally reached the start of the river's dreaded rapids. The waterway, which had been as wide as two and a half kilometres, now narrowed dramatically to just a few hundred metres.

Crazy as it may sound, I hadn't bothered to pack any maps of the river. I assumed that if I managed to get this far I'd be able to more or less figure things out. Plus, I had to travel as light as possible, and the weight of printed topographic maps adds up surprisingly fast. I did have my GPS, which, although limited, gave a basic indication of things. Of course, the nice thing about rivers is that there's usually no need to worry about getting lost—you just keep going in one direction. As for rapids, the maps aren't anywhere near accurate enough to show the kind of detail needed to navigate them anyway. These first rapids didn't look too treacherous, so I cautiously entered into their foaming waves on the right side.

The fast current sped me along as I dodged rocks and waves, once more sticking close to the shore so that I could escape if anything more dangerous materialized. I kept thinking that I'd reached the end, only for the river to curve and yet more wild water to glisten ahead. It was one of the longest rapids I'd ever paddled, stretching over three kilometres. At last the rapids emptied into a quiet little lake.

On this lake I was surprised to see an object moving quickly across the water in the distance. It was a small motorboat with two men on it. They were the first humans I'd seen in the almost two weeks since my brief stop at the hydro dam. So much solitude had made me feel almost like a wild animal, wary of human presence. When they zoomed in my direction I felt almost skittish.

"Hello there, bonjour," said a grey-haired man in hip waders at the front of the boat. At the engine was a much younger man, also in hip waders. Both were wearing mesh bug nets to defend against the blackfly and mosquito clouds. On the opposite shore were some cabins, which they'd evidently come from.

"Hello," I said.

"Where did you come from?" asked the older man.

"A long way from here," I replied.

"Where's the rest of your party?"

"This is it."

"You're alone?"

I nodded.

They introduced themselves: the older fellow, Pierre, owned the cabins, which was a fly-in fishing camp. The younger one, Chad, was one of Pierre's new guides who he was training in preparation for the upcoming season. The rapids were impassable for motorboats, keeping them confined to the lake. But the trout fishing in it was apparently so excellent that this didn't matter. They were curious about my journey, and asked how I handled the loneliness of travelling all by myself in such a remote place. Once my rustiness with human conversation had worn off, I explained that I wasn't lonely because my canoe and tent kept me company.

They nodded, and proved as kind and willing to assist me as anyone I'd met. But I was eager to press on.

"When you head downriver," explained Pierre, who'd been a guide on the lake for years and knew it well, "make sure you stay to the right. The left side is dangerous, with huge waves this high." He gestured to his chest to indicate five-foot waves. That did seem alarming. "And big ledges too," he added.

"Thank you," I said. Without Pierre's valuable tip I would have had to either paddle not knowing which way to go down, or else spend long hours hiking ahead through boulder fields and alder thickets to scout things out.

"Should I stay right the rest of the way? Or just for the part up ahead?" I asked.

"Just for this part."

"What about after?"

Pierre shrugged. "It's different all the way."

"Thank you," I said again. I was grateful for this tip, even if didn't help much with the remainder of the river. Still, any advantage, even for one rapid, was valuable. With a nod and a wave, I paddled off toward the river's outlet.

"Good luck!" they shouted, then roared off in their motorboat.

The river's pace increased quickly as it squeezed below barren mountains. It was a rare sunny day, which normally I'd welcome, except in this case the sun glinting off the water made reading the rapids difficult. I paddled cautiously, sticking as close to the right shore as I could without banging into rocks. Soon, as Pierre had warned, the river's centre and left side transformed into a dangerous vortex of massive whitewater. I zoomed by in a blur on the fast current, focusing my eyes on any hidden rocks submerged beneath the surface. I'd snatched up my wood paddle and was now using it as an anchor to slow my pace, jamming it into the rocky shallows to try to decrease my furious speed.

A boulder looming out of the water forced me to make a hard left. This shot me closer to the turbulent waves in the middle. My heart was pounding, but some determined strokes drove me back to the right shore. More hazards followed, some of which I skirted around on the right, others could only be avoided by nerve-rackingly edging left. It was a wild ride, with the river constricting at first, then widening, but rapids roaring all the while, even in the widest part. I couldn't breathe easy again until almost five kilometres of continuous churning water had passed, hundreds of rock hazards scattered through it. All it would take was one mistake to ruin the three thousand kilometres of effort it had taken me to get this far.

At last I reached calmer water, relieved to have made it through without having to resort to portaging, wading, or lining. The rest of the day continued in similar fashion, with numerous lengthy stretches of whitewater. As before, the key was to avoid the most dangerous parts, where deadly ledges or violent waves lurked, and instead seek out the less hazardous passages. Sometimes these were on the left, sometimes on the right, and sometimes in the middle, but very often it was a shifting combination of each like a black diamond ski run.

The rare clear skies, aside from making it a little more challenging to read the rapids, were a welcome relief, especially in the tranquil pools or small lakes between the whitewater. As I paddled I pulled off my wet gloves, socks, and boots and let them dry in the canoe. My small solar panel, which I'd hardly had a chance to use, I set up in the canoe too, so that I could charge my camera. The falcons were getting close—I could feel it—and I wanted to make sure I had my camera ready for them.

The swift current meant that without any overly strenuous effort I managed to paddle seventy-eight kilometres, making camp for the night below yet another stretch of rapids. My tent I was forced to pitch on gravelly rocks, as there weren't any better options.

The next day I encountered more long rapids interspersed with calmer sections, where trout were visible in the clear waters. The sight of them made me hungry. Given the clearly large number of bears around, I'd been cautious about fishing, since if I did catch a trout its strong scent would linger on my clothes for days, acting as a magnet for any bears within miles. But my ravenous hunger and dwindling rations at last overcame my hesitations, and as I drifted on the current I cast a line into the water. On my third cast with a yellow spoon I felt a strike: the line went taut and the rod bent round like a horseshoe. A few minutes later I landed a seven-pound brook trout. My mouth watered at the sight of it. Back in Norfolk County we had brook trout too, which now seemed like minnows compared to this giant one. Normally, I didn't stop for lunch, but this trout was worth the exception. I canoed to shore to prepare a fire. By cooking it now instead of when I stopped for the night, I wouldn't have to worry as much about the scent.

With my fillet knife, I quickly gutted the fish and roasted it up on some green willow shoots. Then, when it was good and ready, I devoured it. The head and guts I tossed far out into the water so that no bears might find them and associate my scent with food.

After lunch I continued racing downriver through more sets of rapids, a few of which roared on for kilometres. This made paddling them tricky, as sometimes at the start nothing too threatening would be visible. I'd plunge in, zigzagging down whichever side seemed safest, only to discover farther along some looming hazard: the waves might be too big, or there might be a drop-off over a ledge. Then I'd have to slow down, reverse, and tack left or right to escape the danger. Compounding the hazard were the frigid water temperatures. In places along the rocky shores sat huge slabs of melting ice, heaved up by the force of the river during the spring breakup. Some of these ice chunks were over a hundred metres long and taller than me. It was a reminder of how recently the river had been frozen and how icy cold the water beneath me still was.

By late afternoon the friendly skies had clouded over, with thunderstorms gathering above the encircling mountains. Rain began to fall just as I approached some roaring water that, from the sound of it, was bigger than anything I'd encountered so far. I was on the right, the fast current speeding me along, but ahead lay what looked like a partial canyon. Cliffs meant that I couldn't edge down the side, as I might find myself trapped in something deadly. I'd have to hike ahead to scout things out.

I steered the canoe into some weathered granite rocks, leaping onto them and hauling it up. Then I set off along the river's edge. The steep cliffs soon blocked my progress though, and prevented me from seeing what lay ahead. My only choice was to climb the cliffs to gain a better perspective. The steel-toed rubber boots the hydro workers had given me weren't exactly designed for climbing, but there were some shrubby spruces, and so grasping these, I hauled myself up to a ledge, then cautiously ascended the remainder of the way to the top.

From above I could see fearsome standing waves below the cliffs and in the middle of the river: if I hit them, they would sink my canoe. On the opposite shore were low, undercut rocks that looked equally menacing; if the canoe were swept into them, it'd be deadly. The rapids went on for a long way, over a kilometre, and the sheer cliffs meant there'd be no way to wade along the shore or guide the canoe with ropes. If I didn't paddle the rapids, the only option would be a portage. Given the steep incline and my three loads, it promised to be long and difficult. The bugs, too, were swarming me relentlessly, and the deteriorating weather made me uneasy—a storm looked certain to roll in soon.

The decision weighed heavily on me: I knew the stakes were high. Studying the river carefully from my perch on the cliff, there did seem to be a possible passage through the violent rapids, though it would require very tight, precise manoeuvres, with no room for error. I turned from the river and surveyed the boulder-strewn landscape around me, visualizing how time-consuming and arduous the portage would be, especially with the steep terrain. At last, I made up my mind.

Before a seed of doubt could enter my head, I dashed back as quickly as I could to the canoe, carefully descending the cliffs to the water's edge. "All right," I said to the canoe, "we'll run them."

28

TORNGATS

THERE WAS NO doubt they'd be the biggest rapids I'd ever attempted. I had to get to the middle in order to avoid the dangerous whitewater along the cliffs. Under dark skies, I canoed out from shore into the swirling water. But the rip-roaring current proved stronger than I'd anticipated: it was sucking me downriver before I could even reach the midway point. My frantic strokes were of no avail—I was trapped in a thundering current that was hurling me sideways into the rapids.

All I could do was spin the canoe so that it pointed downstream into the standing waves. I cast a fearful glance at the maze of obstacles ahead: the right side below the cliffs was deadly, the left not much better. I sped by the first big, wild waves, the current so powerful that it gave little chance to manoeuvre. Before me roared a huge foaming cataract where the river rushed over a submerged boulder. I was headed straight for it.

I tried to angle around it, but an icy wave surged over the canoe, hitting me square in the face and flooding the boat. I exhaled at the shock and instinctively grabbed onto the canoe's gunwales to try to keep it from flipping over. My heart was pounding: somehow I kept the canoe upright, though now I was knee-deep in water that was sloshing around in the canoe. More rapids loomed, so I snatched the paddle back up and steered the flooded canoe as well as I could. It was tipsy and harder to control—like paddling a sinking bathtub—but I kept it going downriver through the rapids, avoiding more rocks and standing waves.

I let out a sigh of relief as I reached calmer waters, then paddled into shore to bail out the canoe. The drenched backpack and barrel I lifted out so I could flip the canoe over. My boots, too, I pulled off and emptied. It had been an uncomfortably close call. To sooth my nerves, I ate a granola bar. I find there's something wonderfully soothing about them.

Feeling much better, I relaunched the canoe and paddled off. After such a close call, getting back in the saddle was the only thing to do. Sitting on shore stewing about things wouldn't help.

In any case, the wild scenery was so enchanting that I felt almost spellbound paddling down the river in the sight of such lofty rockfaces and weathered, pyramid-shaped mountains. Majestic waterfalls tumbled down the ancient cliffs like white ribbons, while in one place three peaks overlooked the river—the Three Sisters, to use the impromptu name I gave them. The trees were really thinning out now, with the upper slopes little more than exposed, rocky tundra. It was a sign that I'd nearly reached the end of the subarctic forests, which eventually cease to grow altogether, as permafrost—ice beneath the ground that lasts year-round—prevents trees from taking root.

Here, in this remote corner of Canada, I was well over two hundred kilometres from the nearest inhabited place: the tiny Inuit village of Kangiqsualujjuaq. But that was in a straight line. In practice, with all the bends in the river and other obstacles, it was much farther, making the isolation feel all the greater. My plan was to climb into the mountains, find a peregrine falcon's nest, then finish my journey by paddling out to the frigid ocean and Kangiqsualujjuaq.

For miles the river's shore had been nothing but steep slopes and chaotic boulder fields, without a single patch of ground big enough to put a tent on. Exhausted, when at last I came to a gravelly slope that was at least a little less cluttered with boulders, I took it. While it wasn't the softest or most level ground, the view from my camp was one of the most spectacular I'd ever seen, so I couldn't complain. Looking back in the direction from which I'd come I could see the blue thread of the river twisting between dramatic grey cliffs and green mountains.

I gathered up some driftwood for a fire and cooked one of my last freeze-dried meals. So far I'd seen quite a number of birds, ranging from sandpipers to loons, but no falcons. Tomorrow I'd begin my quest into the mountains to search for their nests. Then I turned in for the night, dreaming of finding falcons and pizza.

✳

A THICK FOG rolled in overnight, cloaking the river and mountains. When I woke in the morning, I could barely see the water's edge from my tent, though it was only ten feet away. Eager as I was to continue, paddling in such thick fog was out of the question: I'd never be able to make out the rocks and rapids. I took my time breaking camp, hoping that by the time I was done packing everything up, the dawn would have cleared things at least enough to cautiously depart. By a quarter after six, it had.

The George's rapid current made paddling easy, letting me make up for lost time. At first, the lingering fog made me cautious and kept me close to shore, as it was still impossible to see across the river. It felt a little like paddling through clouds. After I'd made it about twelve kilometres downriver, the mist had dissipated from the water and valleys, but still clung heavily about the mountains on either side. It was these misty mountains I was headed into.

I landed in a little rocky cove and hoisted my canoe up the bank. It looked as good a place as any to set off after a falcon's nest. I didn't know how long I'd be gone, and it seemed unlikely the water levels would rise much more, but still, my advice is, when going off to search for falcon nests, always tie up your canoe. I hauled mine a good distance above the water, then tied it with rope to a sturdy spruce tree. From the barrel, which by now was nearly empty, I took granola bars, a bag of nuts, and my last freeze-dried meal to stash in my backpack. Then I switched from my rubber boots into my hiking ones.

While I hadn't packed maps of the river, I did pack a topographic map of the mountains to the northeast. I fished it out now from the barrel and carefully unfolded it on a rock to study. The densely packed contour lines indicated the foothills of the mysterious Torngat Mountains, which was where I wanted to go. The Torngats form part of the Arctic Cordillera and are among the oldest mountains on earth, eons older than the Rockies. They date back nearly four billion years to when the planet was a lifeless wasteland. Parts of them, in fact, still look like that. There are no permanent settlements anywhere in the Torngats, which spread across a vast area roughly triple the size of Cape Breton, extending north into the frigid, iceberg-laden seas south of Baffin Island. Their lofty summits are the highest peaks in mainland eastern Canada. The very name, Torngats, derives from an Inuit word meaning "place of spirits."

The falcons nest all across these isolated, windswept mountains, wherever they find high, forbidding cliff faces. My plan was to hike northeast into the foothills on the Torngats' southwestern fringe. There were no trails or paths, of course, but I'd follow whatever way looked most promising.

From the water, I'd deceived myself into thinking it'd be relatively easy to scale the steep, rugged hills up out of the river valley into the surrounding mountains. But like a lot of things, it proved harder than it looked. The chaotic jumble of lichen-covered boulders on the slopes up from the river made hiking difficult. I had to balance carefully, stepping from rock to rock, to avoid twisting an ankle. The boulder field led to a forested slope, where spruces and thick shrubbery slowed me down. These shrubs were dwarf birch, a miniature birch tree that grows in dense tangles in the Arctic and subarctic. I had to claw my way through them until I reached a rockface. Here the real climbing began. Carefully grasping whatever handholds I could, I pulled myself up to more spruce groves and birch and willow thickets above.

The bushes seemed to grab at me, holding me back, as I tried to squirm and wriggle my way through. My backpack would catch on branches, or else my bootlaces on shrubs. Meanwhile hordes of blackflies and mosquitoes issued forth to assail me. "Just a little farther," I said to encourage myself, "once I get above the treeline, things will be much easier." Whether or not that was actually true I didn't know, but sometimes you just have to motivate yourself with upbeat thoughts—the power of positive thinking makes all the difference.

I pushed on with renewed energy, plunging into another thicket, clawing and squirming across it, then grasping the small, scraggly spruces to pull myself up the increasingly steep slope. Weathered boulders and rock outcrops loomed ahead on the hillside, while growing in great profusion around the rocks were mats of Labrador tea shrubs with little pink flowers. These shrubs were surprisingly well-anchored in the hillside, such that I could grasp them to pull myself up. As I was doing so, panting from the effort, I stumbled upon a treasure trove: lingonberries. I greedily grasped at such gems, stuffing them into my mouth without a thought for the mosquitoes I swallowed alongside. Their juicy tartness tasted like heaven. My luck got even better when I found some little black crowberries too; they were the first ripe ones I'd seen. Catching the sunlight on the higher slope, they'd ripened sooner than the ones I'd been seeing down in the valleys and swampy forests.

A little farther up the slope I came upon something that made me excitedly exclaim to all the mountains—ripe blueberries! I never would've dreamed of finding any this early in the season. In the far north, blueberries don't typically ripen until August, and I knew well the feeling of waiting patiently for weeks watching the green berries slowly turn to blue perfection. But to find these ripe ones now was a welcome surprise. Evidently, like the other berries, they'd ripened earlier on account of their exposed location on the slope.

More climbing brought me out of the valley enclosing the George River, onto a boulder-strewn plateau stretching away to distant mountains. I had to stop for a moment to take it all in. The mists had lifted, revealing rolling waves of mountains as far as the eye could see. Below them were sheltered valleys, where spruces still clung. It was as epic a landscape as any I could imagine. Better yet, some steep mountains to the west looked promising for peregrines. I cut across the plateau diagonally, weaving between the ancient rock outcrops and weathered boulders.

On the windswept plateaus, the tundra-like conditions made hiking easy. There weren't any thickets to slow me down. The harsh conditions on these high, rocky plateaus prevent most vegetation, aside from miniature berries and shrubs huddled close to the ground for protection from the fierce winds. The only trees to be found were dwarf spruce scattered few and far between, growing in little clumps in sheltered nooks beneath rock outcrops. I pushed on for several kilometres, using the encircling peaks as markers to guide me. Eventually I came to the foot of a high peak, which was part of a line running toward the horizon. In the shadows of this barren summit, I set down my pack and looked around. It seemed ideal for a base camp.

I set up my tent on the grassy tundra, carefully anchoring it with guy lines in case the wind should pick up later. Given the elevation and lack of tree cover, if it wasn't staked down, a passing gust could easily blow it away. Some friendly little warblers came to keep me company, fluttering and singing their cheerful songs among the dwarf spruces. "You're a good sign," I said cheerfully to the birds, "a falcon would definitely eat you. If you're here, falcons can't be far."

After my camp was secure, I headed up the slopes to search for any sign of falcons. All afternoon I searched among the mountainsides, which rose to rocky upthrusts and cliffs with ledges that looked perfect for peregrines. I'd first find a good vantage point, then carefully scan the cliffsides for any hint of them. The mountain's shadows partially concealed things, but I knew that if any falcons were around, I'd likely hear their high-pitched calls. At this time of year, the third week of July, their eggs were likely just about ready to hatch. After searching for several hours, I didn't see any signs of them, but I wasn't discouraged. I'd just have to venture a little farther into the mountains.

I returned to my camp with the plan of getting an early night's rest, so that I could save up my energy for a longer trek in the morning. Luckily, the rains had formed little pools on the rock plateau, allowing me to gather up water to boil. The dead, lichen-covered spruce roots in the sheltered nooks made for excellent firewood.

As I cooked the last of my freeze-dried meals (an unparalleled vegetable lasagna), I watched the sun set over the ancient landscape. These lonely, uninhabited mountains marked a dramatic contrast to the farms, towns, and shimmering cities on the earlier part of my route. Of all my campsites, this one had by far the most isolated feel.

✳

I WOKE IN the early morning, chilled from the mountain air. Poking my head out the tent I saw that the mists had returned. It made the rocky plateau and surrounding peaks appear like some ghostly dreamscape, too ethereal to be real.

I ate two granola bars for breakfast, then laced up my hiking boots. The silence felt a little uncanny, and I found myself almost tiptoeing about, as if I were afraid of making a sound. I left the tent up, shouldered my pack, and headed off toward the fog-shrouded peaks. My plan was to venture into more isolated valleys, then climb the lower slope of another misty mountain to gain a lookout point. The flatness of the plateau and scarcity of vegetation made it easy to cover ground, though the drifting mists partially concealed the peaks, which made navigating more challenging.

It was a strange, wonderful feeling to quietly hike over such a remote and untouched landscape, feeling almost as if I were on another planet or in some mythical place far removed from the modern world. I felt reluctant to disturb anything, carefully stepping around vegetation where I could, and trying not to upset even the scattered rocks that had lain as they had for untold ages.

After a few hours, I began to gain elevation, picking my way up the slopes of a mountain. Its summit was hidden in fog, but lower down I could see weathered cliff faces that looked ideal for peregrine nests. A grassy slope led up toward tumbled rocks and boulders, which at first I could weave between but soon had to scramble over. I had to be careful: if I twisted an ankle here, or slipped and smashed my head on a boulder, my sun-bleached bones would become a new addition to the landscape. In the shadows higher up were occasional patches of snow and ice.

Lightened as my backpack was with only a handful of food items and no tent, as the slope got steeper, I could feel the ache in my legs. There were luckily some clumps of nicely ripened crowberries and lingonberries to snack on. I devoured as many as I could. At this point, my clothing hung loose about me, and I was starting to feel like little more than skin and bones.

Just as I went to pluck another berry I caught sight of something passing overhead on my left that sent a chill down my spine. A bird had flown by, and buzzing with anxious excitement, I thought it had been a falcon. But I was so excited that I half doubted it, thinking my imagination was playing tricks on me. I set down my backpack and dug out my camera.

Then I edged a little farther along the steep, rugged slope to a better vantage point against the weathered rock. From here I scanned the cloudy skies for any sign of life. Patiently

I waited, and waited, and waited—minutes feeling like hours. The mist was slowly dissipating, gradually revealing more of the ancient cliffs.

Then, like a phantom, something flapped across the sky.

29

TREELINE

THERE WAS NO mistaking the graceful sweep of its exceptionally long wings, which seemed almost too big for its body as it powered across the sky—it was a peregrine falcon all right. They are the monarchs of the air—the fastest animal on the planet, dive-bombing their avian prey at speeds of up to two hundred miles an hour. The peregrine made a high-pitched shriek, repeating it several times. I followed its movements as well as I could with the camera as it flew back toward the mountain cliff and then vanished from view.

Again I had to wait patiently, this time for the drifting mists to lift and reveal the cliffs. When they did, I scanned the craggy rocks carefully, scrutinizing all the ledges for any sign of a nest. Some falcons will nest in the same spot all their lives; then, when they're gone, the site will often pass to the next generation. It's thought that some falcon nesting sites have even been used for centuries. Unlike eagles, falcons don't normally use sticks to construct a nest. Their nests are normally just a ledge on a precipitous cliff, where no animal could possibly disturb them.

I wished I had a pair of binoculars, but the necessity of travelling light had forced me to forgo them. In a pinch, though, my camera served as one: I used its zoom finder to scan the cliffs. I felt there must be a nest somewhere.

Then the falcon issued out again, flapping high, and I watched its movements carefully to see where it might land. The falcon flew back toward the precipitous mountainside— and there, perched on a rock shelf on the cliff, was the nest.

It felt surreal to see it, and I stared at it for a minute wonder-struck. What an excellent piece of real estate. In the distance, I caught the silhouette of a second falcon gliding high in the sky. Falcons mate for life, and in the wild live about ten to fifteen years. Most of the incubating is done by the female, but when she flies off for food, the male will cover. Falcon eggs hatch in about a month, after which it takes roughly another six weeks of the chicks clinging to the cliffside with their parents bringing them food until they're big enough to fly.

As I watched the falcon perched on the crag, I thought back to that April morning when I'd seen a falcon out our porch window—and dreamt up the idea of following it here, to this most distant of mountain ranges, at the end of the continent. I reflected on all that I'd seen on my journey—the same journey, more or less, that the falcons make, albeit from the air. In my mind's eye I visualized the protected waters of Long Point, the time-capsule-like forests of the Niagara River, the surprisingly rich greenspace hidden away in the GTA, the wonderful wildness of eastern Lake Ontario, the sanctuaries among the

Thousand Islands, Montreal's preserved forests, the swamps of the St. Lawrence, Cap Tourmente's gems, the mountains of Charlevoix, and all the other places I'd seen leading up to these almost untrodden mountains. They were a reminder that all those little pockets of wildness are crucially interconnected, islands of habitat that falcons and other species depend on in order to make their annual journeys. Once the eggs hatch and the chicks are reared, by the end of summer the peregrines will begin their journeys south for the winter, as do most other arctic birds.

Thinking of which, as much as part of me wished to linger—I still had to make it to the arctic coast. I'd come and found the thing I'd sought, and I knew I would cherish forever the memory of the nesting falcons. It was the kind of thrill that I felt sure would always give me a smile whenever I thought of it, however many years might elapse. Any time I saw a falcon again, I'd picture this awesome place and feel transported back to it.

After a little while longer of silent watching, I bid farewell to the falcons, wishing them safe travels on their journey south. Then I shouldered my pack and began the return trek to my camp. Descending was faster and easier than ascending, and I wasn't slowed down by stopping to scrutinize the cliffs for nests. Still, the majestic feel of the landscape exerted a hypnotic allure, and determined as I was to get back, at times I found myself almost subconsciously halting to stare with a sense of awe at the wild, lonely peaks all around me.

When I got back, I was relieved to find my tent still standing and not disturbed by any animal. I contemplated remaining another night. But I couldn't help feel a little apprehensive about my canoe. I'd secured it as well as I could, yet the mere thought that if anything should happen to it, I'd be stranded, was not a comforting one. Plus, I'd eaten all the food I'd stashed in my backpack. There was still a handful of granola bars and some nuts back at the canoe, which now constituted all my remaining food. If I didn't delay, I could reach it before dark.

I pressed on across the windswept plateau, then started down the steep mountainous river valley, plunging through waist-high thickets of dwarf birch. These made it difficult to see exactly where I was descending, and once or twice I had to catch myself when I suddenly came out above a vertical drop. Then I'd have to shimmy sideways and find a less precipitous path downward. But in one place I misjudged the steepness of the terrain on account of the tanged bushes, and fell down a half-dozen feet, landing smack in front of a big hole of freshly dug earth. Alarmed, I sprang to my feet—it was clearly a bear den, and I'd almost fallen right into it. It looked occupied, but I wasn't going to stick around to find out. I dashed down the slope as fast as I could, clawing through the thickets to escape.

I couldn't breathe easy until I was farther away. A short while later I was doubly relieved to spot in the distance my canoe resting on the rocks. I climbed the rest of the way down to it, telling it the good news about the falcons. There was still a bit of light left, and since the shore here was nothing but rocks, I repacked the canoe and shoved off into the river. A short way downstream I landed at a more hospitable spot to camp.

✳

AS I CONTINUED downriver the next day I could see increasing amounts of ice on shore, often in enormous piles. Snow clung to the higher slopes and shaded valleys, while the trees became ever smaller and sparser, with more and more tundra— all telltale signs that the arctic coast wasn't far. But there were still rapids to navigate before I could safely get there.

Some of these rapids were too large to canoe. I bypassed one dangerous, roaring stretch of fearsome water by climbing along boulders and lining my canoe along the edge with a rope tied to the bow. Then came another very long stretch of rapids, which I entered into on the right, zigzagging around rocks, slowing down into eddies, pivoting around hazards. I thought I'd had it just about navigated when I encountered something more menacing hidden at the bottom: massive Class 4 cataracts that could swallow a canoe whole. Spirited paddling let me escape on the right in the nick of time—but these rapids, I could well believe, had claimed the lives of some earlier travellers. What made them particularly deadly was their deceptiveness—the long, relatively benign sets of easy rapids effectively concealed the danger waiting at the end. To avoid it, I portaged my gear over some boulders, then relaunched below the thundering whitewater.

Since my freeze-dried meals were all gone, when I came upon a little tributary stream gushing into the main river I stopped to fish. The mouths of these little creeks make perfect pools for brook trout. Almost every cast brought in a trout, and when I had five nice ones—not too large, about a pound each, which made them better for cooking—I resumed my travels. As for bears catching the scent, that was a risk I'd just have to take. I found a nice spot in a small clump of forest to spend the night, and roasted up my trout on willow sticks. Crowberries and lingonberries were at hand, and even a few edible bolete mushrooms, which I tossed into my pot. That night I dined like a king, listening to the sounds of the river surging along while I sat with my back against a spruce tree and watched the smoke curl up from the fire.

Early the next morning I reached the most dangerous rapids of all—a long, violent set of powerful cascades known as Helen Chutes. I landed just above them on a small beach where fresh bear tracks cut across the wet sand. A three-kilometre-long portage through the mosquito-filled forest was required to bypass the chutes. With my three loads, this took nearly four hours, and I camped, exhausted, at a small hill in the woods at the end of the portage.

A heavy rain rolled in overnight, soaking everything and keeping me in my tent in the cold morning. On the bright side, the rain was so torrential that I found I could put my cooking pot outside the tent fly and have it fill up in no time, providing me with a supply of drinking water without having to even leave the warmth of my sleeping bag. When the rain eventually let up, a thick fog rolled in. But I set right off; the fog couldn't stop me now, and it gave the river's islands a wonderfully mysterious air. As I paddled down the river loons cried unseen from out of the mist, while little sandpipers hopped along the rocky shores.

I had to carefully line my canoe down a few more big, treacherous rapids. One had an abrupt drop-off into a roaring whirlpool where shrieking seagulls hovered above, attracted by the abundant fish. It was a little nerve-racking, but I managed to balance on the slippery rocks along the shore and guide my canoe through the turbulent water with a rope.

Tucked away on wooded hillsides or below rapids stood the odd cabin or fish camp, but I didn't see any people. In any case, I was determined to keep pushing on. A few more rapids I ran gingerly, while at others that seemed too dicey, I lifted my canoe and gear over the rocks on shore, before putting back in below the roaring waves. Knowing that the river would soon become salty, I filled every container I had—water bottle, thermos, and cooking pot—with freshwater.

As I resumed paddling downriver I caught my first whiff of a sea breeze, which was an exhilarating feeling. Then, testing a few splashes from my paddle, I detected a salty taste. By this time the trees had all but disappeared, and I could appreciate the traditional Naskapi name for the river, Mushuan Shipu, meaning "River Without Trees." Kelp was now visible in the water, whereas upriver the underwater rocks had been free of weeds. One last set of tidal rapids I had to line around cautiously, as the boulders here were slippery from being washed by the high tides and had a green sea algae on them.

Then, just past these rapids, the river seemed to suddenly widen and deepen, with cliffs rising abruptly out of the water. In the distance were spectacular fjords and desolate-looking mountains. This was true Arctic now, the home of polar bears and beluga whales.

It was a bit anxiety-inducing to contemplate that I was now paddling across deep saltwater connected to the Arctic Ocean, in which swam sharks, whales, and most notably, polar bears—the largest land carnivores on earth. They have little fear of humans, with big adult males measuring ten feet long and tipping the scales at over fifteen hundred pounds.

I'd feel my heartbeat quicken whenever I'd see the outline of something large and white beneath me in the water. The terrifying thought that a huge white bear was rising up to flip my canoe and tumble me into the icy water would seize me . . . then, with a massive sigh of relief, I'd realize that it was only a giant, sunken white boulder lying far below, distorted in size and shape by the water. Polar bears are excellent swimmers and can easily outpace a canoe. But I reassured myself that at this time of year, they'd likely all be on ice floes far offshore, hunting seals.

I paddled below high cliffs and across fjords, catching in the distance the sight of a seal surfacing, the favourite prey of polar bears. The incoming tide slowed my progress, but luckily, the winds were light, or else with the cliffs waves could be a serious problem. Late in the day, when I came across a little waterfall, I carefully landed on some slippery, barnacle-covered tidal rocks to replenish my freshwater supply. At this stream I caught another trout for my dinner, then paddled off to find what I figured would likely be my journey's last campsite.

The landscape had become quintessentially arctic—windswept tundra and fjords with snow clinging to the cliffsides. The name "arctic" derives from the Greek word for "bear," a reference to the Great Bear constellation visible in northern skies, so originally *arctic* was just a vague term for anywhere north.

Some think the Arctic is anywhere north of the Arctic Circle, an imaginary line that runs around the top of the world.

But natural environments don't run in straight lines. Forests occur hundreds of miles north of the Circle in some areas, whereas in other places the arctic tundra occurs far south of it. The most widely agreed-upon definition is based on the Arctic isotherm, which isn't a straight line but rather an ecological one where the average temperature for the warmest month is below 10°C, which roughly corresponds to the treeline and permafrost, a definition that includes Ungava Bay's shores. All of the rugged mountains of the Torngats are classified as part of the Arctic Cordillera.

I pushed on up the fjord toward the rocky coast of Ungava Bay, nearly within sight of the isolated Inuit settlement of Kangiqsualujjuaq. The tide had gone out, leaving mudflats with barnacle-encrusted boulders extending far offshore. This made camping something of a challenge—I had to haul my three loads across the mudflats, sinking in knee-deep as I went. I wasn't sure just how high the tides reached. But I examined the rocks carefully for signs of kelp or other seaweed, and once I found some without any, I set up my tent beside them. To celebrate the end of my journey, I made a driftwood fire and a cup of tea. The trout I roasted up and soon devoured, throwing the remains in the fire to destroy the scent.

Then I watched a marvellous sunset over the fjord as I sat on a rock and savoured the solitude of untamed nature, basking in the beauty of it all. With a deep breath I inhaled the exhilarating sea air and the wild sense of freedom that comes with wide-open spaces. It felt a bit surreal to have come so far, and I was filled with a deep sense of gratitude—for the beauty of the scene, for the things I'd experienced and the animals I'd encountered, and last but not least, for all the help I'd received from the many kind people along the way. I felt if the night passed without a polar bear eating me, there was really nothing more I could ask for. As the sun dipped below the horizon I crawled into my tent for the last time.

✳

THE MORNING DAWNED calm and clear, but I took my time packing things up. The tide had come in, bringing the water nearly up to my tent, which would make relaunching easy. When my canoe was good and loaded, I bid farewell to my final campsite, thanking it for an excellent night's stay.

The icy water was clear as crystal with large salmon and arctic char swimming in the depths below. The outgoing tide carried me along, gulls and terns squawking overhead as I aimed the canoe's bow at a small collection of buildings and houses on the horizon: Kangiqsualujjuaq, population nine hundred. It sits nestled beneath low, encircling mountains. In Inuktitut the name means "the very large bay," a reference to the salty inlet I was paddling across.

A pier stood along the coast with a boat launch beside it. I glided in, the canoe's bow skidding up onto the gravelly shore. Then I stood up, smiled, and stepped out. It'd been three months and nearly 3,400 kilometres from Long Point to the arctic coast. My journey was over.

A man in sunglasses stood leaning against a pickup truck just above the launch. After watching me pull up my canoe, he came down.

"Need a ride?" he asked.

"Sure."

"I'm Willy." He offered his hand.

"I'm Adam."

"You're alone?"

I nodded.

"Where did you come from?"

I explained as Willy helped carry my canoe and gear up to his waiting truck. He drove me into town while we chatted about adventures. I mentioned that I hadn't been too concerned about polar bears, since I figured there weren't any nearby at this time of year, and that they'd be far offshore on ice floes hunting seals.

Willy looked over at me and smiled, chuckling to himself. "Two big polar bears," he said grinning, "were spotted swimming upriver just a few days ago."

I was flabbergasted. "Really?"

"Yeah." He nodded. "When the ice melts on the bay in July, they go upriver to look for fish."

"Oh," I said, feeling lucky and also grateful that I didn't know this beforehand. If I had, I wouldn't have slept very well at all. "Do they ever attack anyone?"

"Oh sure," nodded Willy. "There's a woman in town, she was attacked out berry picking. Luckily her husband was there and he shot and killed the bear."

"Goodness," I said, feeling even more strongly that my sleep would have suffered if I'd known this.

It was a short drive into the little community, where Willy dropped me off at the co-op hotel, a dormitory-style accommodation. I thanked him for his help and the stories. Then, thinking of all the kindness so many people had shown me on my journey, it felt nice to be in a position to do some of my own: I made a gift of my canoe to Willy. He seemed very surprised and happy. Shipping it back would be difficult in any case, and I figured Willy would give it a good home.

There's an airfield on the community's outskirts where small planes fly west to Kuujjuaq, the largest community in Nunavik. After flying there, I could catch a flight south to Montreal, then make my way home. But the next flight out of town wasn't for five days. So I spent the time in rambles about the town and up the surrounding mountains, admiring the views of the fjord and frigid ocean. I also satisfied my ravenous appetite, although at first I found that one good meal a day was enough to fill me, until my body readjusted.

It wasn't long before I made more friends. One of whom, Jaiku, a local hunter who was very knowledgeable, shared my interest in birds. He told me that, besides hunting belugas and the occasional polar bear, he had a great interest in gyrfalcons, the largest falcons in the world. Unlike peregrines, the mighty gyrfalcons aren't migratory; they're so hardy that they overwinter in the Arctic—one of the very few birds able to do so. I'd never seen one, but Jaiku offered to take me along the coast to a spot where he'd seen them. With his cousin Nicholas, we set out in his boat, first to check their whale nets for belugas, then off down the coast.

We didn't end up finding any gyrfalcons, but Jakiu did point out a polar bear track. Even without a gyrfalcon, I was grateful for the chance to see more of the rugged Ungava coastline, which was as bleak a shore as any I could imagine. Weathered cliffs rose out of the ocean, while icebergs glistened in the distance. It seemed a very different coastline from what I knew back in Norfolk County on Lake Erie, and yet somehow not so different. Drifting on the sea offshore were mergansers, gulls, terns, and many other birds that I'd see each spring in the weedy bays of Long Point. I asked Jaiku if it was common for ducks and the other birds to drift out on the ocean like that, and he nodded. Just like on the bays back home, I mused. I smiled at the thought of how diverse yet interconnected Canada's many different natural habitats are—and how there were still more of them I wished to explore.

But those were adventures for another day. It was time to head home. I dearly missed my family, and I had a lot to tell them, and they me.

On the morning of my flight, I compressed my things down to a single pack, then began the walk to the airfield outside town. But, as ever on a journey it seems, no sooner had I set off than a stranger pulled up in his truck and kindly offered me a ride.

A short flight took me to Kuujjuaq, and then another flight to Montreal, then a third flight on to Ontario. I made it home by the first of August, in time to watch the falcons and other arctic birds on their return journeys—a reminder that the Arctic is often closer than we think. And that right outside our door, adventures await.

Black bear tracks in wet sand. I found bears very numerous in northwestern Labrador and Nunavik.

Lining my canoe through some rapids while balancing on slippery rocks. Note the mosquitoes in the air, and the damaged canoe yoke.

Running some rapids on the wild George River.

Ice heaved up on the banks of the George River.

As my food supply dwindled, I caught more fish to eat, such as this brook trout on a misty day on the George River.

Roasting a trout on a green willow stick over a fire.

"Exhausted, when at last I came to a gravelly slope that was at least a little less cluttered with boulders, I took it. While it wasn't the softest or most level ground, the view from my camp was one of the most spectacular I'd ever seen. . . . Looking back in the direction from which I'd come I could see the blue thread of the river twisting between dramatic grey cliffs and green mountains."

Trying not to slip while lining my canoe through more rapids on another rainy day on the George River.

A view of the George River, winding through deep valleys and surrounded by weathered mountains. "More climbing brought me out of the valley enclosing the George River, onto a boulder-strewn plateau stretching away to distant mountains."

Hiking in the foothills of the Torngat Mountains. "On the windswept plateaus, the tundra-like conditions made hiking easy. . . . The harsh conditions on these high, rocky plateaus prevent most vegetation, aside from miniature berries and shrubs huddled close to the ground for protection from the fierce winds."

Making camp in the mountains. "I set up my tent on the grassy tundra, carefully anchoring it with guy lines in case the wind should pick up later. Given the elevation and lack of tree cover, if it wasn't staked down a passing gust could easily blow it away."

Scanning the cliff face through the drifting mists for any signs of falcons. "After a few hours, I began to gain elevation, picking my way up the slopes of a mountain. Its summit was hidden in fog, but lower down I could see weathered cliff faces that looked ideal for peregrine nests."

The falcon. "Then, like a phantom, something flapped across the sky. There was no mistaking the graceful sweep of its exceptionally long wings, which seemed almost too big for its body as it powered across the sky—it was a peregrine falcon all right."

Hauling my canoe across mudflats at low tide on Ungava Bay, where polar bears roam.

Day 90: Paddling on the saltwater of Ungava Bay at the end of my journey.

My canoe resting on the rocks at high tide in the fjord, at my journey's final campsite, just a short distance outside Kangiqsualujjuaq. "I sat on a rock and savoured the solitude of untamed nature, basking in the beauty of it all. With a deep breath I inhaled the exhilarating sea air and the wild sense of freedom that comes with wide-open spaces."

AFTERWORD

A REMOTE ARCTIC mountain might seem very far from
a skyscraper in Toronto. But in a certain sense it's not, really.
No matter where you are in Canada, if you happen to look out
your window at certain times of the year, you can see a part
of the Arctic. There's almost nowhere in the country where at
least a few birds heading to or from there don't pass over, from
Vancouver Island to Newfoundland, and even in the heart of
our biggest cities. It's a wonderful illustration of the ties that
bind Canada's diverse landscapes, from the southernmost
Carolinian forests along Lake Erie to the windswept tundra of
the High Arctic.

Much attention has understandably been placed on saving
the Arctic's pristine spaces. But less appreciated is the fact that
to save wild places and wildlife in Canada's North, we must also
save them in Canada's south. Pockets of wildness in southern
Canada form not only critical stopover places for birds on their
annual journeys, but are also in many cases their winter homes.

Yet in recent years we've paved over more of these natural habitats than ever before.

Imagine, though, what those birds might say if they were given a seat at the table and could talk. They'd probably ask us, if it's not too much trouble, to stop paving over, polluting, and otherwise eliminating their homes (and to give them crackers). This seems reasonable enough, but if we need extra motivation to do so, numerous studies now show what common sense long suspected: that when we preserve or rewild greenspace, it's not just wildlife that benefits; we all do, including benefits to our mental and physical well-being.

Plus, if you should happen to paddle and hike several thousand kilometres across the country, an abundance of parks comes in handy. If my journey taught me anything, it's that no matter where you go in Canada, you can't fail to find fascinating natural spaces, even under the Burlington Skyway or below the bluffs of Toronto. These little nature oases further offer a place for kids to play, to fall in love with nature, to cut school to build forts and learn life skills. In fact, people of all ages benefit from nature nearby—just as every person I met in Scarborough proudly told me about their fondness for local places far from the hustle and bustle of the city. Personally, I think there ought to be a policy whereby at least one nature park lies within a ten-minute walk of everyone's residence. Besides providing habitat for migratory birds, these natural areas on our doorsteps remind us of our connection to those vast, untrodden wild places that lie beyond the horizon, faraway lands of enchantment for the mind to dream over.

Another benefit of getting outdoors in nature is that you'll often cross paths with people you've never met before—and on balance, I think we're likely to find that rewarding. Too much time spent cooped up inside staring at digital screens is apt to make us a little too cynical about the world, but getting back outdoors with some old-fashioned travel is a pretty good cure for that. Along the way you're bound to spot some awesome birds and other wildlife, breathe in the fresh air, enjoy the simple charms of the wild, and experience a little adventure. And that, I think, is something well worth pursuing.

ACKNOWLEDGMENTS

BOOKS SELDOM COME together on their own, and this one certainly didn't. I've been extremely fortunate to benefit from the expertise and support of an excellent team at Penguin Random House Canada. First and foremost, I must thank my editor, Nick Garrison, whose early encouragement was instrumental in making this book a reality. Nick's keen insights always improve my books, and this one is no exception. For that, I'm grateful. I must also sincerely thank Nicole Winstanley, Penguin Canada's publisher, for her continued belief in the value of my little adventure stories. Without her, they might never have appeared in print.

Zainab Mirza, publishing assistant at Penguin Canada, also played a hugely valuable role in steering this book to completion. Karen Alliston, the copy editor, scrutinized the manuscript with a keen eye and made many helpful suggestions. Catherine Dorton proofread the book. Any errors that remain are mine alone. On the publicity side of things, Dan French, Penguin's Associate Director of Marketing and Publicity, and Stephen Myers, the book's publicist, brought their expertise to bear. The talented Emma Dolan designed the beautiful cover, while Brittany Larkin and Carla Kean handled things on the production side, along with Noah Kahansky. Helping oversee all of this is Penguin Canada's superb managing editor Alanna McMullen. To each of them, I extend my thanks for their efforts.

Outside the Penguin team, I want to thank Rebecca Nickerson, who created the map of my route that appears at the start of the book. I must also thank my literary agent, Rick Broadhead, for his tireless work, expertise, and attention to detail. Rick is truly the best in the business, and everything an author could want in an agent.

As for the journey itself, I hope that the story I have recounted within these pages has already made clear the debt of gratitude I feel to a great many kind-hearted people who aided me on my journey. The generosity I was shown astonished me, all the more so given that most didn't even know at the time I was on a long journey. I regret that I can't thank every individual who showed me kindness. In many cases I never learned their names, but my sincere thanks are due to all of them.

Of those whose names I do know, I must thank several of them again. Brad and Jillian Wood, and their sons Daniel and Joel, for their exceptional hospitality in letting me camp on their beach (and Jeff Wood, too, for his encouraging words).

Brad I also thank for capturing the shots of me with his camera and for permission to reproduce those photos in this book. A little farther along the lake is where I came across Ed (whose last name I never learned), and he, too, I especially thank for letting me portage up his property and for giving me a hand with my canoe. There were others on the Great Lakes who also granted me permission to camp or cut across their properties, but regrettably I don't know their names. At the Burlington Skyway, I want to thank again Stuart Mills, Carla Hosseini, Tom Karcz, and Eileen McDonald-Karcz for helping me. It was much appreciated on a cold, rainy day, and especially the Tim Hortons from Tom and Eileen. I'm also indebted to Chris Prater for first giving me a first-rate paddle, and then later mailing me his own personal one. Several years ago Chris founded the paddle company, Ripple FX Paddles, and if you ever want an absolutely perfect paddle for racing, I can't recommend them enough.

That brings me to my aunt and uncle, Frank Hummell and Anne-Marie Bulbeck (who graciously received the paddle and my expedition resupplies at their house). My thanks go to the both of them for not only the safe-keeping of my mail, but for providing me with an excellent campground and a wonderful breakfast. I want to further thank my entire welcome party at their place, and for the generous care packages they loaded me up with. For that, I thank Dianna Moore, Grant Moore, Matt, Amanda, and Jocelyn Moore, Jason Garner and Liam, Lucas, and Addison Garner, Audrey Hummell, and Sandra and Charles Durant.

Later I met more perfect strangers, who nevertheless treated me like family. Foremost among them was Muriel at the campground at Les Coteaux. All I can say is that I hope our paths will cross again the next time I'm in the neighbourhood. I also want to thank Marc, who gave me permission to camp outside Trois-Rivières and a refuge in the event of a tornado. I further owe a very special thanks to Camille Vigneault. Camille kept my canoe safe in his horse barn and was as supportive of a stranger who just happened to knock on his door as anyone could be. After my journey ended I paid Camille a second visit and retrieved my canoe. He and his wife, Isabelle, were very hospitable hosts on my return and treated me to a wonderful lunch. Both of them I thank for all their help and especially for looking after my canoe.

On the hike north, I encountered so many kind people whose names I don't know, that should any of them ever happen to read this book, all I can say is that I deeply appreciate your kindness. In particular, Steve, who pulled over and gave me an apple, water, and bug spray did me a favour I'll never forget. Later, the water and kind words from Vincent and Tinesha (my apologies if I spelled that wrong) were also much appreciated.

In Labrador City, my luck surely could not have been better than to have met Ken Manstan and Cindy Ward. Ken was not only good enough to sell me his canoe, he went beyond that—by giving me extra food, first aid supplies, bear bangers, and even his belt (which I'm still wearing today). Cindy and Ken further treated me to a hearty breakfast and their kind well-wishes, as well as Cindy's dad Steve, all of which put wind in my sails. Later, when I reached the hydro dam, the support from everyone I met there, but especially Paul and Blair, meant a lot. For the food and boots, I'm in their debt.

I was already lucky before my journey began to have the support of Peter and Brigitte Westaway. Their incredible support has helped enable me to undertake expeditions, and I'm thrilled since 2020 to hold the title of Westaway Explorer-in-Residence at the Royal Canadian Geographical Society, named in their honour. Life, it seems, is full of strange coincidences, and one of them in this case was that I had already started planning my journey from Long Point to the Arctic before I met Peter and Brigitte and learned that they owned and had restored the Old Cut Lighthouse. To have then first dipped my paddle in the water beside their lighthouse at the very start of my journey, made my starting point feel extra meaningful. I am deeply grateful for their kindness, support, and encouragement.

I'm also grateful for the ongoing support of the Royal Canadian Geographical Society, and especially for John Geiger's support and encouragement. Shortly before embarking on my journey I further had the good fortune to cross paths with Dr. Peter Fritz, who shares my passion for canoeing. Dr. Fritz has since also helped support my expeditions, and I'm excited for us to collaborate more in the future.

Last but certainly not least, I must thank my parents, Mark and Catherine, for always putting up with my adventures and for their helpful suggestions with this book.

Finally, I must especially thank my wife Alexandria (Aleksia) for not only supporting the idea for the journey (even after the arrival of our son Thomas), but for helping me get organized to do it, pushing me out the door, and then later mailing my resupplies—all the while raising our son single-handedly. For that, and a thousand other things, I'm very lucky and grateful.